The Women's Camp in Moringen

Gabriele Herz

The Women's Camp in Moringen

A Memoir of Imprisonment in Germany, 1936–1937

Gabriele Herz

Translated by
Hildegard Herz and Howard Hartig

Edited and with an introduction by
Jane Caplan

Berghahn Books
NEW YORK • OXFORD

Published in 2006 by
Berghahn Books

www.berghahnbooks.com

© 2006 The Estate of Gabriele Herz
Introduction © 2006 Jane Caplan

Library of Congress Cataloging-in-Publication Data

Herz, Gabriele, b. 1886.
　　The women's camp in Moringen: a memoir of imprisonment in Germany,
1936–1937 / Gabriele Herz ; translated by Hildegard Herz and Howard Hartig ;
edited and with an introduction by Jane Caplan.
　　p. cm.
Translated from German.
Includes bibliographical references.
ISBN 1-84545-077-9 (alk. paper)
　　1. Herz, Gabriele, b. 1886. 2. Moringen (Concentration camp) 3. World War,
1939–1945—Prisoners and prisons, German. 4. World War, 1939–1945—Concentration camps—Germany. 5. World War, 1939–1945—Personal narratives,
Jewish. 6. Jews—Germany—Biography. 7. Political prisoners—Germany—Biography. 8. Women concentration camp inmates—Germany—Biography.
I. Caplan, Jane. II. Title.

D805.5.M67H47 2005
940.53'1853595—dc22

2005041090

British Library Cataloguing in Publication Data

A catalogue record for this book is available from
the British Library.

Printed in the United States on acid-free paper

Frontispiece photograph of Gabriele Herz taken in 1941 by Arthur Herz.

Contents

Acknowledgments

The PUBLICATION OF Gabriele Herz's memoir was initiated by members of her family, and three generations have participated in bringing this edition into existence. Hildegard Herz, the wife of Gabriele's surviving son, Arthur, undertook the first translation of the text. Together with his sisters, Gertrude (Gertrud) Kracauer and Ly (Elisabeth) Brettler, Arthur Herz provided indispensable information about their mother and father and about the family's life in and after Berlin. In the next generation, Ellen Kracauer Hartig, Gabriele's granddaughter, was another invaluable informant and correspondent. Her husband, Howard Hartig, who carried out the initial research into the provenance and historical context of the memoir, collaborated in the translation and editing at every stage. Finally, Howard and Ellen's son, Joel Hartig, helped transcribe his great-aunt's initial handwritten translation, researched many of the footnotes that were inserted in the editing process to explain references in the text, and compiled the index. The book is therefore primarily a tribute to the family's collective work in honoring Gabriele's dignity and endurance.

Beyond the family circle, Howard Hartig and Ellen Kracauer Hartig wish to acknowledge with deep gratitude the pivotal role played in the genesis of this edition by Ursula Krause-Schmitt, director of the Studienkreis Deutscher Widerstand and author of pioneering research into the history of Moringen. Her support was especially important in the earliest days of the project, when Howard and Ellen were struggling to discover any information at all about this forgotten camp—a task made all the more challenging by Gabriele's understandable but confusing use of pseudonyms for its inmates and staff. Without Ursula's initial encouragement and her commitment to the project, the memoir would never have had a chance to reach a wider readership. Her contributions included assembling relevant archival materials, arranging for the Hartigs to visit the Moringen memorial site, and setting up meetings with survivors of Moringen, who were able to test and confirm Gabriele's descriptions of the camp against their own recollections.

In my own subsequent work on the memoir, I have been the beneficiary not only of the generous participation of members of the Herz and Hartig families, but also of help from other friends and colleagues. Renate Bridenthal and Marion Berghahn first brought the memoir to my attention, thereby setting me off on an unexpected and rewarding journey of scholarship and friendship. The members of the German Women's History Group in New York offered their usual vigorous and constructive commentary on an early version of the introduction, and I also benefited from Marilyn Young's comments. Wolfgang Ayass and David Crew helped me with their expertise in the history of German workhouses and welfare, and Hans A. Schmitt assisted with the history of Quaker relief in Nazi Germany. Dietmar Sedlaczek, director of the KZ-Gedenkstätte Moringen, and Ursula Krause-Schmitt read through the final draft of the introduction and corrected a number of errors. I owe special thanks to two other colleagues. Bob Moeller worked through successive drafts with his now legendary generosity and keen eye, while Jan Lambertz, equally generous with her time and knowledge, sent me numerous useful documents and references as she came across them in her own work on concentration camp history. My archival research was made possible by the staff of the Niedersächsisches Hauptstaatsarchiv in Hanover and the Bundesarchiv in Berlin; by Jack Sutters at the American Friends Service Committee archive in Philadelphia; and by Josef Keith at the archive of the Friends House Library in London. Nicholas de Libero assisted with the bibliography. Bryn Mawr College funded my research in Germany. It is in gratitude for this and also for over twenty years of support and friendship from the faculty, secretarial staff, and librarians of Bryn Mawr that I dedicate my share of this book to them collectively.

— *Jane Caplan*

Introduction

Jane Caplan

ON AN OCTOBER day in Berlin, Gabriele Herz, a fifty-year-old housewife, reported to her local police headquarters to start serving a three-month custodial sentence. Her crime was that she had returned home after a long absence in Italy—hardly an offense deserving a prison term. But this was Germany in 1936, and Gabriele Herz was a German Jewish woman who had left her homeland a few months earlier to explore how her family could make a new life in Italy, beyond the reach of the Nazis. She had come back home in September 1936: prospects in Italy looked doubtful and her husband Ehm (Emil) had not managed to wind up the family's affairs in Berlin. By returning to Germany from her six-month stay abroad, Herz fell afoul of regulations issued in 1935 by the Prussian Gestapo,[1] which allowed "protective custody" (*Schutzhaft*) to be imposed on German nationals, including German Jews, who returned to Germany after more than a three-month absence in a foreign country.[2] The police treated these returning émigrés (*Remigranten*) as a danger to national security, and detained them pending investigation into their activities abroad. While other detainees were often set free within weeks or months if nothing incriminating was uncovered, Jews were released only when they undertook to leave Germany once and for all—a release, in other words, into forced exile.

The Gestapo sent Herz to the workhouse in Moringen, a nondescript village in the quiet countryside between the provincial capital of Hanover and the university town of Göttingen, where some of the thousands of prisoners arrested by the Nazi regime since January 1933 were incarcerated. In the course of the twelve-year history of the Third Reich, the Moringen workhouse was to be successively a concentration camp for men, a concentration camp for women, and a so-called Youth Protection Camp (*Jugendschutzlager*)—all the while continuing to function as a workhouse for its few remaining inmates. By the time Gabriele Herz arrived in October 1936, Moringen was in its third year

---

Notes for the introduction begin on page 45.

as a camp for women detainees, and she joined about a hundred other women already in detention in one wing of the extensive workhouse buildings. Very few of them were Jewish; most were Communists or Jehovah's Witnesses, along with a handful of Social Democrats, a number of prostitutes and women convicted of criminal offenses, and a few more who had been arrested for making "derogatory" (*abfällige*) remarks about the Nazis, or for violating the Nuremberg Laws' criminalization of sexual relations between Jews and "Aryans." Among this unexpected company quartered in bleak attic dormitories and increasingly crowded day-rooms, Herz endured six months of discipline, deprivation, boredom, and anxiety, until her sudden release in March 1937. By the end of that month, Herz and her husband had finally left their native land, forced into a circuit of travels that eventually took the family, via Italy, Switzerland, and Cuba, to a new life in the United States, in the city of Rochester, New York.

By the standards of persecution and extermination that ruled Germany and Europe under Nazi domination between 1933 and 1945, Gabriele Herz's prison experience, however rigorous and undeserved, was hardly the most horrendous—though, as we shall see, that is not the only context in which we should view it. Neither she nor her fellow inmates suffered severe physical violence while they were in Moringen, and although they had to work, the labor was neither heavy nor unremitting. As one of the early inmates, the Communist Hanna Elling, put it in a later interview: "The conditions under which the women had to live here were certainly hard, but they were not subjected to the kind of terror to which so many women later fell victim in the concentration camps."[3] On the whole, between the camp's opening in October 1933 and its closure in March 1938, the women in Moringen were treated strictly but "correctly." In this sense the Frauen-KL Moringen (Women's Concentration Camp Moringen) was, paradoxically, a place of relative respite during a history of terror and suffering that had begun for some of its inmates with the Nazi seizure of power, and that would resume in 1937–38 when they were transferred to new and more brutal camps.

As a Jewish woman, Gabriele Herz had suffered the harassment and discrimination that were making Jewish lives increasingly unlivable in Nazi Germany after 1933, but she had been spared the worst torments visited on some of her fellow prisoners. A number of Moringen's detainees had already undergone months or years of appalling treatment at the hands of the police and Nazi paramilitaries before their admission to the workhouse camp. They were among the many thousands of Germans, largely members of left-wing parties and trade unions, who had been arrested during the Nazi seizure of power in early 1933 and imprisoned without trial in police cells or improvised detention sites. Most of those who survived this early detention were eventually released to pick up their lives in the Third Reich or in exile; but others were only at the beginning of a relentless twelve-year odyssey that was to take them, and eventually hundreds of thousands of others, through the emerging concentration camp universe of the Third Reich.

When Gabriele Herz reached Moringen in October 1936, the foundations of this concentration camp system were already in place. By then, national procedures for arrest and detention had replaced the indiscriminate raids of the early months of Nazi rule, and a system of state-administered camps had supplanted the haphazard improvisations of 1933. In some ways these measures had the effect of restraining the initial orgy of Nazi violence against their opponents, but they also contributed fatally to the development of the bureaucratically organized police state, as I will explain more fully below. By the winter of 1936–37, six official concentration camps for men were under the control of Himmler's merged police-SS administration. Of these, Dachau, the original "model" concentration camp, was now the largest, with about 2,500 inmates quartered in barracks and ruled with punitive discipline.[4] The new men's camps also applied versions of this vicious Dachau regime, but it was not in force in Moringen. Uniquely, Moringen, designated in October 1933 as the sole official concentration camp for women, was nominally under the control of the SS (Schutzstaffel, or security guard). In practice it was run by the workhouse director, Hugo Krack, who remained a civil servant in the employ of the local administration.[5]

As in the men's camps, most of the inmates of the Moringen camp after 1933 were *Schutzhäftlinge* (literally, "protective detainees") interned by the Nazis in order to crush opposition to the new regime. The largest groups in Moringen were Communists and Jehovah's Witnesses. But by the time of Herz's detention, the police had already been empowered to extend the policy of mass arrest to other "undesirable" groups, notably, recidivist criminals and so-called asocial offenders, such as beggars, prostitutes, drunkards, and hooligans. Increasing numbers of these men and women were hauled into the camps as German society was "cleansed" of its socially marginal members. Within a year of Herz's departure, the expanding SS camp system was beginning to catch up with Moringen, now too small for its swelling population. The women's camp was closed and its prisoners transferred to new SS women's camps. First, they were taken to a decrepit castle in Lichtenburg/Prettin on the Elbe River and then, in 1939, to the newly built camp of Ravensbrück, near Berlin. By this time, the concentration camp population was launched on a rapid process of growth, accompanied by a systematic degradation of conditions. The culmination was the immense wartime system of concentration camps, forced labor camps, and death camps that were intended to house prisoners of war, to crush resistance to the German occupations, to supply huge amounts of forced labor to the German war economy, and, most heinous of all, to support the collection and wholesale extermination of entire populations of the racially, biologically, and morally "unfit."

When we think of the camps, it is to this ultimate and catastrophic tragedy of exploitation and mass murder that most people's minds turn. The Nazi camps, as Hannah Arendt famously argued, were "the laboratories in which the fundamental belief of totalitarianism that everything is possible is being verified ... the true central institution of totalitarian power."[6] As such, they command our fullest attention, and they have become fixed in public memory through thousands of books, both academic and popular; through feature films and documentaries; through diaries and memoirs; through commemorative sites, museums, and monuments. "Concentration camp" is now a term linked indissolubly to Nazi oppression, its terrible power embodied in names like Dachau, Bergen-Belsen, and Buchenwald. Auschwitz has become the universally recognized shorthand for the Nazis' exterminationist project, a symbol for the cataclysm of persecution and mass murder that engulfed Germany and Europe between 1933 and 1945.

Still, brief though those twelve years were and ineluctable as their terrible destination may sometimes seem, if we interpret National Socialist Germany only from this pinnacle we risk ignoring much that we might learn about the character and history of the regime. Perversely, the ultimate horrors of the wartime years can become a kind of unintentional alibi, a curtain drawn over the earlier phases of the regime, when its victims were counted in thousands rather than millions and when they were primarily German nationals, not the populations of conquered countries. In the pre-war years, the concentration camps already held thousands of German political prisoners, criminal offenders, and transgressors of social norms. Until 1938, few of these victims of Nazi oppression were Jewish; fewer still were detained solely because of their race. This early history of the Third Reich, including the emergence of its prison camps, contains answers to the largest questions of what National Socialism was, as well as insights into the smallest scale of broken and extinguished individual lives. The new regime sought public confidence by promising to solve old problems of public order and national decline with more effective methods. In doing so, it released the radical new energies that eventually ran unchecked through German society and government.

The term "camp" covered a multitude of institutions, with differing origins and purposes. The German historian Gudrun Schwarz has counted more than ten thousand camps at the wartime zenith of this system and has divided them into no fewer than seventeen different categories: from the twenty-two core concentration camps and the eight extermination camps to the hundreds of ghetto camps, forced labor camps, prisoner-of-war camps, special camps for Jewish workers, psychiatric institutions, euthanasia sites, work training camps, and more.[7] If we want to understand the character of National Socialism and its impact on Germany and Europe, we must come to grips with not only the extent but also the diversity of this immense structure of incarceration. We need to inquire exactly how each element of it came into existence, as well as examine the internal relations among these parts. A decade ago Schwarz concluded that there existed a "great deficiency of knowledge about not only the system of National Socialist concentration camps but also the number and types of camps."[8] Although an enormous amount has been accomplished in the intervening years—the identification and commemoration of camp-sites, research into individual camp histories, the emergence of a strategic understanding of the camp systems—the sad fact is that the field is almost inexhaustible.[9]

The women's camp at Moringen constituted one small building block in this system, and Gabriele Herz's imprisonment there was one particle in the physics of Nazi terror. This history of one woman in one camp can teach us about both the overarching structure of incarceration in Nazi Germany and how individuals experienced it. We can learn from it what was new after 1933 and what was inherited from existing institutions and practices; which Germans were immediately identified as enemies of the regime and which others were targeted as its grasp extended; what was specific to the treatment and experience of female prisoners compared to male prisoners; and which state employees, by operating the early machinery of custody, however "correctly," gave their consent to an emerging hierarchy of discrimination, persecution, and exclusion. The purpose of this introductory essay is therefore not only to provide a context for understanding Gabriele Herz's memoir of her imprisonment, but also to use her story as an opportunity to explore and explain this lesser-known early history of the Nazi concentration camp system.

To grasp the institutional evolution of the camps, we need to locate them laterally in the character of the Nazis' political and social objectives between 1933 and 1945. To understand Moringen, we have to cast our vision back chronologically and consider the changing use of the institution and its buildings since the early nineteenth century. These may seem like surprising detours to make around one woman's six-month journey into the Nazi prison system, but they will reveal otherwise invisible insights into the causes and character of that journey.

Gabriele Herz and Her Family

The woman whose memoir launches this story was born Gabriele (Yella) Berl in Vienna on 26 April 1886, as the second daughter of a blanket manufacturer and his wife. She received a secondary school education and before her marriage worked as a private tutor in English and French.[10] On a visit to her married sister Marta in Berlin, Gabriele met a young editor, Emil Herz, whom she married in 1910. The marriage brought Gabriele into the heart of assimilated Jewish bourgeois society in Berlin, where fully one-third of Germany's half million Jewish citizens resided. While she preferred Berlin to Vienna, she also felt uncomfortable with some of the privileges that her new life conferred.

Her husband Emil had his own roots in a long-established middle-class Jewish community in the small town of Warburg, between Kassel and Paderborn, where his grandfather Juda Oppenheim was a rabbi.[11] His father had died before his son's birth, and Emil, the only surviving child, remained extremely close to his mother and the Warburg family home.[12] After a university education in Bonn, he found his way into the publishing profession and moved to

Berlin in 1903 to join the up-and-coming firm of Ullstein.[13] Leopold Ullstein had founded this company in 1877 with the acquisition of a Berlin daily paper, and together with his five sons he expanded it rapidly before World War I by establishing or buying a string of other liberal and popular newspapers in Berlin. By the time Emil Herz joined the enterprise, it was already enormously successful and was continuing to expand its newspaper division and to diversify into magazine and book publishing. Herz's job—a tremendous vote of confidence in an inexperienced young man—was to help launch Ullstein's new book publishing division.

In the 1920s, Ullstein was one of Germany's most dynamic publishing houses, as famous for its commercial innovations and advertising as for its authors, who ranged from politicians such as Bernhard von Bülow and Gustav Stresemann to the successful novelists Erich Maria Remarque, Vicki Baum, Leon Feuchtwanger, and Carl Zuckmayer. Capturing Bülow's memoirs for Ullstein was in fact one of Emil Herz's first editorial coups, and he was a prized member of the company. Hermann Ullstein described him as "that genius in the art of starting new projects."[14] Among Herz's successes were a new line of mass-market novels and non-fiction books, the lavishly illustrated Ullstein Universal History series, and, in the 1920s, the top-line Propyläen imprint, which published enormously profitable volumes in art, history, and literature.[15]

Emil Herz's successful editorial career at Ullstein enabled his wife and four children to live the comfortable life of the city's cultured Jewish bourgeoisie, with a villa in the fashionable Dahlem quarter, a friendship circle among Berlin's writers and intelligentsia, and an art collection that included paintings by Max Liebermann, Lovis Corinth, and Max Pechstein and even a small Renoir.[16] The memories of her surviving children record the kind of woman their mother was.[17] For one thing, she was not entirely at ease with her comfortable lifestyle. Modest and unpretentious, she disliked being the mistress of the fine house on the corner of the Griegstrasse, with its cook and its maid and its round of social activities, while so many of her fellow citizens went hungry in the harsh post–World War I years. On her own territory she balanced privilege with self-denial. Although the family had access to a company car and chauffeur for Sunday outings and holiday trips to Warburg or the seaside, Gabriele always chose to travel third-class when she took the train on her own. She reared her children on strict principles—"don't spoil the kids," "eat what you're given," "don't feel sorry for yourself"—and she ran a domestic regime they described as "spartan," certainly more modest than the family finances required. Like her husband, she was somewhat of a disciplinarian, impatient of childish misbehavior and "fast with a slap."

Yet if this suggests severity or stinginess, nothing seems to be further from the truth. The parents' traditionalist views about disciplining children were tempered by kindness. They were also generous in helping, materially and emotionally, needy members of their extended family. Gabriele herself was sensitive and selfless rather than severe. A cultured, well-read, and musical young woman, she brought "Viennese charm" into the Herz household; in fact, Emil's mother had thought Gabriele "too flighty" for her beloved son. On the birth of Gabriele's first child, a daughter (Gertrud), her mother-in-law had remarked disapprovingly: "Warburger Töchter haben Söhne" (Warburg's daughters bear sons), as if Gabriele's light spirits disqualified her for the serious business of reproduction. A mother of four—Gertrud (1911), Erwin (1912), Elisabeth (1916), and Arthur (1921)—Gabriele did not stint on her children's intellectual and cultural upbringing. As far as religion was concerned, the family had a deep-seated Jewish identity but was not particularly observant, despite Emil's background. The boys became bar mitzvah, of course, and the family celebrated the Jewish High Holy Days, but they did not attend services on the Sabbath nor did they keep a kosher home.

Gabriele and Emil prepared their children for life in the real world of post-war Germany. The girls as well as the boys received a good education and training for employment: Gertrud became a Montessori teacher, Elisabeth a designer and textile specialist, Erwin a journalist, and Arthur eventually a photographer and chemist. Gabriele also saw to her children's cultural education. She took them to concerts and occasional films, and she included them in fondly remembered communal play-readings of Schiller and Shakespeare at home with her friends. She entertained her own friends at informal teas in the Griegstrasse, but she was also well able to hold her own in larger gatherings with Emil's celebrated clients. Along with Feuchtwanger and Remarque, these included the playwright Gerhard Hauptmann and the theater director Max Reinhardt. Above all, Gabriele's unpretentiousness expressed itself in her refusal to put herself forward and in her warmth of personality, to which everyone responded. Her genuine interest in others and her ability to get along with everyone proved a reservoir of strength in her Moringen experience.

In all these ways—in terms of economic status, cultural avocations, religious practices, and educational standards—the Herz family fit the typical profile of the Jewish urban bourgeoisie in Germany. But their security was to vanish soon after the Nazis seized power in January 1933 and launched their first campaigns of political discrimination and physical violence against Germany's Jewish population.[18] The regime did not set out immediately to destroy the economically important operations of Ullstein or other Jewish-owned enterprises (Ullstein alone employed over 9,500 people in a time of deep economic depression). Instead, the Nazis aimed to take over ownership of these companies and to keep them going under new management, while continuing to exploit their prestigious names.[19] Like other firms, Ullstein was put under pressure from Nazis within and outside the company in an ultimately successful attempt to force the expulsion of its Jewish employees and the termination of Jewish ownership. "At the close of two months of Hitler's reign," according to Hermann Ullstein, "our firm had been turned from a well-run organization into a battlefield of hatred. Once a place where a publisher felt it his duty to stand by his principles, to seek out the evildoer, and to expose injustices, it had become a tomb, brooding in silence over crimes and monstrosities."[20] Through a series of forcible sales culminating in June 1934, all Jewish ownership of the company was eliminated and the remaining Jewish employees were purged.

Like many other Ullstein editors and authors, Emil Herz had already been forced to abandon this intolerable workplace, in his case in March 1934. The family history he wrote after World War II loses its confident narrative fluency at the point of the Nazi seizure of power and collapses into a few fractured pages of pain and shock. "The shame and horror that ensued [after Hitler's appointment as chancellor] is beyond my scope and descriptive powers. Suffice it to record a few personal observations."[21] One of these fragments masks the complex process by which the family decided its future: "For a long while we ourselves, my family and I, could not bring ourselves to leave home, the ties were too strong. But in the end, after painful experiences, and hearing the footsteps of the Gestapo at our heels, we left Germany. A long trek led us through Switzerland and Italy to Cuba, till finally America opened her doors and took us in."[22]

These attenuated sentences hold in abeyance the family's failed emigration history before 1937 and only hint at their tortuous path of emigration after that date. The full story includes a short and unproductive exploratory trip to Palestine that Gabriele and Emil made over the new year in 1935–36, leaving their youngest child Arthur in boarding school; then Gabriele's longer but equally fruitless investigation of possibilities in Italy over the spring and summer of 1936, while Emil stayed in Berlin to settle the family's affairs; Gabriele's return to Berlin in September, followed by her incarceration in Moringen from October 1936 to March 1937; and after that the family's final flight from Germany. Only Emil's dedication of his book to the memory of "Meine tapfere Frau" (My courageous wife) gestures at what this middle-aged woman had endured by the time they left Germany for good in March 1937.

These divergent reactions, in which Emil appears reluctant to leave and it is Gabriele who seems to take the initiative, mirror the experience of many German Jewish families in the 1930s. As Marion Kaplan writes in her study of German Jewish life after 1933: "Men's role and status as breadwinners made them hesitant to emigrate and gave them the authority to say no."[23] Even though Emil Herz had forfeited his position as breadwinner by March 1934, he was still apparently unable to steel himself for the rupture with his native land. He saw no future for himself outside Germany, least of all in Palestine. The reasons for the subsequent failure of the Italian venture are unclear—possibly Emil's hesitation played a part, or he failed to get a visa. More likely, Gabriele was unable to find any openings for the family to make a new life.[24] But failed emigration was far from unique at the time, as Kaplan also points out: "Statistics may give the false impression that Jews smoothly managed to leave Germany and enter the country of their choice. They cover up the individual stories, which show complicated emigration attempts, failures, and new attempts."[25] Of about 60,000 Jews who left Germany in 1933 and 1934, about 10,000 had returned by 1935, most because they had been unable to support themselves abroad, others because their visas and entry permits had expired. Between 20,000 and 25,000 Jews left each year between 1935 and 1937, and 40,000 more did so when anti-Semitic persecution hit a new crescendo in 1938. But emigration opportunities were often limited by other countries' immigration rules, so that even when a family had resolved to leave, it might not be able to do so in practice.[26]

What was unusual about the Herz family's emigration experience was not its vicissitudes but its timing and consequences. Emil and Gabriele had spent no more than a few weeks in Palestine before concluding that they could never make a life there, but Gabriele did not reveal this trip in her police interrogation. Nor of course did she mention that Emil and Arthur had visited her in Italy in the summer of 1936.[27] Her Gestapo file simply records her location as "Meran[o], Italy" from December 1935 to May 1936 and from June to September 1936 (the gap between May and June remaining unexplained), and states that she was "arrested as a returnee [*Rückwanderin*] on her return to Berlin."[28]

When Gabriele Herz returned to Germany in September 1936, she and Emil were apparently unaware that she was courting arrest as a *Remigrantin* even though the Prussian secret police had begun to detain some returning émigrés as early as January 1934. Identified as they crossed back into Germany, these returnees were supposed to be taken into custody pending investigation of their activities while abroad, unless they were expelled outright. Initially, this worked more as a propaganda move intended to deter exiles from returning than as a practicable policy of detention. As the regime's policy of forcing Jews into emigration became more pronounced, however, the procedures were toughened and took on a more assertive anti-Semitic cast. In the course of 1935, a series of decrees issued by the Prussian police and the Reich Interior Ministry stated that all returning political and "non-Aryan" émigrés were to be regarded prima facie as suspect and undesirable in the new Germany. Those who were not immediately deported were to be taken without trial into protective custody while their cases were reviewed. Detainees were supposed to be sent to "instructional camps" (*Schulungslager*), but since these did not exist as such, the rule in practice meant (and was later specified to mean) internment in Dachau for men and Moringen for women. There, like other political detainees, they ostensibly underwent a regime of ideological instruction and political surveillance before being returned to the community. Their release, at the pleasure of the Gestapo, was contingent on positive behavioral reports from the camp authorities.[29] However, since the regime had no interest in reclaiming Jews for the *Volksgemeinschaft* (the German national community), Jewish *Remigranten* were released only when they could present a guarantee that they would leave Germany permanently within two weeks.

How many Jews were arrested and detained under these regulations is unclear. The Herzs' ignorance of them is understandable, and in any case they were not the kind of people who knowingly broke the law in ordinary circumstances. When the Gestapo caught up with her, Gabriele Herz unwittingly shouldered the burden of responsibility for the couple's unsuccessful attempts at emigration. If she had any sense of what awaited her as "instruction," she might perhaps have imagined it to amount to compulsory enrollment in a political training course of some kind. Taking the idea of instruction with a teacher's seriousness, she was quite unprepared for the six months' imprisonment that she finally experienced.[30] No wonder that Emil acknowledged his wife's courage.

Police Custody and the Concentration Camps after 1933

When Gabriele Herz arrived in Moringen in October 1936, she was swallowed into a machinery of incarceration that was already in full motion. To understand Moringen's place in this—to see what it was *not* as well as what it *was*—we need to review briefly the history of the Nazi concentration camps. This history can best be understood as a sequence of stages between 1933 and 1945, in which the transition to each new phase marked a qualitative change and a process of differentiation in the scope and status of the camp system as a whole, even as individual elements in it persisted.[31] The historian Johannes Tuchel has argued: "As a mechanism of National Socialist power, the concentration camp cannot be seen as a static instrument of terror; it must be analyzed in its total context, as a means of power that was subject to considerable alterations and changing political pressures and functions."[32] Initially a means of political repression, re-education, and deterrence (the phase in which the Moringen women's camp belongs), the camps became after 1936 the nexus of the Nazi power structure, which pivoted on the SS. In this capacity, they were the focus for the Nazi vision of German social and racial "improvement" through the elimination of "harmful" elements. As such, the camps were the fatal point at which the initial project of political terror and coercive reformation converged with emerging Nazi programs for mass social and bio-political engineering, for the mobilization of slave labor, and for physical extermination on a gigantic scale. Although the concentration and labor camps remained conceptually and administratively distinct from the wartime death camps devoted solely to mass extermination, by the middle of the war the difference was blurred. The concentration camps themselves had become places where enormous numbers of prisoners were physically annihilated—but here they died slowly, through their labor for the German war effort, rather than immediately as a result of poison gas. Nevertheless, even as the camps changed in scope and character, elements of the earlier phases survived into the next, so that on the eve of its collapse, the Nazi camp system can be seen as an immense palimpsest of its own history.

The vast majority of men and women detained in the first few years of Nazi rule were arrested as political opponents of the new regime, under the provisions of the Reichstag Fire Decree of 28 February 1933. The first article of this "Decree for the Protection of People and State" suspended the constitutional prohibitions against arbitrary arrest and detention, leaving each state to decide exactly how to implement this provision. In Prussia, Germany's largest state, about 10,000 people, mostly members of the Communist Party, were immediately taken into custody by the police, or by men in the SS or SA (Sturmabteilung, or Storm Troop Detachment) who had been deputized as police auxiliaries, and were detained without trial. Following the Nazis' success in the Reichstag elections of 5 March and their speedy monopolization of political power throughout Germany, the arrests intensified and spread across the country. The new regime aimed to smash organized opposition on the left, and their primary quarries remained the Communists, along with Social Democrat and trade union functionaries.[33]

Through 1933 and 1934, some 30,000 to 40,000 people, known officially as *Schutzhäftlinge*, were detained for periods ranging from a few days to several months (and some eventually for years).[34] The huge numbers quickly overwhelmed the capacity of Germany's jails and prisons, and the authorities had to look elsewhere for accommodation. SA and SS squads hauled off numerous victims for longer or shorter spans to improvised sites and embryonic camps, where they were subjected to atrocious treatment, unchecked by the residual standards of police conduct or prison regulations that might mitigate conditions elsewhere. Hundreds were murdered or driven to suicide; others suffered permanent injury to mind and body.[35] Several of these camps and jails also had custody of the small number of women detainees, estimated at 300 to 400 in 1933–34, who were usually confined in separate women's sections. Women were mostly spared the physical violence inflicted on the male detainees, but some (including many who ended up at Moringen) were brutally mishandled while in police or paramilitary custody, and those held in detention centers that lacked a separate women's section or female personnel suffered sexual assaults by the guards.[36]

Although the arrest campaign had been expressly initiated by Hitler's new government, its massive scale and the lawless barbarity with which it was being executed soon roused unease among the more conservative authorities. This was partly for reasons of what we would now call public relations, and partly because, even if the detainees were to be held only in temporary custody, their sheer numbers required large and organized facilities and hence some kind of official involvement. State and local administrators in Prussia, Germany's largest state, led the way. They saw the mass arrest of political opponents as only a temporary measure, but one they were anxious to supervise effectively while it lasted.[37] It was in this way that the Prussian administration took over surplus public facilities, including the workhouses of Moringen, Breitenau, and Brauweiler, for use as mass detention centers.[38] By the summer of 1933, Prussia was sponsoring a number of state-financed camps, and in October the Interior Ministry designated six sites as the sole authorized camps for long-term detainees.[39]

Included in this list was the Moringen workhouse, in use since April as a facility for male *Schutzhäftlinge* from the Hanover area. From October it was now reserved for women detainees only, and its remaining male inmates were removed to other sites. In a step to impose further central control, the Reich government issued new national regulations on protective custody in April 1934: powers of arrest under the Reichstag Fire Decree were restricted to the police and civil authorities alone, and detainees were to be held only in the officially designated prisons and concentration camps.[40] These measures not only curbed the freelance terrorism of the SA and SS but also reduced the total number of prisoners in protective custody.

By the summer of 1935, fewer than 4,000 *Schutzhäftlinge* were still detained without trial in all of Germany.[41] But, tellingly, as many as half of these were in the state of Bavaria, where since the spring of 1933 the SS leader Heinrich Himmler had been using his position as chief of the Bavarian political police to establish an integrated system of police-SS power and mass detention, with his own objectives in mind.

The shape of Himmler's police and concentration camp system was determined by intricate power struggles within the regime, which began as soon as the party seized power, regarding the strategy and objectives of the Nazi "revolution." It is beyond the scope of this introduction to examine this process in detail, but the stakes included the concentration and distribution of power in the Nazi leadership, as well as the authority to construct a national police system out of the individual state forces and to control the strategy of extra-judicial custody. In the overarching process of the Nazi monopolization of political power, the crucial political counterpart to the February 1933 Reichstag Fire Decree was the Enabling Act of 23 March 1933.[42] Whereas the former suspended civil rights and legitimated the repression of political opposition, the latter effectively dismantled political pluralism and democratic government. Between them, these measures established the "permanent state of emergency" upon which the Nazi dictatorship rested. While those two measures enthroned executive power above judicial and legislative authority respectively, the third leg of this revolution from above was the remaking of the armed service of the executive, the German police system.

From an initial power base in Bavaria, Himmler managed to extend his police powers across Germany between 1933 and 1936 and, in effect, to establish a police state. Aided by his subordinate Reinhard Heydrich, he gained control of the political police in state after state and established his own priorities for the system of political custody. By mid-1934, Himmler was already in effective control of all the political or secret police forces in Germany and was centralizing them into a national system under his sole authority. The most important force, the Prussian Gestapo, had already been detached from the existing police command structure and, in a further crucial step toward complete autonomy, was statutorily exempted from judicial review in February 1936. The full merger of the SS and the police into a centralized and quasi-independent system under Himmler's command was confirmed by Hitler in a decree issued on 17 June 1936, which appointed Himmler Reich Leader of the SS and Chief of the German Police.[43]

Meanwhile, Himmler had also taken over control of the detention camps and was remaking them in accordance with his own objectives.[44] Starting in April 1933, he had overseen the emergence of a model regime in the Bavarian camp of Dachau, near Munich, supervised by his subordinate Theodor Eicke. In May 1934, Himmler charged Eicke with taking over the remaining camps, transferring their inmates to a smaller number of larger facilities, and making Dachau the template for an SS-run camp system to be established throughout Germany. In July, Eicke's power was formalized and extended by Himmler with his appointment as Inspector of Concentration Camps and Chief of SS Guard Units. Through 1934 Eicke managed to extend SS control to almost all existing camps, thus withdrawing them from any oversight by civil authorities. Finally, following the exclusion of the rival SA in June 1934 and a definitive showdown with his political competitors in the Reich interior and judicial administrations in the summer of 1935, Himmler won Hitler's agreement that an enlarged system of concentration camps, run by the SS, would be a permanent and integral component of the Nazi political system.

Such, in outline, was how the SS-police state came into existence and took control of the camps. In three years Himmler had made himself the master of a power structure of unprecedented scale and autonomy: a linked system of police and extra-judicial custody that was also integrated with his own SS organization and increasingly dominated by Himmler's personal vision for the new Germany. The merger of the SS and the police blurred the distinction between political and criminal jurisdiction. Although a regular judicial process of criminal prosecutions, trials, and sentences to judicial and police prisons did continue to function in the Third Reich, the Gestapo now had ultimate and unlimited executive authority to seize anyone and to hold detainees in custody without trial for an indefinite term.[45] Himmler's objective in the coming years was to exploit these powers to the maximum in service of his vision for a new Germany. Under his authority, the Gestapo used its powers both as a substitute for court proceedings and to rearrest convicts released after serving a prison term, while extending its grasp to ever larger categories of people deemed to be undesirable or unfit on political, moral, or racial grounds. The concentration camps, as we shall see, were the holding pens for the vast majority of these victims.

The SS take-over of the camps for male *Schutzhäftlinge* in 1934–35 had involved an ongoing rationalization of these disparate and often quite small facilities. Eicke's Inspectorate shifted political prisoners into a smaller number of bigger camps, to which all new detainees were also assigned, and the Dachau model of organization and discipline was implemented in all of the SS-run camps. Women *Schutzhäftlinge* fared very differently from men in this period, as we shall see in the next section. The men's Dachau regime was based on a set of regulations prescribing the systematic humiliation of inmates, minimal provision for their physical needs, heavy labor, and ruthless standards of discipline and punishment. These regulations were designed to break the resistance of prisoners detained mainly for reasons of political or religious conviction, and to establish an intimidating public image of the camps. Outsiders were to understand them as daunting but necessary places that were intended to "re-educate" obdurate opponents of the Nazi regime by means of a strenuous but fair regimen of military-style discipline and intensive labor, after which they would return to take their place in the community. Insiders knew that re-education was merely a euphemism for coerced submission, and that daily life in these circumstances was intolerably harsh, physically crushing, and spiritually demoralizing. Inmates stood at the mercy of young SS guards, usually 16- to 21-year-olds, and were subjected to every kind of chicanery. Although violent assaults by guards and unnatural deaths were theoretically frowned on and might be referred to disciplinary courts or even to outside prosecutors,[46] the Inspectorate insisted that the camps stood under its authority alone and that they were exempt from outside jurisdiction. Sanctioned physical mistreatment could range from unofficial beatings to severe corporal punishment, from curtailment of already minimal rations to solitary confinement in an isolation cell, from long hours of heavy labor to punitively extended and exhausting roll calls. Contact with the outside world through letters and packages was permitted but rigidly policed. Visits were exceptional, and release was dependent on a fickle and obscure process of administrative review, with reinternment always a prospect.

The camps had, in fact, a dual face between 1936 and 1939. Their inmates, unlike detainees during the Nazi seizure of power, were less likely to be tortured to death or summarily killed by their captors, and by contrast with the wartime period, the camps had not yet become "sites of mass murder."[47] Conditions remained utterly inhumane, but—for what this relative statistic is worth—prisoner death rates were at their lowest in this period. Because the SS placed some of the lower levels of camp organization—barracks supervision, meal distribution, labor allocation, camp maintenance, and so on—in the hands of an inmate hierarchy (the so-called *Funktionshäftlinge* or prisoner functionaries), a degree of self-administration emerged in the oldest established camps that enabled systems of clandestine mutual support to be sustained among the politically committed inmates, notably the Communists. Yet this system also had a more sinister side. The SS preferred to delegate authority to the criminal population, who ran their own regimes of favoritism, intimidation, and outright terror and earned a vicious reputation among their fellow prisoners. For *Schutzhäftlinge* who had previously served terms in judicial prisons or one of the other institutions run by the police or civil authorities, transfer to the SS camps was likely to mean a precipitate decline in conditions. Discipline, diet, living conditions, hours and types of work—all were now designed to sustain inmates' lives at a minimum, to cut them off from the outside world, and to confront them ultimately with a structure of inescapable domination.[48]

Dachau's system was the grim harbinger of the new generation of SS camps that was established in the wake of Hitler's endorsement of a permanent SS concentration camp system in June 1935. In 1936, a new construction program of purpose-built barracks camps was initiated (built by prisoners, of course), and the economic exploitation of prison labor became integral to the chronically under-financed system. With the exception of Dachau, which underwent a massive expansion, all of the existing smaller camp sites and prisons were closed or turned over to other police or judicial authorities for different uses. Their male prisoners were transferred to a network of new and larger SS camps that opened in relentless succession: Sachsenhausen (1936), Buchenwald (1937), Flossenbürg (1938), and Mauthausen (1938). In 1939 Ravensbrück was established for the expanding number of women detainees, to whom undiluted standards of SS treatment were now applied for the first time.[49]

The new influx of inmates was supplied by the strategic evolution of Nazi plans for the remaking of the *Volksgemeinschaft*. This project underwent great advances, if that is the right word, between 1936 and 1939. The vast majority of *Schutzhäftlinge* in 1933–34 had been the political opponents of Nazism on the left, mostly Communists, who were detained in order to break both the organized power of the working-class movement and the will of individuals to resist. As we have seen, the Nazis cloaked this repressive political strategy in the mantle of "protecting" the German people from its alleged enemies by removing them from the community until they were deemed fit for reintegration. Arguably, the regime had in fact successfully broken the back of the political opposition by 1935 with its policies of violence, terror, and imprisonment, and in principle this might have rendered the camps redundant. But it was precisely at this juncture that Himmler secured Hitler's approval for their retention and expansion. The next step in Himmler's unfolding policy was to proceed from political "protection" to social and racial "prevention"—to the pre-emptive designation of new categories of enemies on the grounds of their unfitness for membership in the Nazi community.

Through policies derived from social and biological theories that were pursued in defiance of elementary human rights, the Nazi regime aimed to preserve and enhance the Germanic *völkisch* community by the wholesale elimination of all harmful elements. "Harmful" meant anyone whose hereditary racial, moral, social, mental, or physical characteristics deviated from evolving Nazi definitions of the normal and desirable. "Elimination" might signify anything from restrictions on the right to marry or reproduce, to coercive sterilization, forcible confinement and labor in the name of "re-education," and ultimately physical annihilation. Large-scale confinement, decided and administered by the police with minimal judicial involvement and with or without the prospect of release, was the crucial mechanism in this megalomaniac invention of the German racial future. The concentration camps became the repository for the tens of thousands of men, women, and children extruded from German society by this machinery of eugenic selection.

The purging of the German social order after 1933 marched forward through three related strategies: designating those to be eliminated; creating the legal—or, more appropriately, executive—mechanisms for their arrest and detention; and establishing the conditions of their custody. These intricate processes need not be told in detail here.[50] The main point is that by 1937–38 the concentration camps were starting to fill up with newly defined groups of non-political inmates, detained by the police and held under newly created powers of "preventive detention" (*Vorbeugungshaft*).[51] These groups included "habitual" and "hereditary" criminals, and the so-called asocials (*Asoziale*), a proliferating category that encompassed (to use a list drawn up by the Bavarian political police in August 1936) "beggars, vagabonds, gypsies, vagrants, work-shy individuals, idlers, prostitutes, grumblers, habitual drunkards, hooligans, traffic offenders, and so-called psychopaths and mental cases."[52] To this largely traditional list of the socially deviant—now defined as congenitally damaged—were added newly persecuted groups such as Jehovah's Witnesses. In the case of male homosexuals, an old history of victimization was now intensified as a new policy of outright repression.[53]

The terms of arrest and detention for these groups were tightened at every turn, so that by 1938 prisoners could be held in custody for an unlimited period on a variety of political, criminal, and "social" grounds. In theory, they were subject to regular conduct reports and administrative reviews; in practice, procedures were more capricious than reliable. Still, before 1938–39 the majority of prisoners could expect to be released at some point, though the process was sporadic and unpredictable. Most spectacularly, 2,300 prisoners (none of them Jewish) were released from Buchenwald in honor of Hitler's birthday in April 1939. Thereafter, only a trickle of individuals emerged from the camps as the system of indeterminate detention expanded.[54] According to one estimate, by 1943 some 110,000 Germans had been committed to concentration camps under the various available procedures, two-thirds of them as "asocials"; the number of women in this category is estimated at 6,000 to 8,000 (1933–39).[55] The whole process can be understood as an immense net of regulation extended over Germany's criminal and "deviant" populations and their transfer, whether from the streets or from penal and welfare institutions, to a few preferential sites of long-term confinement, at the head of which stood the concentration camps. Though the camps never achieved a full monopoly of incarceration, they dictated the national standard of institutional misery.

The timing of these measures was far from arbitrary, for it was closely tied to the changing state of the German economy and to the Nazi conception of work. By 1937, the economy had emerged from depression and was revealing sectoral shortages of labor. Control of labor allocation and workplace discipline assumed increasing prominence in economic and social policy, as the pace of rearmament intensified.[56] The Nazis also made it an ideological priority, integral to their conception of the new Germany, to cultivate a work ethic through the mobilization of labor. Not by coincidence, the annual rally of the NSDAP (Nationalsozialistische Deutsche Arbeiterpartei, or National Socialist German Workers' Party) at Nuremberg in 1937 was designated the "Parteitag der Arbeit" (Party Rally of Labor). In the same year, the official title of the concentration camps became "state reformatories and labor camps," and the slogan "Arbeit macht frei" (Work means freedom) was first attached to the main gate of the Dachau concentration camp during its 1937–38 reconstruction.[57] These views were affiliated to a deep-rooted cultural belief in work as a moral virtue and, more specifically, to nineteenth-century *völkisch* ideas of "national work" (*nationale Arbeit*) as necessary to the preservation and defense of the German national community.[58] Those whose lives fell short—criminals, the "work-shy," people physically or psychologically incapable of work—now felt the full brunt of this concept in its perverse reworking by Himmler. The antinomies of work as ennobling, reformative, punitive—and ultimately exterminatory—were to be pursued to their bitterest end in the Third Reich.

The pre-war camp construction plans envisaged a system capable of holding 30,000 to 50,000 inmates, of whom some 25,000 were in custody by the outbreak of the war in September 1939. This figure included the 2,000 women now concentrated in Ravensbrück.[59] These camps were linked to SS-run industrial installations such as quarries and brickworks, and they eventually spun off hundreds of satellite camps (*Aussenlager*) to provide prison labor for all kinds of public and private economic enterprises.[60] Once the war began, Himmler suspended all reviews of prisoners' cases and ordered that no inmates were to be released except into military punishment battalions. Occasional releases did continue to take place, but they were massively outnumbered by new admissions; for most inmates, death was likely to be the only way out.[61] Foreign inmates began to overwhelm the number of Germans (*Reichsdeutsche*), as the Nazi regime imported and mobilized prisoner labor for its increasingly demanding war effort.[62]

Supplying labor for German industry and armament became the overriding purpose of the camps, now largely under the supervision of the newly established SS Central Economic Administration Office (Wirtschafts-Verwaltungshauptamt, WHVA).[63] A dense and intricate network of WHVA camps snaked out across Germany and Europe, with the core concentration camps linked in a chain of suffering to thousands of smaller labor camps and sub-camps of every kind. The number of prisoners held in these camps, and the number who perished in them, reached staggering proportions—literally uncountable, since we do not know the figures for each of these many camp-sites.

By the end of the war, on top of those millions of people who had been systematically annihilated in the mass actions of shooting and gassing, the Nazi concentration camps had claimed the lives of two million more citizens of every European nationality, most of whom perished in desperate conditions of brutality and suffering.[64] Yet the camps never entirely forfeited their ostensible identity as sites of "reformation" through labor, at least for non-Jewish German prisoners (less than 10 percent of the inmate population at the war's end). Cynical though that appellation was, it was not always meaningless in its implications. At Himmler's insistence, "reformable" German inmates received some protection from the outrageous death rates that awaited foreign and Jewish prisoners, and this secured them a privileged status in the camp as far as food, discipline, and other life chances were concerned.[65] This established the divisive camp hierarchies that figure so prominently in the memoirs of camp life after 1939, but which were only embryonic and indeed barely yet visible among the women of Moringen.

Moringen

To fully understand the place of Moringen in this complex history of mass incarceration and the character of Gabriele Herz's imprisonment there in 1936–37, we need, perhaps surprisingly, to go back not just to 1933, but to 1818, or even to 1738, when an orphanage was established in the village. That modest foundation inaugurated a history of institutional confinement in Moringen that has persisted virtually unbroken for more than 250 years up to and including the present day.[66] This is a history that deserves closer attention, for it contains the seeds both of Gabriele Herz's experience in 1936–37, and, arguably, of what she might have faced if she had not finally managed to leave Germany in 1937.

The Moringen orphanage buildings were acquired by the state of Hanover in 1818 for use as a *Straf- und Korrektionsanstalt*, that is, a penal and correctional institution. By 1838, Moringen was being described as a police workhouse (*Polizeiliches Werkhaus*) for "depraved and dangerous" persons of both sexes, and had a mixed character as both prison and workhouse. Although the administration and status of the buildings underwent various changes in the course of Hanover's legal and political history (notably as a result of its incorporation in Prussia in 1867), Moringen remained essentially a workhouse for almost the next hundred years.[67]

Most of Moringen's nineteenth-century inmates were consigned there not as paupers or convicts, but under court or police orders that permitted the detention of certain destitute petty offenders, who eked out a living in the informal economy beyond the workplace as tramps, prostitutes, or beggars. Their detention in Moringen was intended to "correct" their negligent and work-shy habits by subjecting them to the discipline of a harsh regime of daily life and work: hence their designation as *Korrigenden*, which can be translated as "correctional inmates." These inmates had committed victimless crimes— or rather, the "victim" of their offenses was taken to be a society injured by their rejection of its norms. Through detention in the workhouse, they were removed from society, and society was also protected from them, until they were deemed ready to rejoin it on the authorities' own terms. At the same time, the workhouse acted as a grim deterrent to others outside its walls. In this way, Moringen served the linkage drawn between the control of vagrancy, and poor relief, work, and moral "improvement" that had underwritten state policies on pauperism in Germany and Europe since the seventeenth century.[68]

In the imperial period (1871–1919) Moringen was used exclusively for correctional inmates committed under specific provisions of the penal code, and was typical of such workhouses throughout Prussia and Germany. By 1890, its inmate capacity reached eight hundred, though the actual number in detention fluctuated according to the state of the economy and the opportunities for employment. The vast majority of men—80 to 90 percent—were committed as vagrants or beggars, and many of them had been repeatedly detained. When a women's wing was opened in 1908, the female correctional inmates (*Korrigendinnen*) were typically described as prostitutes. For all inmates, daily life was strictly regulated and had much of the discipline of a prison. The workhouse overseers, as in Germany's prisons, were usually ex-soldiers and NCOs; their relations with inmates were harshly authoritarian, if not outright punitive. Work, the ostensible mechanism of moral improvement, was compulsory. Remunerated at a nominal rate, it included activities such as cigar-making, straw-plaiting, weaving mats and chair seats, and tailoring military uniforms, as well as agricultural labor for local farmers. Although working hours may not have been much longer than in the free market and living conditions were marginally less punitive than those in prisons and jails, terms in the workhouse were said to be even more feared and disliked than prison sentences, owing to their length and the uncertainty of discharge.

In both Hanoverian and Prussian law, the right to commit vagrants and suchlike to detention in institutions like Moringen had been variously apportioned between the courts and the police since the end of the eighteenth century. Although only the courts could sentence offenders to terms in jail or penitentiary, the police enjoyed certain powers to consign petty offenders to the workhouse for a period of corrective *Nachhaft*, a subsequent or probationary term of up to two years' workhouse detention that could be attached to a shorter prison term. This police power was incorporated in the imperial penal code that was adopted in unified Germany in 1871. At their discretion the police could commit not only the types of offenders already mentioned, but also anyone who "misused" their relief payments (for example, on alcohol or gambling) or who refused to take up the work they were offered, as well as women who broke the police regulations on licensed prostitution.[69]

The Prussian workhouse system, in other words, established a narrow normative concept of work, drew punitive boundaries around entitlement to poor relief, and embodied a highly authoritarian construction of moral character and the social good. These principles were by no means peculiar to Prussia or Germany in the nineteenth century, but ruled social policy to a greater or lesser extent throughout Western Europe. Moreover, the relationship between these older practices of "correction" and the modern concept of "welfare" was the subject of complex negotiation in the course of European mass urbanization and industrialization. In every society, elements of authoritarianism combined in some form with more democratic standards of social policy making. They also merged with new scientific principles of social welfare and public health that themselves overlapped with penal policy and potentially presented new openings to coercion.[70]

In late nineteenth-century Germany, this mix arguably included an unusually close relationship between concepts of medical health and social welfare, as well as legal provisions for workhouse detention that reflected an older conception of "police" as the broad maintenance of social order. And just as earlier ages had attempted to distinguish between "sturdy beggars" and vagrants on the one hand and those in genuine need on the other, or between the "deserving" and the "undeserving" poor, so one of the watchwords of social and penal policy in the later nineteenth century was the distinction between the "corrigible" and the "incorrigible." Whereas the corrigible might be restored to society through strict corrective discipline, some argued that the incorrigible—whether habitual criminals or merely social misfits and incompetents—were best segregated and held in permanent confinement, where they could do no harm. While Germany was by no means the only country to debate social and penal policy in these terms, the widespread circulation of these ideas in German penal, criminological, and social-welfare circles before 1933 carried some dangerous principles into the intensified detention policies of the Third Reich.[71]

The social and public order policies of the democratic Weimar Republic (1919–33) added further elements to this German mix, though whether this period should be understood as part of a continuum or instead as an interregnum remains a matter of debate.[72] At any rate, by the 1920s, the number of inmates in Moringen and Germany's other workhouses had fallen dramatically. Most male inmates had been conscripted or amnestied during the war, and afterwards the workhouses remained thinly populated for a number of reasons. The immediate post-war employment boom was followed by changes in the law and in welfare policy in the new republic that were aimed at making it less punitive, but also by the state's post-war fiscal problems, which had mounted into a full-scale crisis by 1930 and bedeviled further attempts at reform. In Moringen, the number of correctional inmates barely rose above a hundred in the 1920s, though some of the empty places were filled by new welfare cases, including young people in need of foster care, adults who failed to support their dependents (*säumige Fürsorgepflichtige*), and others in receipt of poor relief. Work remained the primary activity, but sources of employment were limited because low-wage workhouse labor was seen as unfair competition with the local free labor market. The institutional rule book was relaxed somewhat in 1926, and began to include more provisions for leisure and educational activities, a less repressive daily regime, an improved diet, and so on, as well as recommendations that overseers should adopt a more humane and respectful attitude toward their charges.

Another sign that a new dispensation was struggling to emerge was the appointment in 1930 of a new workhouse director, Hugo Krack, whose background lay in pedagogy rather than the penal system or the military. Born in 1888, Krack had trained as a teacher and worked as an educational administrator until his posting to Moringen.[73] Until 1933, he belonged to the liberal

Democratic Party (Deutsche Demokratische Partei, DDP); however, in May 1933 he joined the NSDAP and in the following autumn the SA. By 1939 he had also signed up for the usual Nazi mass-membership organizations, including the civil servants' association (Reichsbund der Deutschen Beamten) and the Air Raid Precaution League (Reichsluftschutzbund), among others.[74] Krack remained director of the Moringen workhouse until 1954, though he was on leave to the military and the reserves during the war years. In this position he became a significant figure in Moringen's history as a women's concentration camp, as we will see.

Krack's appointment in 1930 may have represented a new commitment on the part of the provincial administration to social welfare and public assistance rather than correctional detention and workhouse relief, but this distinction was by no means absolute. While some groups such as prostitutes and needy young people were no longer likely to be consigned to the workhouse after 1918, new ideas for the extension of institutional controls to other groups were also in circulation.[75] The ambiguities of Weimar social policy were signaled most clearly by the growing public and professional discussion of policies for "compulsory care" (*Zwangsfürsorge*) for those physically or mentally in need of public assistance, as well as for the "preventive detention" (*Bewahrung* or *Verwahrung*) of potential offenders.[76] Both concepts foresaw the long-term or even permanent detention of non-offenders in custodial institutions, and would have extended the reach of the authorities over larger categories of potential inmates. These plans may have been intended to shift the ground of the older disciplinary conception of workhouse and correction toward a progressive reformist model. But these proposals also conveyed an unmistakably disciplinary message. They represented a new and potentially repressive model of social regulation that further blurred the boundaries between social and penal policy. Still, in the 1920s reform on a national scale remained elusive, and although workhouses were widely seen as obsolete, they limped along in the absence of any consensus about an alternative.

As the Nazis began their political take-over in Germany in the early spring of 1933, the situation of the Moringen workhouse was perilous. Germany was in the grip of economic depression: the fiscal crisis had left state and municipal administrations struggling to cut expenditures to the bone and police forces unable to pursue petty offenders and vagrants, their numbers now swollen by the hordes of unemployed. Paradoxically, in this period of massive social disruption and poverty, Prussia's workhouses held hardly more than 1,000 inmates between them in 1932. Moringen's capacious buildings sheltered about 150 inmates of all kinds, male and female, young and old, correctional and voluntary.[77] But now, perversely and dramatically, the Nazi seizure of power produced a rapid and unexpected turnaround in this situation of decline and depopulation. The empty halls of Moringen and other workhouses found the first of a series of new deployments, as the political priorities of the German government underwent their massive shift of emphasis.

The new factor was the urgent need for space to house the thousands of political prisoners now falling into the hands of the triumphant Nazis. Across Germany, workhouses seemed to offer a convenient solution to the problem, and Moringen was no exception. The Hanover provincial administration quickly seized the opportunity to exploit their costly and under-used resources in Moringen, and by the end of March had negotiated to make some of its buildings available to their colleagues in the provincial police to house up to three hundred male *Schutzhäftlinge*. The remaining workhouse inmates were segregated in a few rooms, leaving secure sections of the buildings for the new political detainees, most of them Communists and Social Democrats. The first consignment arrived at the beginning of April, and the numbers quickly grew to fill the agreed-upon capacity. Through the spring and summer of 1933, turnover was rapid: some inmates were released (many, for example, in an amnesty issued on 1 May), but more were newly arrested, while others were transferred to larger labor camps. The maximum held in Moringen at any one time was 394, shortly before the men's camp was closed in October. To begin with, the camp was supervised and guarded by armed police with SA and SS auxiliaries, but Krack remained in overall administrative charge of the work-house site. The camp regulations were a combination of workhouse and prison rules. Among other provisions, letters and parcels of food, underwear, and other necessities were permitted. While penalties for infringement of the rules excluded corporal punishment, the armed guards were authorized to shoot attempted escapees on sight.[78]

The status of the detention camp in Moringen remained uncertain. Was it to be a temporary or permanent facility? Prussian and Reich authorities were trying to juggle the need for immediate detention facilities for inmates under temporary investigation against the prospect that some of them would have to be detained for a longer period, though for how long was unclear at this point. The costs of detention, shared by the police and provincial administration, were a critical factor, given that Germany's economic situation did not improve overnight and state budgets were still massively squeezed. Throughout this process, Krack's priority was to keep his workhouse open by emphasizing how many additional inmates it could accommodate, each of whom represented a potential net contribution to the provincial budget and a guarantee of the workhouse's future and his own.

Krack's motives seem mixed—perhaps a combination of bureaucratic con-scientiousness and professional self-interest that made it difficult to keep more principled considerations in view.[79] In 1933, the use of the workhouse for "pro-tective detention" (*Schutzhaft*) might have seemed to him more like a reversion to its older usage or an implementation of the newer concept of "preventive detention" (*Bewahrung* or *Verwahrung*) than a first step toward something much more barbaric. At any rate, Krack was initially inclined to treat the *Schutzhäftlinge* as just another group of correctional inmates, even imagining they ought to be paid for their labor. But a hunger strike mounted in June, which was broken only by shutting off water supplies and eventually force-feeding the inmates, could be seen as the beginning of his perhaps unwilling descent into an agency of political repression, since he took an active, if ambivalent, role in suppressing this act of defiance. In July, conditions in the camp took a decisive turn for the worse as SS commanders and guards took over direct control. They not only tightened camp discipline but began to subject detainees for the first time to repeated brutalities, including savage beatings.[80] Krack was still nominally in charge, but he increasingly distanced himself from the SS regime, had poor relations with the SS commanders, and was troubled by the complexities of running an institution that served so many different purposes.[81]

These new uses now included the detention of women, for in June the first three women *Schutzhäftlinge* arrived in Moringen. Two of them—the Communists Marie Peix, wife of a local Communist leader who had gone underground, and Hannah Vogt, a 23-year-old student activist at the University of Göttingen—had been picked up in the first arrest wave in March and held in a local jail.[82] By August, twenty-six women were in detention in Moringen.[83] In these summer months, before Moringen became exclusively a women's camp, the women political detainees came under the same SS command as their male comrades and suffered similar humiliations and punishments, though apparently not violent physical abuse. Hannah Vogt has described the collective punishment imposed on all detainees in revenge for an act of political protest in Berlin (opponents destroyed an oak tree that had been planted in honor of President Hindenburg on the Nazis' first "Day of Labor" on 1 May), as well as the three days she suffered in the punishment cell for refusing to give the SS commander the Hitler salute.[84]

At first the women were quartered in the infirmary, but soon the workhouse buildings were reorganized to make additional segregated space available, and Krack began pushing for the assignment of more women detainees to his newly enlarged women's wing or *Frauenhaus*.[85] Prompted or not by Krack's efforts to play up his facilities and by the financial advantages of the situation, discussions between the provincial authorities and the Prussian Interior Ministry over the next few months resulted in the decision to reserve Moringen exclusively for women *Schutzhäftlinge*.[86] The male inmates were gradually transferred over the summer and autumn (the last group left for Oranienburg at the end of November 1933)[87] as additional women detainees were admitted. In October, Moringen entered its four-and-a-half year life as a women's concentration camp, with facilities for up to 400 inmates. The SS guards were gone. In their place, local members of the Nazi women's association (the NS Frauenschaft) were recruited as overseers of the arriving women detainees, under the supervision of the erstwhile matron of the women's workhouse. Neither Krack nor the overseers were uniformed.[88]

The administrative status of the Moringen women's camp, formalized in the spring of 1934, was somewhat anomalous.[89] The camp was in effect leased by the Prussian Gestapo from the Hanover provincial administration and nominally stood under the oversight of Himmler in his capacity as chief of all Länder political police forces. However, until he visited the camp in May 1937 (after Herz's release), Himmler does not appear to have directly intervened in its administration. Instead, with Krack as director, it remained under the supervision of the civilian provincial authorities, who were responsible for the relatively humane conditions that prevailed in the camp. In Herz's memoir, Krack appears as "cool, correct, and businesslike," neither particularly harsh nor particularly lenient. Still, formally speaking, he was running a political detention camp on behalf of the SS, and he had the authority to punish any infringement of the camp's regulations. On occasion he could be strict in maintaining discipline and imposing punishments. Herz reports the indefinite suspension of mail privileges as one extremely harsh collective penalty, as well as a particularly egregious case of solitary confinement for a half-witted old woman who had resisted having her locker searched.[90] She records another episode in which the male workhouse guards brutally beat up two workhouse inmates who attempted to escape.[91] An event that stuck in the mind of several inmates was the failure of the workhouse doctor to give a pregnant girl proper treatment, with the result that her baby was born prematurely and died.[92] The part played by Krack in these last cases is unclear.

Other inmate memoirs and surviving documentation that includes a number of grateful letters from released inmates convey a more benign image.[93] Krack seems to have gone out of his way to help some of the detainees, even maintaining contact after their release, at least in the early years. A Jewish physician, whose case was taken up by the British Friends Committee for Refugees and Aliens in 1935, reported that Krack had personally taken her papers to the Gestapo in Berlin and had finally secured her promised release. For this woman, Krack was no Nazi, and she asked that the Friends (Quakers) "should neither mention the name of the camp direktor [sic] nor praise him. Because if the Nazis would know about his kindness, they would dismiss him at once. The loss of his position would be very bad for his family as well as for all the women in the camp."[94] In another case reported by the Friends, who were active on behalf of concentration camp prisoners throughout Germany, Krack chose to employ a released detainee as governess to his children, then living in Göttingen, "although he knows that she is a keen political opponent."[95]

The personal and political principles that motivated Krack's behavior are not easy to discern at this distance. Social status seems to have played some part, since he did not extend the same sympathy to the Jehovah's Witnesses, his social inferiors. Many of the middle-class political detainees seem to have impressed him as his social equals, unlike the usual run of workhouse inmates and girls in "moral danger" that he was accustomed to. A more powerful motivation was his professional commitment to rehabilitating his charges, whether political detainees or workhouse inmates, so that they would be ready for reintegration in society. This ruled out the unshakably committed Witnesses and presumably complicated his attitude toward the Jewish women, but it helps to account for his treatment of the political activists. He genuinely hoped that these women could indeed be "re-educated" by the radio broadcasts of political speeches and the daily readings of the Nazi press, though Herz's account indicates that few women took this program seriously.[96] At any rate, through his quarterly conduct reports to the Gestapo, Krack seems to have actively worked for the women to be released.[97]

Krack's record vis-à-vis the prostitutes, "asocial" women, and workhouse women is more mixed. Most of the prostitutes and so-called asocials did not have the status of *Schutzhäftlinge*: they were being held in "preventive police custody" (*Vorbeugungshaft*) and had been admitted to Moringen by arrangement with the criminal police in a number of states.[98] In Krack's view, these women belonged in the workhouse, not in a concentration camp, and he apparently helped to prevent these categories of inmates from being sent to Lichtenburg when the *Schutzhäftlinge* and so-called career criminals were transferred there in 1937–38. In doing so, he saved them from the deteriorating conditions of Lichtenburg and then Ravensbrück, and he seems to have hoped that his workhouse could become the central custodial institution for such women. But in the perilously changing context of welfare practice after 1933, he had to bow, even for these women, to the new Nazi priorities, which included unprecedentedly coercive eugenic and preventive measures. Perhaps to him the new policies of compulsory sterilization and potentially unlimited detention seemed no more than the latest advances in welfare practice. These cases involved the type of morally "unfit" women who had always come into his hands for professional rehabilitation, and it was under Krack's authority—with his approval and possibly at his prompting—that some of them underwent forcible sterilization after 1933.[99]

On the one hand, then, Krack was allowed to run the camp and his workhouse as something like a custodial rehabilitation unit, and he may have protected at least some inmates from the kind of treatment they might have suffered if a more convinced National Socialist had been named director. On the other hand, he does not appear to have grasped the extent to which Nazi policies were remaking the meaning and purpose of custody and rehabilitation, not only in his own workhouse but in the institutions beyond its walls that became the ultimate destination for some of his temporary charges.[100]

The number of women detainees fluctuated during the first two years, from 128 as the women's camp was established to 141 in mid-November 1933 and back down to 75 in January 1934 following a Christmas amnesty.[101] The arrivals in 1933–34 included newly detained women as well as transfers from jails and detention centers in northern and central Germany, notably a large group after the Brauweiler workhouse camp was terminated in March. In March 1935 came the first returning emigrants, the category that would include Gabriele Herz. In January 1936, the south German states started to transfer their women detainees to Moringen, beginning with a group of Bavarian and

Swabian Communists. These women were installed together in the "Bayern-saal," or Bavaria Hall, where they formed a particularly close-knit collective. Anyone who had been transferred from a jail or other custodial institution was likely to be in terrible physical condition, after months or even years of debilitating confinement and ill-treatment. As Herz notes of the group that arrived in December 1936, many could barely walk, while two others, hardly more than girls, arrived in a state of utter mental collapse after their experiences of interrogation and imprisonment.[102]

Given the continuing rate of turnover, the number of Moringen's inmates remained far below capacity until early 1937. It was only then that the numbers began to shoot up, fueled by the intensified repression of Jehovah's Witnesses and the round-up of so-called habitual criminals. Herz noted the increasing population in January,[103] and by November the number of detainees reached 446, exceeding the camp's official capacity.[104] In the meantime, however, Himmler had initiated a review of provisions for women detainees, following a visit he had made to Moringen in May. Protracted negotiations had ensued between the police and the provincial authorities about the future of the women's camp, and in October it was agreed that Moringen would be closed and its inmates transferred by stages to the old castle at Lichtenburg, the much larger and grimmer camp where they were to come under the direct control of the SS for the first time. The transports began in December, and by March 1938 Moringen had been emptied of its women prisoners and was once again exclusively a workhouse.

A total of 1,350 women detainees passed through Moringen between 1933 and 1938.[105] As we shall see, the departure of the final prisoner transport to Lichtenburg did not spell the end of Moringen's long history as a custodial institution, but by March 1938 Gabriele Herz's own term of detention was long past. She had left both Moringen and Germany behind her.

Women in Detention: Gabriele Herz's Prison World

As soon as Herz entered her cell in the "Alex" (the police jail on the Alexanderplatz in Berlin) to await transport to Moringen, she encountered a group of women typical of those longer-term companions who came to feature so prominently in her account of Moringen. These included two Jehovah's Witnesses (popularly known in Germany as "Ernste Bibelforscher," or "Bible Students," the term they themselves used until 1931), and a young Communist. "Fränze," as Herz noted, was not the first Communist she had known, given her friendship circle in pre-Nazi Berlin. The two Jehovah's Witnesses, on the other hand, were the first she had ever met. That women from these two groups were her earliest prison companions is not surprising, for in their different ways both groups were among the most prominent victims of the Nazi terror, and they formed the largest categories of Moringen inmates.

Of 676 Moringen detainees between 1933 and 1938 whose cases have been studied in detail, some 46 percent were Jehovah's Witnesses and 22 percent were members of the Communist Party (Kommunistische Partei Deutschlands, KPD), although during Herz's time in Moringen in 1936–37, these proportions were more equal. Herz's own group, the returning émigrés (the only group in which Jews were a majority), constituted no more than 6 percent of the total, and the other prisoner categories were approximately as follows: those imprisoned for derogatory remarks, 14 percent; prostitutes and violators of the Nuremberg Laws' ban on sexual relations between "Aryans" and "non-Aryans," about 4 percent each; "habitual criminals," 3 percent; members of the Social Democratic Party (Sozialdemokratische Partei Deutschlands, SPD), less than 2 percent.[106] These figures are based on rough categorizations drawn from surviving files, since Moringen women were not officially categorized or designated by the triangular identification marks in different colors that were used in the concentration camps.[107] Indeed, the *Schutzhäftlinge* did not even wear prison uniforms (unlike women consigned as criminals, who wore black prison-issue clothing).

As a group, all of the *Schutzhäftlinge* were segregated from the male and female workhouse inmates and from some of the criminal detainees, though these distinctions became blurred as some prostitutes were assigned to the detainees' accommodations. The women worked in separate day-rooms: the "Bavaria Hall" for the group of south German Communists, the small "Jews' Hall" for the handful of Jewish women, and the "Great Hall" for the rest of the inmates, including the Jehovah's Witnesses until their segregation in November 1936.[108] Despite regulations that attempted to keep the Jewish and non-Jewish women from visiting each other's day-rooms, the women seem to have circulated fairly freely among the different rooms. In any case, they all continued to meet during the twice-daily exercise periods in the courtyard, so communication among the different groups always remained possible. At night the women were crammed into increasingly overcrowded attic dormitories, freezing in the winter and boiling in the summer, where they slept in bunks on straw mattresses.

Herz has left us vivid portraits of the women in all inmate categories, but above all of the Jehovah's Witnesses and the Communists. As far as the character of women's resistance to Nazism is concerned, these two groups stood at different ends of the spectrum. Among the tens of thousands of Communists incarcerated between 1933 and 1945, women were only a small minority, about 10 percent, which matched their share in the membership of this overwhelmingly male party.[109] By contrast, proportionately more women were involved in the resistance of the Jehovah's Witnesses than in any other group.[110]

The experience of Jehovah's Witnesses under the Nazis was in some ways more complicated than that of the Communists, who suffered the earliest and most relentless repression after 1933. Severe and sustained repression of the Witnesses did not begin until 1935, when the sect was officially dissolved by order of the Interior Ministry and two of its leaders were arrested.[111] But this followed years of intermittent harassment that had started well before 1933. Since their emergence in the US in the 1870s, the Witnesses had attracted a certain following in Germany, profiting especially from the climate of spiritual turmoil that characterized the post-war years. By 1926, the sect numbered about 22,000 in Germany, compared with 3,000 to 4,000 in 1914: still a modest figure, but one that represented one-fourth of the Witnesses' worldwide membership. They were already subject to a low level of persecution in the 1920s. The Protestant churches pilloried them as a false religion, while nationalists and Nazis attacked them as an unpatriotic freemasonry and targeted them in anti-Semitic propaganda on account of their invocations of the Old Testament, the Jewish nation, and Zion and not least because of their ambiguous name. There was pressure to ban or limit the sect, and the police disrupted its public activities, such as mass meetings, leafleting, and energetic proselytization. As soon as the Nazis came to power, several Länder initiated more stringent measures against the Witnesses under the provisions of the Reichstag Fire Decree, but until 1935 the sect managed to exist in a shaky limbo between harassment and legality. The sect was torn between its German and US leaderships' defensive protestations of loyalty to the new regime and a swelling grass-roots belief that the Witnesses had been launched in the 1920s on a testing time of persecution that would soon culminate in Armageddon and the coming of the Kingdom of Jehovah.

The Nazi regime eventually cracked down hard on the Witnesses for ideological reasons. In origin they were a chiliastic sect—that alone was bound to set them at odds with the prophets of the secular Thousand Year Reich—and since the end of the 1920s, they had become more uncompromising and exclusive doctrinally. With their belief in total subordination to divine authority as revealed in the Bible, they were on an inevitable collision course with National Socialism's secular claims to total authority. The Witnesses interpreted any demands of the civil authorities that conflicted with their own principles—for example, that they give the Hitler salute or that their children join Nazi youth groups—as the work of Satan. To resist was to withstand the divine test, but to concede was to invite damnation. Although the Nazi authorities tried to associate the Witnesses with organized Communist subversion, the character of their resistance was often far more personal and local, though nonetheless adamant—refusals to vote, to use the Hitler greeting, to display flags, to join Nazi organizations, to take oaths. Once the regime formally dissolved the sect in April 1935, even such quiet recalcitrance attracted the vicious consequences experienced by political detainees, including loss of employment and pension, arrest, brutal interrogations, internment in camps and psychiatric institutions, and, most bitter of all, removal of children into foster care. The date for the intensification of repression was significant: 1935 was the year when military conscription was introduced, and Witnesses refused en bloc to serve. After this date, Jehovah's Witnesses constituted perhaps 10 percent of all concentration camp inmates of German nationality, a vastly disproportionate figure compared to their insignificant numbers in the population.[112]

Gabriele Herz's observations about the Jehovah's Witnesses give a lively sense of how these women's stubborn and ostentatious beliefs were both impressive and infuriating to fellow prisoners and warders alike.[113] The Witnesses were on average older than the other inmates; they came from modest, often rural backgrounds; and they were less educated or worldly. In many respects, these were model prisoners—indeed, they might have been model citizens, if not for their unshakable religious convictions. (Even Gabriele Herz described one of her Berlin cellmates, with telling ingenuousness, as "the personification of the best German characteristics."[114]) Not only had their religious activity caused their arrest in the first place, but it was the source of continuing trouble in the camp, where they insisted on proselytizing among the other inmates. This was provocative to fellow prisoners, who found the Witnesses' piety tedious and self-absorbed, and to the camp authorities, who did not know how to break their unflinching solidarity. When the Witnesses refused to work for the Winter Relief Campaign (Winterhilfe), a camp-wide task of sorting and mending old clothes for the annual national welfare drive, on the grounds that this supported a state whose existence they rejected, the workhouse director reacted by segregating them into a separate room. Intended as a punishment, the move backfired since it allowed the women yet more scope to pursue their scriptural studies without interruption.[115]

Striking in Herz's account are the Witnesses' perpetual invocations of appropriate verses from the Bible, which form an elegiac chorus of commentary on the political challenges of Nazi Germany and the insults and strains of prison life. But it was not only the Witnesses who seemed to Gabriele Herz to be insulated by ideological certainty. In their Berlin prison cell, the young Communist Fränze had offered Gabriele Herz her counter-Bible: a wall scratched with quotations from Marx, Engels, and other members of the Communist pantheon, including Lenin, Stalin, Rosa Luxemburg, and Maxim Gorky, embellished with their portraits.[116] In Herz's eyes the Moringen Communists were equally radiant with faith, "firmly convinced of the ultimate victory of the communist ideal ... Moscow is the sun around which they orbit and from which they receive their light."[117] Yet although she disagreed with their political beliefs, Herz warmed to the Communists in a way she never did to the Witnesses. The Witnesses struck her as "unrealistic ... with their air of rapture and their belief in the imminent end of the world." For the Communists, however, she had "the greatest respect for [their] strong and principled personalities, for their steadfastness and their moral integrity."[118]

The Communist Party and its individual members had been the primary target of Nazi repression after January 1933. Unprepared for the violence of the Nazi onslaught, the KPD cadres were dangerously exposed to arrest when they tried at first to organize open resistance to the Nazis, before being forced underground.[119] These men and women—parliamentary deputies, party and

union officials and activists—were the most likely to suffer from Gestapo brutality. Many of them had been sentenced by the courts to lengthy prison terms,
usually for treason, after which they were held in detention as *Schutzhäftlinge*
for months and years rather than weeks. The Moringen Communists—most
of them single women in their thirties[120]—included five women who had had
seats in the federal (Reich) or state (Land) parliaments, as well other party
officials and activists. Other women who were not themselves members of
the party had been arrested because they were married to prominent Communists. In many cases, a husband or other male family member was held in
Dachau or another camp, or had already been murdered by the Nazis.

Herz's close observation of the Communist women is the hallmark of
her memoir. Though she was candid about what she saw as their failings,
only a genuine and sympathetic interest in the women and their politics can
account for the attention she gave them and the care with which she sought
to reconstruct their political discussions. One explanation lies in Herz's own
left-leaning political attitudes. Another, more personal reason was the close
relationship she developed with Herta Kronau (Herta Kronheim),[121] one of
the two Jewish Communists assigned to the Jews' Hall, whom she described as
"one of the most intelligent and most cultured women in the camp."[122] Kronau
aroused her curiosity and eased her access to the other Communist women
living in the Great Hall and the Bavaria Hall, which enabled her—a member, as
she says, of the "bourgeoisie"—to listen in on their political conversations. The
Great Hall's eighty residents included members of every inmate category, but
when Herz arrived, the Bavaria Hall was inhabited exclusively by a group of
seventeen south German Communists whose shared political background and
years of imprisonment since 1933 gave them unusual cohesion. Herz was obviously profoundly impressed by these women and their political commitment.
She interpreted their unshakable sense of solidarity in spiritual rather than
political terms that are revealing of her own moral philosophy and her essentially non-political outlook: "They all speak the same unpretentious Bavarian dialect, but in their mouths this dialect is more than a merely superficial
manner of speaking; it is the expression of a common spiritual outlook, of an
ancient, indigenous, venerable tradition. A pure and unpolluted atmosphere
reigns here—mountain air from the inland peaks."[123]

The acknowledged leader of the "Bavarians" was Zenta Baimler, Herz's
thinly disguised pseudonym for Centa Herker-Beimler, the wife of the Bavarian Communist leader and Reichstag member Hans Beimler.[124] The Beimlers
had gone underground in March 1933 but were arrested within weeks of each
other in April. Hans was sent to Dachau, Centa to the prison at Stadelheim,
where a number of other Communist women were in detention. In May 1933,
Hans succeeded in escaping from Dachau into Switzerland—a daring flight
that made him an instant hero of the Communist resistance—and he even
managed to spirit their children out of Germany.[125] While Hans was running clandestine Communist opposition from his exile in Czechoslovakia

and France, Centa remained under close confinement in Stadelheim. She was among the first south German Communists transferred to Moringen in January 1936—the founding members, so to speak, of the Bavaria Hall.

Centa Herker-Beimler's status among the Communists was further enhanced when news reached the camp that Hans had gone to Spain to fight for the Republic as one of the first members of the International Brigades and even more when he fell in battle defending Madrid against Franco's rebels in December 1936.[126] Still, Herz's account does not show Centa as much of a participant in the political debates, even though she had been an activist herself before 1933. Her authority seems to have derived more from her husband than from her own political engagement. In any case, politics assumed more prominence in camp life with the arrival (dated by Herz as January 1937) of a new contingent of some twenty Communists, who were honored by their Moringen comrades as veterans of the Nazi prisons. They were followed by a number of women who had returned to Germany after living abroad for years, including in Spain and the Soviet Union. Their fresh perspectives animated political conversations, in which the lead was usually taken by one of the ex-members of parliament. These included the former Reichstag member Anna Löser,[127] a defender of Stalin and an optimist in her belief that German public opinion was shifting away from Hitler. Also reliably on the side of Stalin was former Bavarian Landtag member and tobacco worker Dora Doebel (Viktoria Hösl),[128] who argued valiantly to justify the Soviet leader's strategies against the criticisms and sense of betrayal voiced by some of her younger comrades.

In part, the memoir can be read almost as a contest between two groups of believers, with Gabriele Herz as audience and rapporteur. The counter-point to the Witnesses' biblical incantations were the declaratory statements of Communist belief, staged by Herz in an oddly formal way that evokes the stilted record of a parliamentary debate more than the flow of recollected conversation. But however awkward in style, these political discussions are of the utmost interest. No other record has conveyed the interactions among Communist women during this time in such detail: this alone would make Herz's Moringen memoir an unusually valuable document. According to one historian, Moringen gave the Communist women their first sustained experience of community and solidarity—in contrast with the outside world, where they had lived in constant fear of spies, double agents, and denunciations.[129] Perhaps for the same reason they may have felt freer to exchange ideas and express their political doubts openly. Herz's account of these intense conversations recalls the fact that not only were the Communists the first and most enduring victims of Nazi repression, but that the very foundations of their resistance—their political principles and their expectation that Russia would come to their rescue—were being put to a severe test.

The Communists monitored political events inside and outside the Soviet Union with close attention, often with misgivings and even dismay. They were especially alert to developments in Soviet social and family policy, which the

KPD had tended to treat as women's affairs. In the early 1930s, the KPD made women's rights in the workplace and maternal rights the centerpiece of its attempt to win more female voters, and the party led the political battle to legalize abortion.[130] Herz shows the women engaging in lively debates about Soviet policy shifts in these fields in the mid-1930s, shifts that the women (like subsequent historians) saw as reviving a more "traditional" notion of the family after the radical departures of the revolutionary period.[131] Outside of Russia, another topic of discussion was the civil war in Spain, where Germany and Italy were arming General Franco's Nationalist rebels and the Soviet Union was helping the Republican government forces. Like many contemporaries, the women viewed this war as a surrogate or rehearsal for the greater direct clash between fascism and communism that they believed was imminent.[132] At stake for the Communist women was not simply their political beliefs; or rather, to speak of "political beliefs" would be to miss how, as Herz observed, the Communists grasped the world almost exclusively through their ideology and their sense of the stage that Soviet Russia had reached on the road to socialism and universal human freedom. For them, Nazi Germany was the antithesis of everything that communism stood for, and Soviet Russia the only possible source of ultimate salvation for themselves and for humanity as a whole.

At the same time, the women's convictions were severely strained by the news of events in the Soviet Union that filtered in from the outside world. The period of Herz's imprisonment coincided with the great wave of Soviet show trials, in which leading figures in the Bolshevik Party and the military were being publicly vilified and shown confessing to monstrous crimes and conspiracies against the Soviet state.[133] Herz reports that the trials provoked "the greatest anxiety and fear" among some of the Communists, who were "bitterly disappointed [and] find the whole situation incomprehensible."[134] The testimony of women who had returned from the Soviet Union and brought back firsthand accounts of conditions could be especially demoralizing. Herz records one particularly furious dispute of this kind between the critics and supporters of Stalin, a dispute that turned into a painful argument about the achievements of the Russian Revolution and whether Stalin was defending or betraying them.[135] Given the hopes that the women placed in their rescue by the Soviet Union, these arguments were far from abstract and were no doubt inflected with personal optimism or despair about their own fate and that of their families.

Herz describes the loss of family connection as one of the heaviest burdens the women had to bear. Many had been forced to leave their children in the hands of relatives or, worse, the state. Some also had husbands who were incarcerated in the far more fearsome men's concentration camps, where they faced the possibility of torture, injury, and death. Herz paints a moving picture of the tremendous and imaginative efforts the women devoted to sustaining the men's spirits. Within the constraints of limited and censored correspondence, the women sent their husbands encouraging letters and pictures and procured some of the sad necessities that their physical maltreatment required—in one case a set of crutches, in another new dentures.[136] Occasionally, there came the cruel news that a husband had died (meaning that he had been killed) in Nazi custody.

For the Moringen women, everyday life was filled not with physical violence or immediate intimidation and danger but with monotony, deprivation, and deep depression.[137] They lived with inadequate food, space, warmth, and activities and with debilitating insecurity about their release dates, their future in the new Germany, and the fate of family members. The misery of separation from children and family took its toll. As much as the women's shared experience gave them a common bond, it could also be a source of demoralization: day after day it reminded each woman what she had lost. Still, caring at a distance for husbands and children was one way to restore some meaning to lives that, as Herz comments bitterly, had otherwise been evacuated of all value and significance.[138] Even the work the women performed was barely productive, as well as being tedious and often disagreeable. Sorting and mending clothes for the Nazis' Winter Relief Campaign was the main occupation during Herz's imprisonment, but she was scornful of the wastefully inefficient organization of this national volunteer welfare drive. In her view, bureaucratic shortcomings were squandering the goodwill attached to a popular project that "had begun as a great gesture, with genuine idealistic enthusiasm."[139] In the summer months some women would be assigned to labor in the local farmers' fields or in the workhouse garden, a more physically demanding job but one that they appreciated because it took them outdoors into the fresh air.[140]

Like other Nazi prisons and camps, Moringen had its formal list of regulations that set out prisoner entitlements as well as rules of behavior and penalties for their infraction.[141] Herz gives several examples of the warders' petty enforcement of the rules and their often self-important authoritarianism, which seems to have derived more from insecurity than despotism. Unlike in many of the other camps, however, Moringen's regulations were not generally flouted or subject to capricious interpretation by the authorities. Women could receive and send a stipulated number of letters (censored, of course), and they were allowed to accept small sums of money and packages of clothing and food sent by family and friends. Herz describes the flood of packages that poured into the camp at Christmas and the eagerly anticipated Christmas dinner of roast pork and red cabbage—a once-a-year contrast to the otherwise monotonous meals of pasty soup and bread. She also alludes to the hobbies that women busied themselves with in their spare time. Mostly, they did various kinds of sewing and embroidery; some drew pictures and made paper designs, or plaited straw into small items such as purses.[142] They exchanged these objects as gifts with friends both inside and outside the camp, or sold them to raise a few pennies. Through these occupations as in camp life in general, the women actively helped one another to endure their detention, and Herz's memoir, like other camp reminiscences, offers many examples of the mutual help and reassurance that the women offered one another.

It is not entirely implausible that Herz found a degree of satisfaction living among these women, despite the miserable conditions and the debilitating anxieties. Her daughter Elisabeth may exaggerate when she suggests that "Moringen was one of the happiest times [in Herz's life]. She could be on her own, be responsible for herself." But there is also more than enough evidence to support her explanation that her mother "could develop her relations with the inmates ... she was much beloved by them."[143] Similarly, when her son Arthur says that his mother "became a person in Moringen, she could be herself there,"[144] this surely underplays the onerous conditions she was forced to endure, and it certainly misses the despair and disgust Gabriele voiced at the indignities of her daily life. Yet his claim also catches a truth about the kind of woman she was: a woman unreconciled to her elevated status as the mistress of a big house in Berlin, a woman open to unexpected experiences and new relationships, a woman genuinely interested in her companions and alert to the nuances of their lives.

Herz seized on the heterogeneity of her camp companions as a chance "to expand my personal relationships and hence my knowledge of human nature."[145] The original German subtitle of the memoir, *Schicksale in früher Nazi-Zeit* (Destinies in the Early Nazi Period), shows that Herz was especially keen to portray the scattered individual lives that had been tossed together in Moringen. Emblematic of this tangling of destinies was the startling link between the Communist Fränze and Lisa Goldschmidt, two of her fellow prisoners in the "Alex" in Berlin. As Fränze told the story, Lisa, a Jewish physician, had been imprisoned for allegedly helping to print Communist leaflets; and Fränze's husband Gustav had once worked as a chauffeur for Lisa's father: "Strange, isn't it?" remarked Fränze. "The daughter of our former employer and me, here together in the Alex."[146]

In Moringen, Herz's Jewish fellow detainees were mostly her social equals, but she also shared her prison and camp days with women she would never normally have met, including prostitutes, a brothel-keeper, thieves, drunks, and tramps. With a humane and occasionally ironic touch, she took pains to record their stories of love, misadventure, and betrayal, surely exotic to her middle-class ears. Then there were the core groups of Communists and Jehovah's Witnesses, most of whom were working class and deeply committed—Herz might have said in thrall—to demanding ideologies. Precisely this social and intellectual diversity of her fellow prisoners was what appealed to her and inspired her unusual empathy and human warmth. In turn, many of the women opened up to her and came to depend on her qualities as a listener and a teacher. Her record of these encounters evokes the literary genre of social reportage on the habits and views of social inferiors, of which middle-class prison memoirs (for example, the suffragist memoirs from pre-1914 British prisons) form a recognizable sub-category. But Herz was not simply an outside observer. Her stories constantly attest to her gentle curiosity about her companions in misfortune and her generous sympathy for their condition. If Herta

Kronau mocked her for always "hunting" the camp for new women to meet and new stories to hear, the foil was her own camp nickname, "Mutter Herz" (Mother Heart), earned as she comforted the young Jewish girl Anni Reiner in a moment of distress.[147]

Herz's memoir repeatedly reveals not only the pleasure she took in her new companions and her ability to win their trust and intimacy, but also her willingness to put her own skills as a speaker and writer to practical use. In Moringen she got grudging permission from the director to give English lessons to two groups of fellow prisoners with whom she then shared her passion for English literature. As spokesperson for the group of Jewish women, it was Gabriele who asked for official permission to celebrate Hanukkah, who explained the festival's meaning to the non-Jewish inmates, and who led the service. More often, her own didactic inclinations took a back seat as she drew stories of life and loss from the women around her, or listened silently to those heated conversations in which the Communists thrashed out the political issues of the day. While she seems to have aimed at an even-handed and dispassionate record of the political debates, her own emotional stake is much more discernible in other parts of the memoir. Especially unmistakable is her open identification with the bond between mothers and their children, a theme that comes up again and again as the women tell their wrenching stories of parting and loss. A bawdy prostitute whom Herz briefly encounters in Hanover is redeemed the moment she starts to talk lovingly of her daughter.[148] The anguish suffered by the Communist and atheist Dora Doebel, whose son Herbert is being raised by Catholic nuns, runs as a tragic refrain throughout the memoir, culminating in the moment when Doebel learns that the boy is seriously ill with tuberculosis.[149] When Herz records her reserved and melancholy friend Herta Kronau speaking of her own mother, one is unsure whether the sentiments are Herta's or Gabriele's own: "Only one thing remains eternal, through chaos and confusion, in good times and in bad times: a mother's love."[150]

For Herz, human love of this kind evoked her sense of the divine: it spoke of an innate human need for a spiritual home, whether or not clothed in a formal religious creed. She was distressed by the Communists' adamant refusal, as she saw it, to acknowledge the spiritual in any form—even its part in the emotions of happiness and love, or what Herz called "the natural desires of the human heart." Dora Doebel's inability to let a "bridge of yearning" take her from her human emotions to something higher, to "that other shore," saddened Herz immensely.[151] Christmas Eve 1937 provided another striking and poignant demonstration of the gap between herself, a Jew, and the Communists who armored themselves against every infiltration of religious sentiment. "I was very much looking forward to the Christmas Eve celebration itself, with its ancient, beautiful Christmas carols, but, unfortunately, my hopes were dashed," she wrote. Not only were the women forced to listen to a radio speech by Goebbels, but afterwards the Communists "utterly refused not only any kind of religious ritual but also any religious feeling. It's simply not consistent with their Communist ideology." When one of the other inmates began to sing a carol, "no one joined in. On the contrary, an awkward silence prevailed ... I was watching the women around me closely. You could see the stubborn defiance in their faces, on their tightly pursed lips. And yet, and yet. I could feel that some of them would have liked to sing along, would have liked to relax for once and to give themselves over to spiritual exaltation, perhaps also to long-suppressed childhood memories. But apprehension about doing so in front of the others remained stronger than this urge. Anything but publicly renounce the principle of freethinking, which everyone is so proud of, and which now, like a tyrant, robs this one beautiful and rare moment of its true meaning."[152]

Emotions are also close to the surface when Herz and her informants conjure memories of their lives before the Nazis and before their imprisonment, memories bathed in an aura of idealized happiness that is rather simplistically contrasted with the obvious afflictions of the present. These may not be the most compelling moments in the memoir, but in their stylized way they convey a genuine and profound sense of loss. Herz's narratives always imply that personal happiness and political conviction make at best an unequal exchange, and one may surmise that these are her own views as much as her informants'. Her commentary on what the Nazis have taken from her—not only her family but her confidence in the integrity of German culture, her deep-rooted belief in the authority of reason, civilization, and intellect—also has a certain stylistic artlessness. The same shock and grief at the Nazis' betrayal of German culture can be found in many memoirs; however awkwardly, they express a heartfelt sense of anguish and disbelief that the reader is bound to honor. In Herz's case, the familiarity of these sentiments is balanced by her acutely sympathetic ear for the individual tragedies—for the quite ordinary lives thrown into chaos by absurd and outrageous Nazi policies that forbid "Aryan" girls to fall for Jewish men, or that seize on thoughtless jokes and drunken bravado and declare them to be political sabotage. And over all hangs the knowledge that some Germans have paid for their beliefs not only with their freedom but with their health and their lives. Among these are the women who enter Moringen already broken by years of incarceration and ill-treatment, the women whose husbands remain at risk in Dachau and other camps, the women whose husbands have already been murdered by the Nazis.

Surely this sense that other women she met had suffered far more than her helps explain Gabriele Herz's reported reluctance to publish an account of her detention.[153] The stages by which the memoir came into existence are not entirely possible to retrace. As with many such memoirs, it was the desire of a new generation that the story should not be forgotten that led to the rediscovery and translation of Gabriele's typescript. The German typescript was found among Emil Herz's effects after his death in 1971, Gabriele having died fourteen years earlier in 1957. But exactly when she began to record her memories, and how she did this, remains unclear. Although the final manuscript is presented in diary form, with datelines from Berlin and Moringen, this is misleading. Every memoir is to some extent artifice, and Gabriele Herz's literary strategy was to write as if she had been composing her account month by month as events took place, starting in Berlin before her detention in September 1936 and ending there the day before she left Germany for good at the end of March 1937. In fact, she did not begin writing until after her release, but her device creates a simple and serviceable narrative framework. Within it, readers are invited not only to accompany Gabriele on her own journey from Berlin to Moringen and to follow the camp's history for six months, but also to observe its daily life, meet individual prisoners, listen to their stories, and overhear the political debates that were such a constant and vigorous preoccupation of Moringen's Communists. Her excellent memory is well known to her family, who are confident that she would easily have been able to recall events and conversations (even if a stylistic analysis suggests that she rendered the latter into a limited range of verbal idioms). Somewhat more awkward are the passages in which Herz surveys events on the European political stage in 1936 and 1937, which cannot disguise either their didactic tone or their frankly retrospective angle of vision.[154] But even as acknowledged artifice, the memoir cannot reveal the circumstances of its own composition, and here the evidence is incomplete.

Some of the uncertainty stems from the fact that the memoir remained unpublished during Gabriele's lifetime (and for that matter, Emil's). Gabriele's surviving children recall her reluctance to endow her Moringen experiences with any significance once the full story of Nazi atrocities emerged at the end of the war. She dismissed her own ordeal as trivial compared to the enormity of what others had suffered. It seems unlikely (the final pages of the text notwithstanding) that Gabriele began writing it immediately after her release in March 1937, in the middle of the innumerable tasks of departure from Berlin. The composition process more probably began in some form while Gabriele, along with Emil and their son Arthur, were in Lugano, Switzerland, in the fall of 1938, awaiting the visas that would take them to Cuba at the beginning of 1939. It was probably finished in the first year or two after the family gained entry to the US in 1940 and settled in Rochester. Quite likely, Gabriele and Emil were working simultaneously on their two memoirs, hers of Moringen and his of his own family in Warburg. At some stage during this period, she typed out the text that has survived, though we do not know exactly when.

Equally difficult to determine is how the memoir was revised during the course of composition. Married to a highly experienced professional editor, Gabriele appears to have discussed the text with Emil in some detail and to have accepted at least some of his expert advice, though we cannot reconstruct exactly how this was done. A number of amendments and deletions are written into the typescript in Emil's hand (and in one place two numbered pages have simply been removed), but it is impossible to tell whether these changes were made with or without Gabriele's agreement. Stylistically, the memoir reproduces Gabriele's characteristic run-on sentences, familiar to her children from the long letters she wrote them after the war, which have for the most part been preserved in this translation. At the same time, it does have some affinities with Emil's own family memoir, *Denk ich an Deutschland*. Notably, the summaries of political events and the reflections on the rise of the Nazis in each text are somewhat reminiscent of each other in language, tone, and placement. Both Emil and Gabriele also invoke the same line from Richard Beer-Hofmann's 1918 play *Jacob's Dream*—"As a crown I will wear it, not a yoke"—to signify a renewed identification with Judaism.[155] But we are not entitled to deduce joint authorship of Gabriele's memoir from such slim evidence—nor that, if there was indeed some kind of collaboration between the couple in either or both of their memoirs, Emil's must therefore have been the leading hand and not the other way round.

Since no handwritten notes for Gabriele's memoir have survived, the full circumstances of its composition will remain unknown. The best conclusion we can arrive at is that Emil made his contributions to the text as both her husband and an editor, but that Gabriele, the "courageous wife," deserves full recognition as its author. In fact, her memoir fills precisely the gap, the challenge of life under Nazism, that Emil seemed unable to face in his own writing.

With its canny and touching portraits of fellow inmates, its sometimes unexpected anecdotes of camp life, its self-effacing style, and its disarming, even artless judgments, Gabriele's memoir offers a testimony that substantiates and hugely expands the more fragmentary reminiscences by other Moringen survivors. And it is in a real sense a memoir, not an autobiography. Herz makes herself the mouthpiece as much for the stories and experiences of her cellmates and fellow detainees as for her own observations and commentary. She is almost always less interested in relating her own experiences than in hearing what other people have to say about themselves, their lives, and their beliefs. Her "hunter's" ear is more curious than critical, and so her memoir re-creates in sharp and generous detail the human relationships and political passions that flourished in Moringen's stony ground. It offers us a rare outsider's view into both the clarity and the confusion of Communist beliefs at an extraordinarily testing time. It also reveals the perplexity of a woman struggling awkwardly to understand how a civilized country could have sunk so rapidly into such depravity. Brief though Gabriele Herz's detention in Moringen was, she has left us an unrivaled insider account of this long-ignored women's concentration camp.

Conclusion

After Moringen, Gabriele and Emil journeyed with their two younger children through several countries before they finally settled in Rochester in 1940. Emil and Gabriele left Berlin for Italy as soon as Gabriele was released in March 1937. Their younger son Arthur remained at school in Berlin until his parents summoned him in April 1938 to join them in Florence—he recalls having time to pack only a few belongings and the family prayer books. Elisabeth, the younger daughter, rejoined the family in October after they had already moved to Lugano, Switzerland. There they applied unsuccessfully for French visas, but were granted entry to Cuba and sailed for Havana in December 1938. In August 1939, Arthur gained entry to the US and went to Rochester, as an advance guard for his parents, to train as a photographer at the Rochester Atheneum and Mechanics' Institute. Gabriele and Emil joined him there in 1940. Their other daughter Gertrud, married and with a son, had managed to leave Germany in March 1939; she spent the war years in Shanghai and immigrated to the US in 1949. So, apart from the elder son, Erwin, who had moved to Britain in the 1930s and remained there for the rest of his life, the immediate family was able to reconstitute itself in the US.[156]

The life led by Gabriele and Emil in Rochester in the 1940s and 1950s was very different from what they had enjoyed in pre-Nazi Berlin. Gabriele earned the family income by working for many years as a cleaner in a Rochester hospital. Emil, disabled by cataracts, settled back from his once powerful career and occupied himself with his own writing projects. Though he took up his family's claims for restitution for the stolen possessions and the pension he had been denied, neither Emil nor Gabriele indulged fantasies of re-creating their old Berlin life in the US. The couple embraced the adopted land in which they had found refuge and where their children were to make new lives and families for themselves. The principles Gabriele had once schooled her family in—"don't feel sorry for yourself ... you never know what life will bring"—she now applied to herself. According to her children, she neither complained nor compared her modest present life to the prosperous past, but was grateful for her family's survival, security, and renewal in the United States.

Yet the written memoir records a history Gabriele does not seem to have told her children in full: a history of the multiple losses the Nazis inflicted on her and her Moringen companions. Her own sense of what she had lost pervades the memoir, conveyed alike in the stories she tells about others and in what she tells us about herself. Like so many fellow exiles, she had been deprived of her country twice: even before she was finally forced to abandon her homeland, its collapse into barbarity had estranged her from the very fact of its having once been "home."

ALTHOUGH GABRIELE HERZ left Moringen behind her in March 1937, neither the story of the women's camp nor that of Moringen will be complete unless we pursue it briefly down two paths. One follows the women detainees to Lichtenburg and thence in May 1939 to Ravensbrück, while the other traces the history of the Moringen workhouse site after their departure.

The Lichtenburg women's concentration camp was established in December 1937.[157] Lichtenburg's fortress-like buildings, which dated back over four hundred years, had been used as a penitentiary between 1812 and 1928, after which it was closed down on sanitary grounds. In June 1933 it had been pressed back into service as a concentration camp for men, but by 1937 it was too small to house their growing numbers. Once Lichtenburg's thousand or so male inmates had been transferred to the new men's camp at Buchenwald in the summer of 1937, the Moringen women arrived to take their place. By now, Jehovah's Witnesses made up a majority of the contingent.[158] What awaited them in Lichtenburg was something quite different from the institution they had left. Unlike Moringen, their new camp was commanded by an SS officer under the supervision of Eicke's Inspectorate of Concentration Camps. Staffed by women recruited and supervised by the SS, the camp was run according to barely modified concentration camp regulations. Every aspect of daily life—living conditions, diet, work, discipline—was incomparably worse than Moringen. There were uniformed guards, dogs, truncheons, hoses, corporal punishment, and punishment cells. For the women shipped there from Moringen, it was, as one of them said, a transfer "into hell."[159] Further regular intakes of women prisoners continued through 1938, until they too began to strain the holding capacity of Lichtenburg's decrepit buildings. But now Ravensbrück, the first concentration camp built specifically for women, was being readied for its inaugural shipment of prisoners.

If Lichtenburg was hell, it is unclear what word could be used to describe Ravensbrück, the final stage of this institutional odyssey.[160] The Ravensbrück camp had been constructed by prisoner labor from Sachsenhausen on an empty lakeside site near Berlin, which, unlike Lichtenburg's cramped and decaying buildings, was capable of almost infinite expansion. It received its first thousand inmates in the spring of 1939. By now the majority were no longer German political prisoners or Jehovah's Witnesses, but German women designated as criminals or "asocials" and Jewish women. After the beginning of World War II in September 1939, women started to flow into Ravensbrück from every German-occupied country, most of them resisters, foreign laborers, or Sinti and Roma (Gypsies). The camp was run entirely by the SS and was fully integrated in the concentration camp universe, its regime mixing ferocity, humiliation, punitive labor, and mass death in the regular wartime proportions. Release was now increasingly rare. Once admitted, women were likely to remain there until they were transported to some other camp; died of mistreatment, malnutrition, or medical experimentation; or were selected for extermination by gassing. Of the 107,000 women and the 20,000 men (housed in a separate camp) who were registered into the Ravensbrück complex between 1939 and 1945, no more than 30,000 survived.[161] Among those killed in Ravensbrück and in other sites of Nazi murder were women who had been Herz's companions in Moringen.[162]

Meanwhile, Moringen had not come to the end of its own "useful" life under the Nazis. In October 1934, the judicial authorities had taken over responsibility for the workhouse from the provincial civil administration, underlining its future as a quasi-prison.[163] Even as the numbers of women *Schutzhäftlinge* filled out and some prostitutes were quartered with them rather than among the correctional inmates, the Moringen workhouse had also become the destination for new inmate categories. These included vagrants caught up in the first arrest campaigns in 1933–34, who were now liable to indeterminate detention, as well as a group of "recalcitrant" girls sent there in 1938. In addition, the provincial authorities, with Krack's approval, used Moringen after 1937 as a kind of asylum to house all kinds of people unfit for work, collected from various regions of Prussia. The later 1930s give the impression of a constant coming-and-going, as different categories of inmates were shuffled bureaucratically among custodial institutions, from asylum to workhouse to camp in a deadly game of social exclusion.

The workhouse continued to shelter the aged, the infirm, and the incapable almost to the end of the war, but meanwhile, on another front, Moringen had entered the most savage phase of its history. In August 1940, a "Youth Protection Camp" was established in part of the buildings, eventually expanding in 1944 to occupy the entire site and some adjacent land on which a barracks camp was constructed. Himmler and Heydrich had lobbied for this institution (together with a parallel camp for young women in Uckermarck, adjacent to Ravensbrück) as part of a strategy to wrest control over "delinquent" 16- to 21-year-olds from the youth welfare authorities and the courts.[164] The camp was placed under the supervision of the criminal police office of the Reichssicherheits-Hauptamt (Reich Central Security Office) to combat juvenile delinquency, and its director and staff were drawn from the ranks of the police, SS, and SD. It thus marked a decisive step in the police take-over of the custodial care and preventive detention of young people, both delinquents and young political detainees. These inmates were sentenced to detention for every imaginable social and political "offense," including "ineducability," moral delinquency, a predilection for "swing" (the forbidden jazz music that became a magnet for alienated middle-class youth), "work-shyness," homosexuality, eugenic "unfitness," political opposition, disobeying police orders, and refusal to join the Hitler Youth or to accept conscription.[165]

The camp's priority was to foster the "re-education," rather than welfare, of these inmates and to protect society from elements defined as dangerous and incorrigible: in this way it extended the concept of preventive police detention to adolescents. In fact, administratively and practically the Moringen *Jugendschutzlager* was nothing less than a concentration camp for boys, with all the marks of those institutions: barracks accommodation, armed guards, starvation diet, intensive forced labor, brutal discipline. Only in one respect did it differ from the wartime adult camps. Far from being shrouded in obscurity, it seems to have courted publicity and invited official visitors to view the future of juvenile justice in the new Germany. Hidden by the propaganda image, the real face of this future was grim in the extreme. Few inmates could look forward to release, unless to an adult concentration camp or the armed forces. Between 1940 and 1945, eighty-nine deaths were registered among the total of about fourteen hundred inmates, but this figure almost certainly hides many more youths who perished in hospitals or other camps from the ill-treatment, malnutrition, or disease they had suffered in Moringen. This was indeed the most evil phase of Moringen's miserable history in the Third Reich.

So the long history of Moringen converged with the history of incarceration in Nazi Germany in a double sense. It was both a faint precursor to the final murderous outcome and, between 1940 and 1945, itself a tragic site of that outcome. In local memory, however, the twelve Nazi years were soon discounted. After being used between 1945 and 1952 as a camp for some of the numerous "displaced persons" (DPs) uprooted by the chaos of the war, Moringen was reborn as a psychiatric hospital, and was once again known to local inhabitants as "the workhouse."[166] Today the site remains in use as a state hospital for forensic psychiatric patients in compulsory care. These are persons with legally diminished responsibility under the provisions of the penal code who have committed serious offenses, or those who have committed serious offenses under the influence of drugs or alcohol (mostly violent and sexual crimes or arson). Some of the original buildings no longer exist, and the barracks and barbed wire of the youth camp are long gone. It is a secure institution, but visitors are permitted and some residents are allowed to make supervised excursions outside the hospital. Patients, currently numbering about three hundred, mostly live in group rooms or communal apartments, some of them facing onto the spacious garden and low buildings that now occupy the site of the old closed and overshadowed exercise yard.

One part of the original structure that has survived is the imposing eighteenth-century entrance building, which now houses a small and rather dispassionate exhibit illustrating the changing history of the Moringen workhouse since 1738. The main memorial of Moringen's history in the Third Reich, however, has been installed since 1993 in one of the old village gatehouses a few hundred meters down the road. There the KZ-Gedenkstätte Moringen maintains a permanent exhibition and documentation on the history of the camps, runs educational programs for young people in particular, and welcomes visitors from Germany and the world.[167]

This geographical separation—the workhouse site itself still in use, the memorial exhibit displaced into another village building—evokes the displacement of Moringen's Nazi history in post-war local memory. The question this raises is not only how to commemorate Moringen as orphanage, workhouse, and Nazi camp, but also how to understand the lengthy historical relationship between these successive institutions. Was it just administrative convenience that allowed the same nexus of buildings to begin life as an orphanage, to mutate into a workhouse, to confine the Third Reich's political opponents and imprison the youthful victims of its social policies, then to shelter DPs, and finally to house the criminally insane? Or is there a more integral and troubling relationship among these sequential methods of segregating and confining the deviant and the outcast?

The long history of Moringen as an institution of confinement bears witness to the distinctive systems of social discipline that became characteristic of modern Western societies as they emerged into secular statehood and industrial capitalism.[168] The existence of these institutions and the projects of social sorting and segregation that they supported in the name of public order and discipline provided a reservoir of ideas and practices that could be tapped in very different ways. Historians concur that Nazi disciplinary policies emerged from ideas circulating in Weimar and imperial Germany about how to meet the challenges of social welfare and public order, but also that the Nazi regime adopted radically different objectives and methods from the liberal-democratic orders of Weimar Germany and later the Federal Republic—not "rehabilitation and integration," however forcibly, but much more rigorous practices of "exclusion and extermination."[169] In the Third Reich, whoever was not reformable was liable to be physically eliminated on grounds of hereditary unsoundness. This—so eugenics taught—would solve the problems of social disorder and public health once and for all. Between 1933 and 1945, Moringen stood at the crossroads between these two models: simultaneously a traditional institution of confinement and an outpost of the murderous tendencies of Nazi bio-politics.

In recent years, historical research has dispelled the illusion that the Nazi concentration camps were as isolated from history as they were allegedly insulated from the rest of Germany during the twelve-year Nazi dictatorship.[170] The origin of these camps, we must remember, lay in the mass detention of political "subversives" by the new government in 1933 in the name of public order. Although the scale and purpose of these *Schutzhaft* arrests was unprecedented, we have already seen that this was not true of either the powers of arrest or the concept of preventive detention as such, both of which had older histories. Moreover, the new regime launched simultaneous campaigns against the socially marginal, marshaling these ancillary projects of mass detention under the banner of political and social public order. Officials in the federal and state governments, and local administrators such as Hugo Krack, could surely see the policy continuities, which were underlined when—again in the name of good order—the civil authorities moved to transfer *Schutzhäftlinge* out of the hands of the Nazi paramilitaries and concentrate them in more structured institutions under civil oversight.[171] These early months of what became the Third Reich are replete with examples of similar actions by the civil authorities, who aimed not just to impose legal and procedural order on the Nazis' grab for power, but also to seize this opportunity to realize their own stalled projects of authoritarian reform.[172] Local and national publicity given to the early camps indicates that their masters both sought and expected public support for their ostensible objectives of reformation through hard labor.[173] The workhouse camps of Moringen, Breitenau, and Brauweiler, along with the Emsland land reclamation camps, epitomized the corrective purposes of this instructional program.

As we look back now on the full twelve-year history of the Third Reich, it is easy to forget that those who lived through the Nazi seizure of power in 1933 did not know exactly where the new regime would take their country, nor how rapidly it would plunge into the depths of political depravity. Of course, many Germans (and not just the Nazis' declared political opponents) had profound apprehensions about the future of the regime, and those who predicted a disastrous outcome to the Nazi adventure were eventually proved more correct than they could possibly have imagined. But the future is always veiled, whereas people can readily look to the past to make sense of their own times, and the historian needs to take full account of this. For numerous Germans who were not already opposed to the NSDAP in 1933, the impulse to interpret events through what was familiar would have seemed logical and perhaps comforting. The legitimating resources this angle of vision provided can help to explain how Germans could see the early detention camps as reworked versions of the familiar, rather than as novel and unsettling departures.[174] The camps were located in Germany, after all: they were not yet hidden in some mysterious region between the eastern frontiers and the war zone. They were not entirely concealed from public knowledge, even if the information disclosed was strictly controlled and deeply dishonest. And although their public representation as deterrent and reformative institutions was spurious, it was possibly not ineffective in interweaving the familiar and the new in the public mind.

If we consider the Moringen camp by the standards of the eventual concentration and extermination camps, we are likely to echo the views of some its surviving inmates: their experiences were incommensurable with what women (including some of the Moringen detainees) suffered in Ravensbrück and what awaited millions more in the wartime camps. In this history, it is arguable that the Nazi seizure of power in 1933 was not the only significant turning point. For it was not until Himmler achieved mastery over the police and the concentration camps, which effectively withdrew the entire system from any external oversight and made it the playground of his eugenic vision of racial renewal, that Nazi confinement policy was intensified and radicalized. As we have seen, instead of the political detention camps being closed down as most of these original prisoners were released, Himmler's take-over and his reorientation of priorities from political control to social and racial engineering ensured that the camps would continue to be filled with an ever-expanding circle of inmates. The older paths of nineteenth-century authoritarian social discipline and Nazi political detention now merged into immense new projects of coercive bio-politics and intensive labor exploitation.

Even within this radical framework, attempts to normalize the concentration camps persisted. The men in charge of them still wanted Germans to believe that the camps were model reformatory institutions. Around 1940, Oswald Pohl, head of the SS Wirtschafts-Verwaltungshauptamt, instructed camp commanders to commission documentary photographs of their camp buildings and activities in order to make a record of Nazi achievements. A mendacious visual archive of Ravensbrück was assembled, representing it as a clean and orderly prison camp with neat rows of barracks, busy work stations, and traditionally designed housing units for the guards.[175] In this way, Pohl's project invoked familiar imagery drawn from an older disciplinary repertoire, denying both the catastrophic reality and the path that Nazi rule had laid out from Moringen to Lichtenburg to Ravensbrück. It is through following the progressive remakings of "normality" that we can best understand how the ultimate catastrophe became possible.

Notes

1. The Prussian Geheimes Staatspolizeiamt, or secret state police office, was officially abbreviated as Gestapa. The term "Gestapo" (i.e., Geheime Staatspolizei) did not become current until the establishment in 1936 of a national secret police under the leadership of Heinrich Himmler. For the early history of the Gestapo, see Hans Buchheim, "The SS—Instrument of Domination," in Helmut Krausnick, Hans Buchheim, Martin Broszat, and Hans-Adolf Jacobsen, Anatomy of the SS State (New York, 1968), 143–66.
2. See Klaus Drobisch and Günther Wieland, System der NS-Konzentrationslager 1933–1939 (Berlin, 1993), 200–201. For further details on the handling of Remigranten, see Herbert Tutas, Nationalsozialismus und Exil. Die Politik des Dritten Reiches gegenüber den deutschen politischen Emigranten (Munich and Vienna, 1975), chap. 1:3.
3. Barbara Bromberger, Hanna Elling, Jutta von Freyberg, and Ursula Krause-Schmitt, Schwestern, vergesst uns nicht. Frauen im Konzentrationslager: Moringen, Lichtenburg, Ravensbrück 1933–1945 (Frankfurt am Main, 1988), 123.
4. Figures in Drobisch and Wieland, System der NS-Konzentrationslager, 271.
5. Until October 1934, the Moringen workhouse was supervised by the provincial administration (Provinzialverband) based in Hanover. On 16 October 1934, the workhouse was transferred to the supervision of the judicial administration (Justizverwaltung), a provision that enabled the provincial court in Celle to commit criminal cases to indeterminate detention there. See Cornelia Meyer, "Abschreckung, Besserung, Unschädlichmachung: Die Disziplinierung gesellschaftlicher Randgruppen im Werkhaus Moringen (1871–1944)" (MA diss., University of Göttingen, 2000), 161–67.
6. Hannah Arendt, The Origins of Totalitarianism (New York, 2nd ed., 1958), 437–38.
7. Gudrun Schwarz, Die nationalsozialistischen Lager (Frankfurt am Main, 1996), 261–62. See also the exhaustive catalogue of camps assembled after the war by the International Tracing Service, republished in Martin Weinmann, ed., Das nationalsozialistische Lagersystem (CCP) (Frankfurt am Main, 1990).
8. Schwarz, Die nationalsozialistischen Lager, 9.
9. The most recent research can be sampled in three major series: Ulrich Herbert, Karin Orth, and Christoph Dieckmann, eds., Die nationalsozialistischen Konzentrationslager, 2 vols. (Göttingen, 1998), and two ongoing series of volumes edited by Wolfgang Benz and Barbara Distel, Geschichte der Konzentrationslager 1933–1945 (Berlin, 2001–) and Der Ort des Terrors. Geschichte der nationalsozialistischen Konzentrationslager (Munich, 2005–).
10. Herz lacked a university qualification for public employment, and in any case pre-war Vienna offered few opportunities for Jewish women in the educational system; Harriet

Freidenreich, *Female, Jewish, Educated: The Lives of Central European University Women* (Bloomington, 2002), 69–73.

11. Biographical details on Emanuel Emil Herz (1877–1971) from Emil Herz's family history, *Before the Fury: Jews and Germans before Hitler* (New York, 1966), a translation of *Denk ich an Deutschland in der Nacht. Die Geschichte des Hauses Steg* (Berlin, 1951); and from the author's interviews with family members: Gertrud Kracauer and Elisabeth Brettler in New York (25 April 2003; Gertrud's daughter Ellen Kracauer Hartig also present) and Arthur Herz in Exton, Pennsylvania (14 May 2003; Arthur's wife Hildegard Herz also present), and a telephone interview with Gertrud Kracauer's daughter Ellen Kracauer Hartig (4 August 2003).

12. He had furnished a "Warburg room" in his Berlin house with items from his family home.

13. For the history of Ullstein, see Modris Eksteins, *The Limits of Reason: The German Democratic Press and the Collapse of Weimar Germany* (Oxford, 1975), passim, and Hermann Ullstein, *The Rise and Fall of the House of Ullstein* (London, n.d.).

14. Ullstein, *Rise and Fall*, 162.

15. Eksteins, *Limits of Reason*, 111–22.

16. For a brief profile of Jewish women's lives in this period, see Marion Kaplan, *Between Dignity and Despair: Jewish Life in Nazi Germany* (New York, 1998), 10–16.

17. This account of Gabriele's life and opinions is drawn from interviews with family members (see note 11 above). Phrases in quotation marks come from these interviews.

18. Invaluable sources for the experience of German Jews between 1933 and 1937 include Kaplan, *Between Dignity and Despair*, and Saul Friedländer, *Nazi Germany and the Jews*, vol. 1: *The Years of Persecution, 1933–1939* (New York, 1997).

19. Eksteins, *Limits of Reason*, 282–86. For "Aryanization" in general, see Avraham Barkai, *From Boycott to Annihilation: The Economic Struggle of German Jews 1933–1943* (Hanover, NH, 1989); Helmut Genschel, *Die Verdrängung der Juden aus der Wirtschaft im Dritten Reich* (Göttingen, 1966).

20. Ullstein, *Rise and Fall*, 29.

21. Herz, *Before the Fury*, 268.

22. Ibid., 269.

23. Kaplan, *Between Dignity and Despair*, 68. See also Frances Henry, *Victims and Neighbors: A Small Town in Nazi Germany Remembered* (South Hadley, MA, 1984).

24. Up to 1938, Italy was a plausible destination for Jewish émigrés, especially those who had useful professional qualifications, e.g., in medicine or business; see Juliane Wetzel, "Auswanderung aus Deutschland," in *Die Juden in Deutschland 1933–1945*, ed. Wolfgang Benz (Munich, 1988), 481–82; and Klaus Voigt, *Zuflucht auf Widerruf: Exil in Italien 1933–1945* (Stuttgart, 1989).

25. Kaplan, *Between Dignity and Despair*, 73.

26. For emigration history and statistics, see Wetzel, "Auswanderung," and Herbert A. Strauss, "Jewish Emigration from Germany: Nazi Policies and Jewish Responses," *Leo Baeck Institute Year Book* 15 (1980): 313–61.

27. Arthur Herz reports that his father smuggled out an old manuscript that he had hoped, unsuccessfully, as it turned out, to sell in Italy.

28. Niedersächsisches Hauptstaatsarchiv Hannover (NHStA), Hann. 158 Moringen, acc. 105/96, nr. 130 (Herz's personal file in Moringen). The terms *Rückwanderer* and *Remigrant* were used interchangeably. Since Herz's children have no memory of their mother having returned home, possibly the May–June gap disguises the trip made by her husband and son to Italy. Another possibility (suggested by Ursula Krause-Schmitt in a conversation with Ellen Kracauer Hartig and Howard Hartig) is that a sympathetic police official effaced the record of the Palestine trip, which might have attracted a more severe penalty.

29. This account is taken from Tutas, *Nationalsozialismus und Exil*, chap. 1:3; see also Christoph Graf, *Politische Polizei zwischen Demokratie und Diktatur* (Berlin, 1983), 285–93.

30. See *Memoir*, 61.

31. Historians' periodization of the camps has varied, depending on shifts of emphasis between the political and economic functions of the camps, and on whether or not the wartime camps are included. For a survey of the variants, see Karin Orth, *Das System der national-sozialistischen Konzentrationslager. Eine politische Organisationsgeschichte* (Zürich and Munich, 1999), 21. My own periodization follows the four-phase division (1933–36, 1936–39, 1939–42, 1942–45) proposed in Herbert, Orth, and Dieckmann, *Nationalsozialistischen Konzentrationslager*, vol. 1, 24–32. For a short history of the early detention system, see Jane Caplan, "Political Detention and the Origin of the Concentration Camps in Nazi Germany, 1933–1935/6," in *Nazism, War and Genocide: Essays in Honour of Jeremy Noakes*, ed. Neil Gregor (Exeter, 2005).

32. Johannes Tuchel, "Planung und Realität des Systems der Konzentrationslager 1934–1938," in Herbert, Orth, and Dieckmann, *Nationalsozialistischen Konzentrationslager*, vol. 1, 56.

33. See Eric A. Johnson, *Nazi Terror: The Gestapo, Jews, and Ordinary Germans* (New York, 2000), chap. 5; Detlev Peukert, *Die KPD im Widerstand. Verfolgung und Untergrundarbeit an Rhein und Ruhr 1933 bis 1945* (Wuppertal, 1980), chaps. 1 and 2. As well as those detained in *Schutzhaft* without trial, others were tried by newly established special courts (*Sondergerichte*) and sentenced to prison terms for treason; however, on release some were immediately taken back into custody as *Schutzhäftlinge* and sent to one of the camps.

34. For an exhaustive analysis of the evidence and this estimate of the total number of detainees arrested between February 1933 and August 1934, see Johannes Tuchel, *Konzentrationslager. Organisationsgeschichte und Funktion der "Inspektion der Konzentrationslager" 1934–1938* (Boppard am Rhein, 1991), 96–110; for a shorter summary, see Herbert, Orth, and Dieckmann, *Nationalsozialistischen Konzentrationslager*, vol. 1, 24–32. For the concept and practice of *Schutzhaft*, see Günther Wieland, "Die normativen Grundlagen der Schutzhaft in Hitlerdeutschland," *Jahrbuch für Geschichte* 26 (1982): 75–102; Graf, *Politische Polizei*, 255–84; legal analysis in Gerhard Werle, *Justiz-Strafrecht und polizeiliche Verbrechens-bekämpfung im Dritten Reich* (Berlin and New York, 1989), 533–42.

35. For conditions in the early camps, see Drobisch and Wieland, *System der NS-Konzentrationslager*, part 1; and Benz and Distel, eds., *Geschichte der Konzentrationslager*, vol. 1: *Terror ohne System. Die ersten Konzentrationslager im Nationalsozialismus 1933–1935* (Berlin, 2001) and vol. 2: *Herrschaft und Gewalt. Frühe Konzentrationslager 1933–1939* (Berlin, 2002).

36. Renate Riebe, "Frauen in Konzentrationslager 1933–1939," *Dachauer Hefte* 14 (1998): 124–27. See also Anni Wadle's account of her Gestapo interrogation in Hamburg, in *Mutti, warum lachst du nie?* (Dreisteinfurt, 1988), 56–65.

37. The indispensable source for the early political and organizational history of the camps is Tuchel, *Konzentrationslager*; for a summary (now partially corrected by Tuchel's research), see Martin Broszat, "The Concentration Camps 1933–1945," in Krausnick et al., *Anatomy of the SS State*, 400–452; for the earliest places of detention for women, see Riebe "Frauen in Konzentrationslager," 124–27; for individual studies of the early camps, see Benz and Distel, eds., *Geschichte der Konzentrationslager*, vols. 1–3.

38. The use of workhouses and other types of detention sites is summarized in Tuchel, *Konzentrationslager*, 38–45. For Breitenau, see Dietfried Krause-Vilmar, *Das Konzentrationslager Breitenau: Ein staatliches Schutzhaftlager 1933/34* (Marburg, 2000); also see Gunnar Richter, ed., *Breitenau: Zur Geschichte eines nationalsozialistischen Konzentrations- und Arbeits-erziehungslagers* (Kassel, 1993), and Wolfgang Ayass, *Das Arbeitshaus Breitenau: Bettler, Landstreicher, Prostituierte, Zuhälter und Fürsorgeempfänger in der Korrektions- und Lande-armenanstalt Breitenau (1874–1949)* (Kassel, 1992), 262–327. For Brauweiler, see Josef Wisskirchen, "Schutzhaft in der Rheinprovinz: Das Konzentrationslager Brauweiler 1933–1934," in Benz and Distel, *Geschichte der Konzentrationslager*, vol. 1, 129–56.

39. For the camps situated in the Emsland reclamation region, see Elke Suhr, *Die Emslandlager. Die politische und wirtschaftliche Bedeutung der Emsländischen Konzentrations- und Straf-gefangenenlager 1933–1945* (Bremen, 1985), and Dirk Lüerssen, "'Moorsoldaten' in Esterwegen,

Börgermoor, Neusustrum: Die frühen Konzentrationslager im Emsland 1933 bis 1936," in Benz and Distel, *Geschichte der Konzentrationslager*, vol. 1, 157–210.

40. Broszat, "The Concentration Camps," 416–20.
41. Total given by Tuchel, *Konzentrationslager*, 203.
42. Text and analysis in Rudolf Morsey, *Das "Ermächtigungsgesetz" vom 24. Marz 1933. Quellen zur Geschichte und Interpretation des "Gesetzes zur Behebung der Not von Volk und Reich"* (Düsseldorf, 1992); see the English translation in Jeremy Noakes and Geoffrey Pridham, eds., *Nazism 1919–1945*, vol. 1: *The Rise to Power 1919–1934* (Exeter, 1983), 161–62.
43. For a summary of this double process of centralization and autonomization, see Buchheim, "The SS—Instrument of Domination," especially 145–60; for a fuller account, see Graf, *Politische Polizei*, 128–53.
44. Discussed in detail in Tuchel, *Konzentrationslager*, and in Drobisch and Wieland, *System der NS-Konzentrationslager*; for a summary, see Broszat, "The Concentration Camps," 400–456.
45. For the judicial prison system under National Socialism, see Nikolaus Wachsmann, *Hitler's Prisons: Legal Terror in Nazi Germany* (London, 2004).
46. Broszat, "The Concentration Camps," 436.
47. Tuchel, "Planung und Realität des Systems der Konzentrationslager," 56.
48. For camp conditions during this period, see Drobisch and Wieland, *System der NS-Konzentrationslager*, Part 3, and Herbert, Orth, and Dieckmann, *Nationalsozialistischen Konzentrationslager*, vol. 1, section 1; for a critical analysis of the prisoner functionary system, see Karin Orth, "Gab es eine Lagergesellschaft? 'Kriminelle' und politische Häftlinge im Konzentrationslager," in *Ausbeutung, Vernichtung, Öffentlichkeit. Neue Studien zur nationalsozialistischen Lagerpolitik*, ed. Norbert Frei, Sybille Steinbacher, and Bernd C. Wagner (Munich, 2000), 109–34; and Karin Hartewig, "Wolf unter Wölfen? Die prekäre Macht der kommunistischen Kapos im Konzentrationslager Buchenwald," in Herbert, Orth, and Dieckmann, *Nationalsozialistischen Konzentrationslager*, vol. 1, 939–58.
49. For the establishment of Ravensbrück and overviews of its history, see Ino Arndt, "Das Frauenkonzentrationslager Ravensbrück," *Studien zur Geschichte der Konzentrationslager: Schriftenreihe der Vierteljahreshefte für Zeitgeschichte*, 21 (Stuttgart, 1970), and Riebe, "Frauen in Konzentrationslager 1933–1939"; Bernhard Strebel, "Ravensbrück—das zentrale Frauenkonzentrationslager," in Herbert, Orth, and Dieckmann, *Nationalsozialistischen Konzentrationslager*, vol. 1, 215–58; and Helga Amesberger and Brigitte Halbmayr, eds., *Vom Leben und Überleben. Wege nach Ravensbrück. Das Frauenkonzentrationslager in der Erinnerung*, vol. 1: *Dokumentation und Analyse*, vol. 2: *Lebensgeschichten* (Vienna, 2001–2); further discussion and references in Linde Apel, *Jüdische Frauen im Konzentrationslager Ravensbrück 1939–1945* (Berlin, 2003); Christa Schikorra, *Kontinuitäten der Ausgrenzung: "Asoziale" Häftlinge im Frauen-Konzentrationslager Ravensbrück* (Berlin, 2001); Insa Eschebach and Johanna Kootz, eds., *Das Frauenkonzentrationslager Ravensbrück. Quellenlage und Quellenkritik. Tagungsdokumentation* (Berlin, 1997); and Grit Philipp, *Kalendarium der Ereignisse im Frauen-Konzentrationslager Ravensbrück 1939–1945* (Berlin, 1999).
50. See Ulrich Herbert, "Von der Gegnerbekämpfung zur 'rassischen Generalprävention': 'Schutzhaft' und Konzentrationslager in der Konzeption der Gestapo-Führung 1933–1939," and Patrick Wagner, "'Vernichtung der Berufsverbrecher': Die vorbeugende Verbrechensbekämpfung der Kriminalpolizei bis 1937," in Herbert, Orth, and Dieckmann, *Nationalsozialistischen Konzentrationslager*, 60–86, 87–110; Wolfgang Ayass, *"Asoziale" im Nationalsozialismus* (Stuttgart, 1995); Wolfgang Ayass, "Vagrants and Beggars in Hitler's Reich," in *The German Underworld. Deviants and Outcasts in German History*, ed. Richard Evans (London, 1988), 210–37; Robert Gellately and Nathan Stoltzfus, eds., *Social Outsiders in Nazi Germany* (Princeton, 2001); Michael Burleigh and Wolfgang Wippermann, *The Racial State: Germany 1933–1945* (Cambridge and New York, 1991); on women, see Schikorra, *Kontinuitäten der Ausgrenzung*.
51. Powers for the criminal police to order preventive detention of certain categories of criminals and "asocials" were introduced by decree in December 1937; in January 1938 the

existing powers of protective custody (*Schutzhaft*) were extended to cover non-political offenders and centralized in the hands of the Gestapo. (In addition, the courts had had powers since November 1933 to sentence "dangerous habitual criminals" to indefinite prison terms in judicial prisons.) Detainees held in "preventive detention" and those held in "protective custody" were subject to different supervisory authorities and terms of detention, but both groups were now normally sent to the concentration camps. For details see Werle, *Justiz-Strafrecht und polizeiliche Verbrechensbekämpfung*; also Broszat, "The Concentration Camps," 446–56; for implementation, see Ayass, *"Asoziale" im Nationalsozialismus*, chap. 6.

52. Broszat, "The Concentration Camps," 450.
53. For the persecution of Jehovah's Witnesses, see Hans Hesse, ed., *Persecution and Resistance of Jehovah's Witnesses during the Nazi Regime 1933–1945* (Bremen, 2001); for homosexuals, see Günter Grau, ed., *Hidden Holocaust? Gay and Lesbian Persecution in Germany, 1933–45* (New York, 1995); Geoffrey Giles, "The Institutionalization of Homosexual Panic in the Third Reich," in Gellately and Stoltzfus, *Social Outsiders in Nazi Germany*, 223–55, and Geoffrey Giles, "'The Most Unkindest Cut of All': Castration, Homosexuality and Nazi Justice," *Journal of Contemporary History* 27 (1992): 41–61.
54. David Hackett, ed, *The Buchenwald Report* (Boulder, 1995), 56. For a longer discussion of releases, see Eugen Kogon, *Der SS-Staat*, 2nd ed. (Frankfurt, 1947), 254–62.
55. Figures cited in Schwarz, *Die nationalsozialistischen Lager*, 36–37.
56. See Tim Mason, *Social Policy in the Third Reich: The Working Class and the "National Community"* (Providence and Oxford, 1993), chap. 6.
57. Wolfgang Brückner, *"Arbeit macht frei": Herkunft und Hintergrund der KZ-Devise* (Opladen, 1998), 22.
58. Ibid., 26–39.
59. Orth, *System der nationalsozialistischen Konzentrationslager*, 38–39; Arndt, "Das Frauenkonzentrationslager Ravensbrück," 108–9.
60. See Michael Thad Allen, *The Business of Genocide: The SS, Slave Labor, and the Concentration Camps* (Chapel Hill, 2002).
61. For the wartime concentration camps, see Orth, *System der nationalsozialistischen Konzentrationslager*. Matthias Kuse, "Entlassungen von Häftlinge aus dem Frauenkonzentrationslager Moringen 1934–1938" (MA diss., University of Bremen, 1999), 6, cites an estimate that about 1 percent of all KZ inmates were released from 1933 to 1945. One of these exceptions was Nanda Herbermann, a German Catholic activist imprisoned in Ravensbrück from August 1941 to March 1943; see Nanda Herbermann, *The Blessed Abyss: Inmate #6582 in Ravensbrück Concentration Camp for Women* (Detroit, 2000).
62. In Buchenwald, for example, the proportion of German prisoners fell from 33 percent in August 1942 to only 8 percent by October 1944; see figures and other data in Orth, *System der nationalsozialistischen Konzentrationslager*, 102–6.
63. See Allen, *The Business of Genocide*; Ulrich Herbert, "Arbeit und Vernichtung. Ökonomisches Interesse und Primat der 'Weltanschauung' im Nationalsozialismus," in *Ist der Nationalsozialismus Geschichte?* ed. Dan Diner (Frankfurt, 1988), 198–236; Wolf Gruner, *Der geschlossene Arbeitseinsatz deutscher Juden: zur Zwangsarbeit als Element der Verfolgung 1938–1943* (Berlin, 1997); Nikolaus Wachsmann, "'Annihilation through Labor': The Killing of State Prisoners in the Third Reich," *Journal of Modern History* 71 (1999): 624–59.
64. The statistical evidence is discussed by Orth, *System der nationalsozialistischen Konzentrationslager*, 343–50.
65. Orth, *System der nationalsozialistischen Konzentrationslager*, 192ff.; Hackett, *Buchenwald Report*, 54–55, 226f.
66. This description of the early history of Moringen is drawn from Meyer, "Abschreckung, Besserung, Unschädlichmachung."
67. Moringen was one of twenty-four Prussian workhouses in the imperial period, and the sole such institution for the province of Hanover.

68. For the workhouse system and further references, see Ayass, *Das Arbeitshaus Breitenau*, 13–68; for the history of confinement in Europe, see Norbert Finzsch and Robert Jütte, eds., *Institutions of Confinement: Hospitals, Asylums, and Prisons in Western Europe and North America, 1500–1950* (Cambridge, 1996); for comparable policies in Britain, see M. A. Crowther, *The Workhouse System 1834–1929: The History of an English Social Institution* (London, 1981).

69. Details in the 1876 German penal code (*Strafgesetzbuch für das Deutsche Reich*), §§ 361 and 362.

70. See Detlev Peukert, "The Genesis of the 'Final Solution' from the Spirit of Science," in *Reevaluating the Third Reich*, ed. Thomas Childers and Jane Caplan (New York, 1993), 234–52. For further reading on nineteenth-century social policy, see references in David F. Crew, *Germans on Welfare: From Weimar to Hitler* (Oxford and New York, 1998), introduction.

71. For German criminology, see Richard F. Wetzell, *Inventing the Criminal: A History of German Criminology 1880–1945* (Chapel Hill, 2000).

72. On Weimar social policy and the issue of continuity and discontinuity, see Crew, *Germans on Welfare*; Edward R. Dickinson, *The Politics of German Child Welfare from the Empire to the Federal Republic* (Cambridge, MA, 1996); Elizabeth Harvey, *Youth and the Welfare State in Weimar Germany* (Oxford, 1993); Young-Sun Hong, *Welfare, Modernity, and the Weimar State 1919–1933* (Princeton, 1998); and Christoph Sachsse and Florian Tennstedt, *Der Wohlfahrtsstaat im Nationalsozialismus* (Stuttgart, 1992).

73. See Matthias Kuse, "Hugo Krack. Ein 'Zivilist' als KZ-Direktor?" *Dokumente. Rundbrief der Lagergemeinschaft und Gedenkstätte KZ Moringen* 20 (July 2001): 8–11; Hans Hesse, *Das Frauen-KZ Moringen 1933–1938*, 2nd ed. (Moringen, 2002), 96–107.

74. See Krack's file in the NSDAP Partei-Korrespondenz (Berlin Document Center, microfilm roll no. A3340-PA-G206; NARA Rg. 242). Thanks to Jan Lambertz for this material.

75. See Ayass, *Das Arbeitshaus Breitenau*, 245–51; Ayass, *"Asoziale" im Nationalsozialismus*, 13–18; Crew, *Germans on Welfare*, esp. 197–212; Harvey, *Youth and the Welfare State*; Hong, *Welfare, Modernity, and the Weimar State*.

76. Matthias Willig, *Das Bewahrungsgesetz (1918–1967). Eine rechtshistorische Studie zur Geschichte der deutschen Fürsorge* (Tübingen, 2003). Thanks to Wolfgang Ayass for this reference. See also Harvey, *Youth and the Welfare State*, chap. 7; Hong, *Welfare, Modernity, and the Weimar State*, chap. 8

77. Meyer, "Abschreckung, Besserung, Unschädlichmachung," 41, 129ff.; and see Krack to Landesdirektorium in Hanover, 29 March 1933 (NHStA Hann. 158 Moringen, acc. 84/82, nr. 1, 7–9), which lists "about 60 male and 10 female inmates and wards [*Pfleglinge*] and about 30 [male] and 60 [female] voluntary inmates [*Arbeitsfreiwillige*]."

78. See Meyer, "Abschreckung, Besserung, Unschädlichmachung," 154–61; Klaus Mlynek, "Der Aufbau der Geheimen Staatspolizei in Hannover und die Errichtung des Konzentrationslagers Moringen," in *Hannover 1933. Eine Grossstadt wird nationalsozialistisch*, pub. Historisches Museum am Hohen Ufer (Hannover, 1981), 65–80; Hausordnung (undated, 1933) in NHStA Hann. 158 Moringen, acc. 84/82, nr. 1, 35–36. For the comparable uses of workhouses as concentration camps in this period, see Gunnar Richter, "Das frühe Konzentrationslager Breitenau (1933/34)," in Richter, *Breitenau*, 50–95, Krause-Vilmar, *Das Konzentrationslager Breitenau*; and Reimer Möller, "Schutzhaft in der Landesarbeitsanstalt: Das Konzentrationslager Glückstadt," in Benz and Distel, *Geschichte der Konzentrationslager*, vol. 2, 101–10.

79. For an assessment, see Kuse, "Hugo Krack"; and see also below, 24f.

80. See Hans Hesse, ed., *Hoffnung ist ein ewiges Begräbnis. Briefe aus dem KZ Hannah Vogt—1933* (Bremen, 1998), 33–35.

81. See documentation in NHStA Hann. 158 Moringen, acc. 84/82, nr. 1, e.g., 153–54, 160–61.

82. See Hesse, *Hoffnung ist ein ewiges Begräbnis*, 25–29; and Hannah Vogt, ed., *KZ Moringen. Männerlager. Frauenlager. Jugendschutzlager. Eine Dokumentation* (Göttingen, n.d.).

83. See the weekly return of detainees signed by the SS camp commander Cordes, dated 25 August 1933 (NHStA Hann. 180 Hannover, nr. 752, 472).

84. Vogt, ed., *KZ Moringen*, 17–19.
85. Krack to Landesdirektorium in Hanover, 23 June 1933 (NHStA Hann. 158 Moringen, acc. 84/82, nr. 1, 90).
86. The major source for the history of the women's camp is Hesse, *Das Frauen-KZ Moringen*.
87. Memo signed by SS-Sturmbahnführer Flöhr and Hugo Krack, 29 November 1933 (NHStA Hann. 180 Hannover, nr. 752, 556). For Oranienburg, see Günter Morsch, "Oranienburg–Sachsenhausen, Sachsenhausen–Oranienburg," in Herbert, Orth, and Dieckmann, *Nationalsozialistischen Konzentrationslager*, 111–34; and Bernward Dörner, "Ein KZ in der Mitte der Stadt," in Benz and Distel, *Geschichte der Konzentrationslager*, vol. 2, 123–38.
88. See "Bericht über das Frauenkonzentrationslager Mohringen [*sic*] i. Solling," [February 1948], in BA: BY5/V 279/84; Hesse, *Das Frauen-KZ Moringen*, 94–95.
89. See Kuse, "Entlassungen von Häftlingen," 15–17.
90. *Memoir*, 99f. and 114.
91. *Memoir*, 122f.
92. Reported in *Der Strafvollzug im III. Reich. Denkschrift und Materialsammlung*, ed. Union für Recht und Freiheit (Prague, 1934), 98 (thanks to Jan Lambertz for this material). The physician was probably Dr. Otto Wolter-Pecksen (see biographical appendix).
93. See Kuse, "Hugo Krack," and Kuse, "Entlassungen von Häftlingen," 84–94; see also the report "Durchgangslager Mohringen [*sic*] am Solling (Northeim) Ende 1936–Anfang 1937," BA: BY5/V 279/84.
94. Letter from Milli Beermann in New York, 1 November 1935; Friends House Library and Archives, London, Friends Committee for Refugees and Aliens, Political Prisoners, Correspondence 1933–1938, FCRA/19/1. This case is also mentioned by Elizabeth Howard, one of the British Quaker volunteers in Germany, who had visited Moringen in the spring of 1935. Howard and her fellow visitor Marion Fox were allowed to meet and "chat" with other inmates. Howard described conditions as "by no means bad," and claimed that "those who desired kosher food were allowed to have it," though I have not found this claim corroborated elsewhere; see Elizabeth Howard, *Across Barriers* (London, 1941), 89–91.
95. Report by W. R. Hughes, 24 October 1934, Friends House Library and Archives, London, Friends Committee for Refugees and Aliens, German Emergency Committee Papers 1933–1946, FCRA/18/1. For Quaker activities in Germany in the 1930s, see Hans A. Schmitt, *Quakers and Nazis: Inner Light in Outer Darkness* (Columbia, MO, 1997).
96. *Memoir*, 97. Kuse, "Entlassungen von Häftlingen," 45.
97. Kuse, "Entlassungen von Häftlingen," 23–26, 72ff., 87.
98. For "asocial" women in workhouses after 1933, see Schikorra, *Kontinuitäten der Ausgrenzung*, chap. 2.
99. Kuse, "Hugo Krack," 10; Kuse, "Entlassungen von Häftlingen," 87; Meyer, "Abschreckung, Besserung, Unschädlichmachung," 164f. Presumably also involved in these decisions was the workhouse physician, Dr. Otto Wolter-Pecksen (see biographical appendix). For sterilization programs under the Nazis, see Gisela Bock, *Zwangssterilisation im Nationalsozialismus. Studien zur Rassenpolitik und Frauenpolitik* (Opladen, 1986); also Robert N. Proctor, *Racial Hygiene: Medicine under the Nazis* (Cambridge, MA., 1988), esp. chap. 4.
100. This is the judgment of Meyer, "Abschreckung, Besserung, Unschädlichmachung," 168ff.
101. Policy and procedure for release are examined by Kuse, "Entlassungen von Häftlingen." The average length of detention was four months, with some detainees being released within as little as two weeks. Somewhat lower monthly figures are given in Hesse, *Das Frauen-KZ Moringen*, 41–45.
102. *Memoir*, 120; see also Centa Herker-Beimler's account in Hanna Elling, *Frauen im deutschen Widerstand* (Frankfurt am Main, 1981), 107–8.
103. *Memoir*, 139.
104. This figure is given in Jutta von Freyberg and Ursula Krause-Schmitt, eds., *Moringen. Lichtenburg. Ravensbrück. Frauen im Konzentrationslager 1933–1945* (Frankfurt am Main, 1997),

16. But see return of numbers for 1937 sent by Krack to Gestapo, 15 February 1938 (NHStA Hann. 158 Moringen, acc. 84/82, nr. 2, 181).

105. Harder and Hesse, "Die Zeuginnen Jehovahs," 37–38; Hesse, *Das Frauen-KZ Moringen*, 41; see also Riebe, "Frauen in Konzentrationslager 1933–1939," 127–34. Estimates of the total number of women detained throughout Germany in the period 1933–39 vary. A figure of 3,000 is cited in Gabriele Pfingsten and Claus Fülberg-Stolle, "Frauen in Konzentrationslagern—geschlechtsspezifische Bedingungen des Überlebens," in Herbert, Orth, and Dieckmann, *Nationalsozialistischen Konzentrationslager*, 911. Sybil Milton's estimate is 6,000–8,000, of whom about 1,500–2,000 were political prisoners, and about a quarter Jewish; see Sybil Milton, "Deutsche and deutsch-jüdische Frauen als Verfolgte des NS-Staates," *Dachauer Hefte* 3 (November 1987), 5.

106. Harder and Hesse, "Die Zeuginnen Jehovahs," 39–43, relying on two databases from the Moringen archives (personal files and personal forms). Harder and Hesse emphasize both the incompleteness of the sources and the fluctuations of inmate proportions at different times. See also Hesse, *Das Frauen-KZ Moringen*, chap. 4. A somewhat different breakdown, based on about 1,200 cases but without a discussion of the source base, is given by von Freyberg and Krause-Schmitt, *Moringen. Lichtenburg. Ravensbrück*, 16: Communists, 26 percent; Jehovah's Witnesses, 22 percent; derogatory remarks, 17 percent; returning émigrés, 12 percent; prostitutes, 9 percent; Jewish violators of the Nuremberg laws, 7 percent; "habitual criminals," 6 percent; Social Democrats, 3 percent; "asocials," 1 percent.

107. The list given in Broszat, "The Concentration Camps," 452, includes a blue triangle designating émigrés, though Drobisch and Wieland, *System der NS-Konzentrationslager*, 206, list this as assigned to "Arbeitszwangshäftlinge" (forced laborers); see also Hackett, *The Buchenwald Report*, 30–31.

108. *Memoir*, 111. Herz's four companions in the Jews' Hall included one other returning émigré (Gertrud Mannheim), two Communists (Herta Kronau and Ilse Lipinski), and one young woman sentenced for violating the Nuremberg laws (Anni Reiner). For identifications, see biographical appendix.

109. Klaus-Michael Mallmann, "Zwischen Denunziation und Roter Hilfe. Geschlechterbeziehungen und kommunistischer Widerstand 1933–1945," in *Frauen gegen die Diktatur. Widerstand und Verfolgung im nationalsozialistischen Deutschland*, ed. Christl Wickert (Berlin, 1995), 86.

110. Jürgen Harder and Hans Hesse, "Female Jehovah's Witnesses in Moringen Women's Concentration Camp: Women's Resistance in Nazi Germany," in Hesse, ed., *Persecution and Resistance*, 35.

111. This account is largely taken from Detlef Garbe, *Zwischen Widerstand und Martyrium. Die Zeugen Jehovahs im "Dritten Reich"* (Munich, 1994); see also Christine King, *The Nazi State and the New Religions: Five Case Studies in Non-Conformity* (New York and Toronto, 1982), chap. 6.

112. Henry Friedländer, "Kategorien der KZ-Häftlinge," in Hesse, *Persecution and Resistance*, 16.

113. For a more positive judgment see Herberman, *The Blessed Abyss*, 175–76.

114. *Memoir*, 64.

115. Ibid., 110.

116. Ibid., 71f.

117. Ibid., 85.

118. Ibid., 86, 85.

119. See Heide-Marie Lauterer, *Parlamentarinnen in Deutschland 1918/19–1949* (Königstein-Taunus, 2002), chap. 5.

120. See Hesse, *Das Frauen-KZ Moringen*, 137–53.

121. Herz invented pseudonyms for her fellow inmates, which I have used in the introduction and kept throughout the memoir text, followed by the real name when it is known. Further biographical details are give in the biographical appendix. For numerous identifications of

Herz's fellow inmates, see Ursula Krause-Schmitt, "Im 'Judensaal' des Frauenkonzentrationslagers Moringen," *Dokumente. Rundbrief der Lagergemeinschaft und Gedenkstätte KZ Moringen* 19 (2000): 6–12. Some inmates are described category by category in Hesse, *Das Frauen-KZ Moringen*, chap. 4.

122. *Memoir*, 83.
123. Ibid., 87.
124. See Centa Herker-Beimler's account in Elling, *Frauen im deutschen Widerstand*, 105–10; Barbara Distel, "Im Schatten der Helden: Kampf und Überleben von Centa Beimler-Herker [*sic*] und Lina Haag," *Dachauer Hefte* 7 (1991): 21–57; von Freyberg and Krause-Schmitt, *Moringen. Lichtenburg. Ravensbrück*, 34–35.
125. See Hans Beimler, *Four Weeks in the Hands of Hitler's Hell-Hounds: The Nazi Murder Camp of Dachau* (London, 1933), 38–42; see also *Memoir*, 87f.
126. Details in Bromberger et al., *Schwestern, vergesst uns nicht*, 105–7, and von Freyberg and Krause-Schmitt, *Moringen. Lichtenburg. Ravensbrück*, 34–35.
127. See biographical appendix.
128. See biographical appendix.
129. Lauterer, *Parlamentarinnen in Deutschland*, 272.
130. For the Communist Party and abortion politics in the Weimar Republic, see Atina Grossmann, *Reforming Sex: The German Movement for Birth Control and Abortion Reform, 1920–1950* (New York, 1995); for the party's views on women's politics and its appeal to women, see Julia Sneeringer, *Winning Women's Votes: Propaganda and Politics in Weimar Germany* (Chapel Hill, 2002), esp. 208–16, 277; and Mallmann, "Zwischen Denunziation und Roter Hilfe."
131. *Memoir*, 85, 135. For women's situation in the Soviet Union in this period, see Wendy Goldman, *Women, the State and Revolution: Soviet Family Policy and Social Life 1917–1936* (Cambridge, 1993), and Sheila Fitzpatrick, *Everyday Stalinism. Ordinary Life in Extraordinary Times: Soviet Russia in the 1930s* (Oxford, 1999), chap. 6.
132. *Memoir*, 131. Centa Herker-Beimler confirms the existence of "discussion groups" that were fed by information smuggled into the camp; see Elling, *Frauen im deutschen Widerstand*, 108.
133. For the purges and show trials, see Barry McLoughlin and Kevin McDermott, eds., *Stalin's Terror: High Politics and Mass Repression in the Soviet Union* (Basingstoke, 2003), and Robert W. Thurston, *Life and Terror in Stalin's Russia, 1934–1941* (New Haven, 1996).
134. *Memoir*, 121.
135. Ibid., 133–35; see also Riebe, "Frauen in Konzentrationslager 1933–1939," 132.
136. *Memoir*, 91.
137. Apart from the evidence of Herz's memoir and the other memoirs already cited, see the report in the *Deutschland-Berichte der Sozialdemokratischen Partei Deutschlands (Sopade)* (Frankfurt am Main, 1980), vol. 3 (1936), 1013–15.
138. *Memoir*, 151.
139. Ibid., 108. The same views were expressed by Wadle, *Mutti, warum lachst du nie?* 86.
140. See Wadle, *Mutti, warum lachst du nie?* 84–86.
141. Copy of the "Dienst- und Hausordnung für das Frauenschutzhaftlager Moringen" in NHStA: Hann 158 Moringen acc. 84/82, nr. 2, 144–47.
142. Described, with illustrations, in Wadle, *Mutti, warum lachst du nie?* 87–94.
143. Interview with Elisabeth Brettler, New York, 25 April 2003.
144. Interview with Arthur Herz, Exton, PA, 14 May 2003.
145. *Memoir*, 85.
146. Ibid., 73.
147. Ibid., 90.
148. Ibid., 78f.
149. Ibid., 153.

150. Ibid., 96f.
151. Ibid., 126.
152. Ibid., 124.
153. Interviews with Arthur Herz, Exton, PA, 14 May 2003, and Elisabeth Brettler, New York, 25 April 2003.
154. For example, *Memoir*, 121 and 128.
155. Richard Beer-Hofmann, *Jaákobs Traum* (Berlin, 1918): "Herr! Was Dein Wille mir auch auferlege/Wie Krone will ich's tragen—nicht wie Joch!" Cited by Herz, *Denk ich am Deutschland*, 312, and paraphrased in *Memoir*, 78.
156. Although all immediate family members survived, Howard Hartig, the husband of Gabriele's granddaughter Ellen, writes that "there were significant losses throughout the extended family," including several second cousins and Emil's aunt, and that Gabriele's son-in-law Maxim Brettler "lost his mother and younger brother, although no specific documentation of their fates has ever surfaced"; communication to author, 3 December 2003.
157. For the Lichtenburg camp, see Klaus Drobisch, "Frauenkonzentrationslager im Schloss Lichtenburg," *Dachauer Hefte* 3 (1987): 101–15; von Freyberg and Krause-Schmitt, *Moringen. Lichtenburg. Ravensbrück*, 49–74; Drobisch and Wieland, *System der NS-Konzentrationslager*, 272, 297–301.
158. Harder and Hesse, "Die Zeuginnen Jehovahs," 55; Drobisch, "Frauenkonzentrationslager im Schloss Lichtenburg," 103.
159. Quoted in Drobisch, "Frauenkonzentrationslager im Schloss Lichtenburg,"107.
160. For Ravensbrück, see references in note 49 above; Herbermann, *The Blessed Abyss*, includes a bibliography of Ravensbrück memoirs.
161. In the spring of 1942, Jewish and physically handicapped inmates were transported to be gassed in the course of the "euthanasia campaign"; medical experiments began at the same time; a camp crematorium—evidence of rising death rates and of the intention to conceal these from outside authorities—was constructed in August 1943 and a gas chamber in December 1944; see Apel, *Jüdische Frauen im Konzentrationslager Ravensbrück*, chap. 6.
162. See von Freyberg and Krause-Schmitt, *Moringen. Lichtenburg. Ravensbrück*, 37.
163. For this aspect of Moringen's history, Meyer, "Abschreckung, Besserung, Unschädlichmachung," 161–70.
164. For this period, see Manuela Neugebauer, *Der Weg in das Jugendschutzlager Moringen* (Godesberg and Mönchengladbach, 1997); Heinrich Muth, "Das 'Jugendschutzlager' Moringen," *Dachauer Hefte* 5 (1989): 223–52; Martin Guse, Andreas Kohrs, and Friedhelm Vahsen, "Das Jugendlager Moringen—Ein Jugendkonzentrationslager," in *Soziale Arbeit und Faschismus*, ed. Hans-Uwe Otto and Heinz Sünker (Bielefeld, 1986), 321–44.
165. On youth protest and "delinquency," see Detlev Peukert, *Die Edelweisspiraten. Protestbewegungen jugendlicher Arbeiter im Dritten Reich* (Cologne, 1988); Matthias von Hellfeld and W. Breyvogel, eds., *Piraten, Swings und junge Garde. Jugendwiderstand im Nationalsozialismus* (Bonn, 1991).
166. Wolf-Dieter Haardt, "'Was denn, hier—in Moringen?!' Die Suche nach einem vergessenen KZ," in *Die vergessene KZs? Gedenkstätten für die Opfer des NS-Terrors in der Bundesrepublik*, ed. Detlef Garbe (Bornheim-Merten, 1983), 98.
167. The memorial is directed by Dr. Dietmar Sedlaczek and may be contacted at Gedenkstätte im Torhaus, Postfach 1131, 37182 Moringen, Germany, or www.gedenkstaette-moringen.de.
168. See Finzsch and Jütte, *Institutions of Confinement*.
169. Dickinson, *The Politics of German Child Welfare*, 294; see also Detlev Peukert, *Volksgenossen und Gemeinschaftsfremde. Anpassung, Ausmerze and Aufbegehren unter dem Nationalsozialismus* (Cologne, 1982); Christoph Sachsse and Florian Tennstedt, *Geschichte der Armenfürsorge in Deutschland*, vol. 2: *Der Wohlfahrtsstaat im Nationalsozialismus* (Berlin and Cologne, 1992); Ayass, *"Asoziale" im Nationalsozialismus*, 217–25.

170. For the public face of the camps, see Robert Gellately, *Backing Hitler: Consent and Coercion in Nazi Germany* (Oxford, 2001), chap. 3; for the relation between "order and terror," see Peukert, *Volksgenossen und Gemeinschaftsfremde*, chap. 11; Robert Gellately, "The Prerogatives of Confinement in Germany, 1933–1945: 'Protective Custody' and Other Police Strategies," in Finzsch and Jütte, *Institutions of Confinement*, 207–11; and introduction to Herbert, Orth, and Dieckmann, *Nationalsozialistischen Konzentrationslager*, vol. 1.

171. Gunnar Richter emphasizes the continuity in administrative practices as well as personnel in Breitenau; see Richter, *Breitenau*, 12.

172. Examples within our purview here include the June 1933 law on eugenic sterilization and abortion and the new legislation on habitual criminals, both of which enacted policies that had long been under discussion in official circles; see Jeremy Noakes, "Nazism and Eugenics: The Background to the Nazi Sterilization Law of 14 July 1933," in *Ideas into Politics*, ed. R. J. Bullen, H. Pogge von Strandmann, and A. B. Polonsky (London, 1984), 75–94, and Wagner, "'Vernichtung der Berufsverbrecher.'"

173. For examples, see Suhr, *Die Emslandlager*, 209ff.

174. See Gellately, *Backing Hitler*, 51–61.

175. See Sigrid Jacobeit, "Fotografien als historische Quellen zum Frauen-KZ Ravensbrück," in Eschebach and Kootz, *Das Frauenkonzentrationslager Ravensbrück*, 33–45, and Philipp, *Kalendarium*, 214–31.

The Women's Camp in Moringen

A Memoir of Imprisonment in Germany, 1936–1937

Moringen, Mid-October 1936

Barely two weeks have passed since my arrest in Berlin, and only a few days since my incarceration here in Moringen. And yet this brief period seems like an eternity to me. What a difference between the old security of my protected home in Berlin and the insecurity of the present; such a profusion of events and individuals, so many strange destinies.

But let me tell the story as it unfolded.

It was September 29, 1936. We were entertaining friends, as we did so often: an art correspondent, an editor, and a physician. Our garden was in its full fall splendor, the asters were aglow with color, tubs of red geraniums encircled our broad terrace, fruit hung heavy from the tall trellises. Cheerful shouts rang out from the nearby Grunewald, and the wind bore the fragrant scent of the pines. But our friends took no notice of this beauty. They strode pensively across the wide lawn and discussed the political problems of the day: the repression within the country, the constant threat to the independence of Austria and Czechoslovakia, the consequences of Italy's subjugation of Ethiopia, the horrors of the Spanish Civil War, the indecisiveness of the Western powers. Now, three years after he had seized power, Hitler had it all his own way.

After dinner my husband Ehm [Emil] read aloud a series of passages from Nietzsche's *Human, All Too Human*.[1] They showed just how much the Nazis now dishonor the great philosopher by attempting to claim him as a prophet of their own teachings. Nietzsche repeatedly condemns the inherent emptiness of the Germans, their lack of genuine culture, their pursuit of external power with no sense of purpose. Against the narrow-minded "Teutonic-German provincial" cast of thought, he invokes the freedom and breadth of a coming "European mentality." Surprisingly, he sees the Russians and the Jews as the strongest driving forces for a successful transformation of Europe in the future. He urges the German people to free themselves from their spiritual and political ponderousness by embracing a racial mixture with the more dynamic Jewish population.

My husband's restlessness struck me. He was constantly fetching another book, asking new questions, suddenly interrupting the discussion and withdrawing to his study, first with one, then with another of his friends. I assumed that this anxiety was a lingering effect of the illness from which he had only recently recovered. The next morning, however, brought the real

---

Notes for the *Memoir* begin on page 159.

explanation. Ehm handed over a notice, addressed to me, which had arrived the evening before:

Summons

You are hereby required to report to Berlin Police Headquarters, Alexanderplatz, Room 217, between 11 and 12 o'clock on Wednesday morning, September 30, 1936, for the purpose of your interrogation. Passport required.

The Secret State Police [The Gestapo]

"This demand is a bad sign," said Ehm anxiously. "I'm sure the Gestapo wants to hear the details of your stay in Italy. We should get on our way."

At 11 o'clock on the dot we were at Police Headquarters. We were admitted into one of the great portals of the immense dark red building. An iron gate prevented access to the interior. I presented my summons to the guard on duty and was let in. Ehm asked to be allowed to accompany me, but the officer rejected all of his entreaties with a firm "no." And so I had to make my way on my own. I walked through a long corridor that exuded icy cold and a sense of hostility. The few people who scurried past looked intimidated. Eventually, I reached Interrogation Room 217, a room universally recognized and feared throughout Berlin.[2] I composed myself, knocked, and entered. A senior official [Regierungsrat], a tall, well-groomed man, received me coolly but politely, and had me sit down in front of his file-covered desk.

"Frau Herz," he began, "you returned from Italy four weeks ago. Where did you live there, and for how long?"

"I spent about half a year with the sister of my late mother in Merano."

"A stay abroad in excess of three months means that you forfeit your right to return to Germany and is punishable by law."

"That regulation is completely new to me. It did not exist when I left the country."

"Yes, it was issued only very recently, and it is retroactive.[3] What was the purpose of your stay in Merano?"

"I was investigating opportunities for a new life for us in Italy."

"Were your efforts successful?"

"Negotiations for us to take over a tourist hotel or perhaps for my husband to find a teaching position are still pending."

"Why did you return?"

"Because my husband fell seriously ill here in Berlin."

The official leafed through his files.

"Your spouse is the director of a publishing house, correct?"

"My husband was a board member and director of the Ullstein Publishing House.[4] He had to give up his position two years ago."

"Why didn't your spouse leave Germany, too, and follow you to Italy?"

"My husband had made all the preparations for his emigration, but was unable to proceed with it owing to the fact that he fell ill."

The official removed from his files a large sheet of paper stamped with several seals, read it carefully, braced himself, and said: "Since your stay abroad was limited to several months in our ally Italy, only three months of instructional camp [*Schulungslager*] will be required of you."

"Three months of instructional camp," I repeated in terror. "Is there no way around this? Am I allowed to appeal?"

"No. There is no appeal against a decision of the Gestapo. Instructional camp, by the way, is the most lenient type of custody; it does not mean prison. You have one day to put your affairs in order. I will expect you in my office tomorrow at this same time. Your passport will remain here as security against any attempt to escape."

A quick nod. I was dismissed.

EHM REFUSED TO ACCEPT this ruling lying down. He rushed off to see the relatives of Manfred von Richthofen, whose book, *The Red Fighter Pilot*, he had published years earlier. That book had become a kind of national Bible. Field Marshal Hermann Göring had recently written a special foreword to a new edition. Ehm also called on a number of military officers whose writings he had published. Then he went to Air Force Colonel Udet, who had been a long-time colleague at the publishing house.[5]

Ehm found closed doors everywhere. Yet he refused to give in: "We must just abandon everything here and flee straight to Holland tonight, or even better to Denmark."

"That's out of the question," I argued. "My passport has been confiscated." We saw no way out. We had to bow to the inevitable.

OUR CHILDREN TRIED HUMOR to mask our mutual anxiety: "Be careful, Father, once Mother has been properly 'instructed,' there will be nothing to laugh about. She will bring you to your senses with her mighty worker's hands."

I packed a small suitcase. Winter was coming, so I included lots of warm clothing. I felt increasingly uneasy. What might lie ahead for me? During the night I wrote to my friends. Were they farewell letters? I don't know.

Ehm and I again set out early. The train was packed with young people reporting for Labor Service[6] that day, the first of October. Happy laughter, jokes, and humorous exclamations rang from every compartment. At the Alexanderplatz station, an SA band had lined up and was sending off the young people with lively marches: "Muss i denn, muss i denn zum Städtle hinaus, und du, mein Schatz, bleibst hier? [Must I then, must I then go to the town and you, my dear, stay here?]" Does that song also apply to me?

Again we walked through the immense portal, through the wide, echoing passageways, until we reached the doorway of the State Police.

"I shall move heaven and earth to get you out again as soon as possible," Ehm whispered to me.

A long handclasp, a farewell kiss, and Ehm left me. I already knew my way to Room 217. The same official again received me politely, made a few notes to himself in his files, then took me to two police officers in another room, and left.

What a difference. As much as the first official had made a point of treating me like a "lady," the police officer who now began yet another round of interrogation questioned me as if he were facing a hardened criminal. An undisguised malice permeated all of his questions about birth dates, parents, husband, and children.

"Why didn't you leave Germany for good? We don't want you here anyway."

"Because I do not wish to emigrate alone; my husband, in spite of his best efforts, has been unable to arrange his own emigration due to his illness."

"We will send even the blind and the lame on their way. Your husband was the director of a publishing house? Which firm?"

"My husband managed the Ullstein book publishing house and its affiliate Propyläen Publications."

The official jumped as if he had been bitten by a tarantula.

"What, Ullstein and Propyläen? They're the ones who published the works of liberal riff-raff like Erich Maria Remarque, Zuckmayer, Frank, Lion Feuchtwanger, Alfred Neumann, and Vicki Baum.[7] The books we could burn— the authors, unfortunately, have escaped abroad."

As if he needed to engage in dialogue with his Führer, he cast a long glance at the large portrait of Hitler that looked down, defiant and threatening, from the wall.

"And you," the interrogation continued, "did you write for any of the newspapers they published? For the *Vossische Zeitung*, by any chance?"

Ah, the dear old *Vossische Zeitung*, I thought. For two hundred years it had championed freedom, progress, culture. Then after the Nazi takeover, it had refused to prostitute itself by fawning over the new rulers, and decided to cease publication voluntarily.[8]

"No, I never worked as a writer."

"Were you politically active, were you a member of the Social Democratic or Communist Parties?"

"No."

"How long and where did you live in Italy?"

"About six months, with my relatives in Merano."

"What do your relatives think of our new Germany?"

I hesitated. What is the meaning of this unexpected and dangerous question? Is it a trap? The man leaned well forward. Over his thick eyeglasses his malevolent, narrowed eyes observed me with intense concentration.

"What are you waiting for, answer me now."

"We discussed family matters and possible career opportunities for myself. In any case, my relatives are not Germans, but Italians," I answered calmly.

The second officer, an older man who until then had listened to the interrogation silently but with obvious discomfort, interjected very quietly but very firmly: "I hardly think that is relevant. The matter has been completely clarified. I shall draw up the transcript."

He dictated a lengthy record of my interrogation, which I had to sign, then he led me out.

"There are still a few formalities to take care of. Follow me."

First stop: The records department. Again I had to account for my family background and state for the record which of my relatives should be notified "in the event of my sudden demise."

Second stop: The photography studio. I know from other cases that they will take numerous shots of me and show them to my relatives in a few days' time, so that they can confirm my identity yet again and ensure that no one else has impersonated me. A curious idea—as if anyone, however much you paid her, would want to take my place.

Third stop: The fingerprint unit. I winced, but my guide informed me: "We used to do this only with criminals, but recently we have started doing it with everyone we admit."

After the procedure was completed, I was supposed to wipe my hands with a dirty rag, but I used my handkerchief. The constable barked at me angrily: "Don't be so fussy, lady! You're going to have to get used to things being a lot different from now on."

On it went—upstairs, downstairs, through ever more corridors and floors. The fall sun and my inner turmoil brought perspiration to my brow; my little suitcase began to feel heavy in my hands.

Fourth stop: I could not believe my eyes when the long hallway led to an iron gate which bore the inscription, in large black letters: WOMEN'S PRISON. Frightened, I looked at the official: "But yesterday the official told me that 'instructional camp' does not mean prison."

The policeman shrugged his shoulders: "You've held up well so far, Frau Herz. Keep your courage up."

An electric signal light flashes. A prison matron appeared, greeted me: "Body search."

Dulled, listless, I undressed. My dress, the coat and its pockets, the little suitcase were rummaged through, nail file and scissors were confiscated, my fountain pen as well, money counted and locked away, the suitcase taken to a storeroom, a detailed list made of my belongings by number, color, and size. The matron stares at me. Suddenly she asks: "Now tell me, how on earth did *you* get here? What crime have *you* committed?"

"I stayed with my mother's sister in Italy for a few months, that is my crime."

Pensively and ambiguously, she replies: "Well, well, you learn something every day."

Fifth and, for the time being, last stop: A cell, which I was more or less shoved into.[9] In the twilight of the waning day, I could distinguish a woman—no, three women—then iron bedsteads with blue checked covers, a table, and an unoccupied stool, which I sat down on. The women ask sympathetic questions, to which I give monosyllabic answers. Dinner is brought. I am given a tin bowl with soup and two thick, dry slices of bread. Prison and a tin bowl. I begin to grasp my situation. I cannot eat, cannot speak, cannot hear. I want to go to bed, but am quickly warned that this is not allowed before 7 o'clock. Time passes slowly. Finally the wait is over. I try to stretch out, but the hard iron springs press painfully, literally boring into my flesh. One of the women hands me her blanket: "Maybe this will help, it's very difficult at first."

I close my eyes and try to sleep. But sleep is out of the question. The cell is right on the street, on the Alexanderplatz, the center of Berlin. An awful, ever-increasing din rises from below us. Automobile horns, shouts and laughter, the raucous yells of drunks, the elevated trains speeding past, drawing red ribbons on the cell wall with the light from their windows. Their violent motion makes the beds shudder.

In vain I attempt to collect my thoughts. The events of this one short day return only in incoherent, blurred images. If this is the beginning, what will the ending be? Will I ever see my husband and my children again?

From the tower of the Parochial Church, the ancient, familiar chimes ring out:

Üb immer Treu und Redlichkeit	Be ever honest, ever true
Bis an dein kühles Grab	Until your dying day
Und weiche keinen Finger breit	And ne'er a hairbreadth deviate
Von Gottes Wegen ab.	From God's ordainéd way.

I can distinguish the high, sharp tones clearly. Yes, be ever honest, ever true. And the reward for such action? Just don't think about it. Don't think about it.

IF I SURVIVED the prison at the Alex unharmed, it is thanks to the three women with whom I shared my cell. Two of them, Helene and Else, were Bible Students;[10] Fränze was a Communist. In past years I had become acquainted with a number of Communists, but until then I had never met any Bible Students. I had envisioned them as weak, somehow physically or mentally deformed beings. Possibly Else conformed very remotely to my preconceived image: a delicate person, late twenties, with flaxen hair and a pale face covered with freckles. But Helene? I would never in my life have thought that she was a Bible Student. A magnificently developed woman aged about thirty-five, she was the personification of the best German characteristics. Tall, with radiant blue eyes, she wore her luxuriant blond hair like a crown. Despite her modest economic circumstances—she and her husband had been caretakers for a house on the west side of Berlin—she possessed a remarkably good general education and a quite amazing knowledge of the Bible. She could recite any passage in the Old or New Testament from memory, by author, chapter, and verse, and the Word dripped like honey from her lips. She enjoyed pontificating, and was, with all due modesty, quite conscious of her own worth.

There had lately been a lot of news about legal action against the Bible Students, but I didn't know why the Third Reich hounded them so mercilessly and punished them so severely. After all, "Bible Student" sounds so harmless and gentle. I questioned Helene, and she volunteered information willingly.

"We Jehovah's Witnesses—the term 'Bible Students' is misleading—believe we are under an obligation to obey unequivocally every word of the Holy Scripture. We want to re-establish Christianity in its original purity and lead our lives as the evangelists and the apostles did, in communion only with our Lord, without the church, without its pretensions to authority, and without its priests. Our goal is the kingdom of God on earth, a kingdom of peace, without hatred, war, or consideration of race and nationality. We abhor the National Socialist state. We reject Hitler's claim that the Nordic-Germanic 'master race' is superior, we refuse to give the Hitler salute, we do not sing the bloodthirsty 'Horst Wessel Song,'[11] and we steer clear of the Labor Front.[12] The Nazis are enraged by our resistance and are making every effort to break up our congregations and destroy our entire community. I already realized that at my first interrogation: 'Your activities as an individual are of no interest to us,' the police officer told me, 'but the organization as a whole interests us a lot. Start by giving us the membership list of your congregation.'

"'I do not possess any such list,' I answered truthfully. I felt no obligation to add that I had been able to burn it in our basement furnace while the police were conducting a search of our apartment.

"'Then give us the names from memory.'

"'I refuse to perform such a dishonorable act.'

"'You'd get an early release if you give us an exact account of the names.'

"'I am no Judas. I will not betray my Savior for thirty pieces of silver.'

"The police officer pulled out a phonograph record.

"'This record has been distributed in Berlin and in the provinces. It bears the innocuous label "Religious Education" and only has quotations from the Bible on it. But they have been deliberately selected to contradict and subvert our most recent decree on "The Duties of the Hitler Youth." Who assembled these quotations? Who made this recording?'

"'I don't know.'

"'Who produced and distributed it?'

"'I won't say.'

"'We have ways to open your mouth. Near Hanover there are concentration camps with very successful educational methods: hard labor in the moorland and rods and whips have broken the resistance of women stronger than you.'

"A chill went down my spine. Corporal punishment for women! But I answered calmly: 'Matthew says, "It is better for you to enter life maimed or crippled than to have two hands or two feet and be thrown into eternal fire"' [Matthew 18:8]."

Fränze, the beautiful and vivacious 22-year-old Communist, had listened to this report with both approval and disdain. "I didn't oblige the authorities with such fine language," she said. "But otherwise my examination went the same way. In every interrogation they mainly want to identify confederates and accomplices. I couldn't deny that I was a member of an illegal organization. A former friend who had been seduced by the big reward had betrayed me. The jerk. I couldn't deny either that I had contributed illustrations and articles to our newsletter, *The Red Front*. But I was absolutely determined not to give up the names of my comrades. They put me in solitary confinement for three weeks in an attempt to bring me around. It was awful. A cramped, dim cell, gray-black walls. No let-up whatsoever. Days and nights were barely distinguishable. Nothing to do. Always alone with only my own thoughts, which threatened to turn into hallucinations. One night, a prisoner in the cell next to mine went mad. Her screams reverberated horribly along the corridor: 'I'm dead, bury me already, but in a Christian cemetery. A priest should say an "Our Father." But you dogs are letting me rot here in my cell.' The guards had trouble overpowering this madwoman, but finally they dragged her in a sack into the maniacs' cell, which has rubber walls so no sound can escape."

THE CONVERSATION LINGERS uneasily on such depressing memories, the women making a conscious effort not to lose their emotional balance. All activity is forbidden in the prison, to make the experience more grueling, so the women try to relieve this dangerous enforced idleness with "reading" and "games." Neither is permitted, of course, but necessity is the mother of invention. Four times a day, the matron takes the prisoners to the lavatory. She waits at the open doors until her charges leave the private area. But before this, the prisoners tuck away as many sheets of the cut-up newspaper that serves as toilet paper as they can hide under their clothes. If your luck is bad, you rescue a government gazette with official notices; if your luck is good, you carry back pieces of the daily newspapers. These pieces are put back together again in the cell and read with the utmost interest. The news they contain, no matter how outdated, offers the only contact with the outside world and kindles passionate discussions. Crossword puzzles, which generate hours of hard deliberation, are awarded "first prize."

Once that harvest has been exhausted, the "playing cards" are retrieved from the mattresses. They look nothing like regular, colorful playing cards. Instead they are just pitiful gray pieces of cardboard, the imprint "Camelia Sanitary Napkins" still betraying their origin. It was only with great effort that I recognized the primitive pencil sketches as the usual characters: King, Queen, Jack. The "playing cards" come from the previous "owners" of our cell, who had in turn received them from their predecessors. They are passed on as a valuable legacy from one prisoner generation to the next.

Food offered another break in the monotony. It was almost always bad and often inedible, usually consisting of a thick slice of bread spread with margarine or mashed turnips, along with a pasty soup with a minimum of meat and fat. Depending on its handful of other ingredients, it passed itself off as cabbage soup, bean soup, or pea soup. Maggots were often a free bonus. Most disquieting was the absolutely nauseating addition of carbonate of soda, intended as a bromide to curb sexual arousal.

This malnutrition, along with the lack of activity, is the most important element in a system that has been carefully and deliberately developed to weaken the prisoners and break their physical and emotional resolve. It leads promptly to severe weight loss among the newly admitted, which ends only because the stay here is limited to the three to four months of pre-trial detention. Later, after sentencing, the prisoners are sent off to other jails, prisons, or concentration camps. A short time ago, a Communist, the wife of a wealthy manufacturer, had the courage to file an official complaint. She appealed in writing to the director of the prison: "One day we too will be restored to the community. How are we to bear vigorous children? The starvation diet here endangers not only our own health, but still more that of the next generation." None of these arguments met with the slightest success. And for these disgraceful rations the state exacts a "food and lodging fee" of 1.50 marks a day, when they can collect it.

"They'll get nothing from me," gloated Helene. "I invested my little bit of money in warm clothing just in time. But the rest of you will have to pay. The word of the Gospel according to Luke applies to each of you: 'You will not get out until you have paid the very last penny' [Luke 12:59]."

Even so, I did not immediately enjoy my full share of these sumptuous provisions: since I was a "newcomer," there was nothing spread on my bread slices for the first five days. It was difficult for me to resist the generosity of my companions, who kept trying to share their meager rations with me. "Springtime" made a sympathetic remark each time she served me the dry bread, consoling me with the prospect of better times to come.

"Springtime" is in fact the only guard who behaves decently toward the prisoners, whereas her colleagues are malevolent and dangerous. There is "Dear Auntie Anna," so called because she always pretends to be so loving and kind, but isn't; and then there is "The White Poplar," with her silver hair, so incongruous with her vicious nature; "The Radio Tower," who broadcasts her malicious whispers from a height of 1.90 meters [6'2"]; and "The Mushroom," with her fuzzy mop of dyed auburn hair, who takes obvious pleasure in harassing the prisoners in every possible way.

ONCE A DAY all of the prisoners are led outdoors for half an hour of fresh air. "Fall in for exercise" is the command. Cell after cell empties, and behind the matrons a long line of silent women starts to move. Not a word, not a call may interrupt the silence. Violation results in solitary confinement, reduction of the daily food rations, and other penalties. One cannot walk on the wide center of the corridor; it's coated with a glaze, smooth as glass, which offers no foothold, as a precaution against escape attempts. The shoulder along the wall is very narrow, to allow for better control, and has room for just one person at a time.

Down below is the prison yard.

In the midst of a huge complex of buildings, a space of only a few square meters, paved with stone slabs, has been left vacant. Dirty, blackish-red walls, many stories high, compress it. Fresh air has only limited access, the sun none at all. These stone edifices, which threaten to crush the bleak area under their collective weight, feature windows large and small, spaced equidistantly, all barred with thick iron gratings. A place redolent of terror and dread. Once this was the site of supreme corrective justice, the tragic scene of crime and punishment—but no longer. Now it is the stronghold of exultant and derisive injustice, of punishment without crime.

Approximately one hundred women crowd into the cramped space, among them a few prostitutes and a few thieves, but the overwhelming majority are Communists and Bible Students. There are newly admitted women—lively, resilient, almost curious—and inmates into whose features the long ordeal has cut its sharp traces. All social classes are represented, and all age groups. The women's attire remains exactly as it was at the moment of arrest, varying from evening gown, casual dress, or work shirt to the gaudy splendor of the prostitutes.

At the gate to the courtyard and on the top steps of the main stairway, affording a clear prospect, a unit of heavily armed policemen stands guard. They size us up with threatening yet mocking looks; opposite defenseless women, their nightsticks, revolvers, and rifles look crass and absurd.

At two opposite ends of the yard, two matrons share the command. "Forward, march!" commands the one. The women start moving, one by one, in single file. "Move it!" shouts the other one.

Many cannot go on, are left behind, step into the inner circle, which is meant for the weak and the physically handicapped, and walk on slowly.

"Faster, faster!" the voice, curt and shrill, commands. Feet pump, hair flutters, breath is short.

An eerie scene. A dance of death, but danced by living, poor, exhausted, groaning people. I am reminded of the woodcuts of Holbein, the etchings of Goya. Beethoven comes to mind, the immortal music of *Fidelio*, the procession of prisoners who are taken briefly from their dark dungeons into the prison yard and pour out their sorrow in grief-stricken song. Only here there is no singing, no speaking, no lamenting. Here the women run around in circles as if possessed. They run, they race, they surge ahead with all their strength, as if their lives depended on it.

"Faster. Faster!"

ONE MORNING A matron handed Else a note. "Interrogation tomorrow," Else said softly and dejectedly.

"You needn't be afraid of anything," Helene tried to calm her. "You were never in a position of authority. You never spoke in meetings. You were always only an ordinary servant of the Word. Sure, you attended our meetings regularly, and you distributed our journal *Awake*. But that's it. Stay with the truth, but avoid every unnecessary word."

"Yes, you, Helene, you know when to speak and when to be silent, you know how to put words together intelligently. But God has denied me such gifts. I am no match for these people."

"Don't belittle yourself, Else. You know Ecclesiastes says: 'Patience is better than pride' [Ecclesiastes 7:8]."

"But it's not so much about me as the others. The Gestapo is trying to get incriminating information out of me against my wonderful boss, who employed me as a sales clerk in his bakery and introduced me to our movement. Even the customers who bought their bread and rolls from us are suspect. I don't know what I should say to the officer."

"In Luke it is said: 'When you are brought before synagogues, rulers, and authorities, do not worry about how you will defend yourselves or what you will say, for the Holy Spirit will teach you at that time what you should say' [Luke 12:11-12]."

Helene's voice resounded like that of a preacher. Else collapsed onto her stool. Her delicate body became even smaller. There was fear in her eyes.

"Whatever I say, these people will twist my words. They impale every word as if with a skewer, and entangle you in contradictions. They threaten you with awful punishments, concentration camp, physical abuse. I am afraid of them, really afraid."

"In the first letter of John it is said, 'There is no fear in love. But perfect love drives out fear … The one who fears is not made perfect in love' [1 John 4:18]."

Helene pulled her frightened friend from her stool and led her gently aside: "Let us call to our Lord."

To the noises of the metropolis pounding up from the street below, to the indistinct sounds that give our citadel such eerie life—the creaking of a cell door, faint footsteps in the hall, the quickly stifled scream of a prisoner—are added whispered words of prayer. They are taken from that book into which Jewish people, thousands of years ago, put their fears but also their faith in God and their will to live, and which still offers an abiding refuge to the afflicted the world over—the Psalms.

Helene had strung together verses from different Psalms and shaped them into a prayer appropriate to the situation. She recited each verse slowly and Else repeated it after her.

"'In my anguish I cried to the Lord, and He answered by setting me free' [Psalms 118:5].

"'Save me, O God, for the waters have come up to my neck … the floods engulf me' [69:1-2].

"'Save me, O Lord, from lying lips and from deceitful tongues' [120:2].

"'Since they hid their net for me without cause and without cause dug a pit for me' [35:7].

"'Ruthless witnesses come forward; they question me on things I know nothing about' [35:11].

"'Yet for your sake we face death all day long; we are considered as sheep to be slaughtered' [44:22].

"'Defend my cause and redeem me; preserve my life according to your promise' [119:154].

"'Your word is a lamp to my feet and a light for my path' [119:105].
"'Your love, O Lord, reaches to the heavens, your faithfulness to the skies' [36:5].
"'For with you is the fountain of life; in your light we see light' [36:10]."
Else calmed down. That night, however, I heard her moaning. I went to her.
She was lying in bed trembling, her pulse racing, with beads of cold sweat on her
forehead. Only after many hours did she fall asleep again. In the morning "White
Poplar" brought the news: "The interrogation originally scheduled for today has
been postponed until next week. Date and time will be announced later."

Else might well die of fright by then. Yes, they do know how to crush people
in the Alex.

THE NEXT DAY Helene wanted to hold another prayer session, but Fränze was
indignant: "Can't you just give your interminable whimpering a rest. You have
been rattling off your litany for centuries. But in all that time nothing has
changed. Hatred, misery, and exploitation remain. We Communists had to
step in to provide mankind with a new life worthy of the human being."

"You're a bit late," scoffed Helene. "It's a good thing mankind wasn't depending on you. Long before your Lenin and Stalin, Moses, the prophets, and the
other lawmakers of the Old Testament put the practice of charity, social responsibility, the protection of the poor and the weak at the center of every human
and divine order. And they redressed the worst abuses of social inequality by
naming the fiftieth year as the great Hallel [Praise] year, in which all debts were
to be forgiven and all property was to be given back to its original owner."

These arguments made little impact on Fränze. She was completely in her
element and sparkled with the pleasure of combat. "Those were nothing but
paper promises. Faded schemes without flesh and bones, mere fantasies that
have never been realized. It just won't do to pin the hopes of all humanity on
the clouds, on the alleged will of an allegedly supreme being. Our fate is determined here on earth. Our challenge to religion rests on the knowledge that we
must forcibly take your heaven with its God and its saints away from you, so
that we can finally give you our earth with all its riches."

Helene had sprung to her feet, indignant, her voice was suddenly sharp.
"Your earth. How cold and loveless it has become because of you. You destroy
every true value, you suffocate all personal life. You level and regiment everything with your egalitarianism. So and so many cubic meters of living space. So
and so many grams of protein, fat, and carbohydrates. So and so many hours for
work, so and so many for sports—perhaps even half an hour for making love.
You banish beauty, enthusiasm, and idealism from God's wonderful earth. You
turn it into a joyless place for machines and smokestacks. The prophecy of Amos
applies to you and expressly to you: 'The days are coming,' declares the Sovereign
Lord, 'when I will send a famine through the land—not a famine of food or a
thirst for water, but a famine of hearing the words of the Lord' [Amos 8:11]."

Fränze shook her head and made a gesture with her delicate, nervous hands
as if she were trying to push an obstacle out of her way. "The same proverbs

over and over, the same God-ordained subordination. Meanwhile, the Nazi tide is rising higher and higher, but you put your hands in your lap, gaze raptly heavenwards, and make pious speeches."

"That's not true," countered Helene passionately. "We don't just talk, we also fight, but in our own way and with our own weapons. Without priests and a church hierarchy we are freer and more mobile than the Catholic and Evangelical communities. We undermine the Nazi state from within, we strengthen all of the forces of the resistance with our propaganda. We proceed as James recommended in the first chapter of his epistle: 'Do not merely listen to the word, and so deceive yourselves. Do what it says. Anyone who listens to the word but does not do what it says is like a man who looks at his face in a mirror [and, after looking at himself, goes away and immediately forgets what he looks like]' [James 1:22–24]."

Fränze became pensive. "But you leave us Communists to carry on the actual struggle, to commit our blood and our lives. In the end, Hitler will not be dislodged by sermons and prayers, but only by fire and the sword. Maybe we will have to travel a short distance together. But you church ladies are not of much use in the long run."

Suddenly Fränze addressed me: "Frau Herz, I want to make sure that you don't come under the influence of these holy women and become one of them yourself. Come on, I'll show you some pages from *our* bible."

She led me to the long wall opposite the window and invited me to read. It took some time before I was able to see and decipher the hairline etched inscriptions. They were so completely drowned in the gray of the paint on the wall that it would have been impossible for the uninitiated to discern them. It took unbelievable audacity to carry the fight into the bosom of the enemy like this. For a moment I felt that I was not in a Prussian prison cell, but in the offices of a Communist newspaper. There were those pithy declarations from *The Communist Manifesto* of Marx and Engels: "Workers of the world, unite. You have everything to gain, and nothing to lose but your chains."

These were followed by excerpts from essays and speeches by Lenin, Stalin, Gorky.

We will eradicate the ruling class and put an end, once and for all, to the exploitation of any person by his fellow men.

We will transform the crisis of capitalism into a victorious and triumphant revolution. We have the capacity, the organization, and the necessary resolve.

Communism is the leap from the realm of repression into the realm of freedom.

The oppressed people now celebrates its marriage to freedom. Strong and happy people will emerge from this union.[13]

In between were poems by Karl Liebknecht, Rosa Luxemburg's prison letters, and pictures and drawings as well.[14] Some of the portraits were quite artistically executed: Lenin with a friendly face, complete with goatee, suggesting more a comfortable bourgeois than the powerful figure of a world revolutionary; Trotsky, intelligent, elegant, bespectacled, making a grand gesture, archetype of the intellectual; Stalin, short, stocky, cunning, with a thick moustache, archetype of the Asiatic.

In contrast to these portraits were expert caricatures: Hitler, a wide open, screaming mouth; Goebbels, a weirdly elongated clubfoot and a Mephistophelian face; Göring, a broad, manly chest covered with medals.

A great deal of space was taken up by excerpts from Stalin's speeches during the years 1934–35, with ominous references to an inevitable new war:

> Despite the experiences of the World War, the bourgeois politicians have forgotten everything and reach out for war just as the shipwrecked grasp at straws; they have reached a dead end, and they have no choice but to throw themselves headfirst into the abyss.
>
> Amidst this stormy sea of disaster and ruin, amidst this preparation for a new war, for a division of the world, towers the single rock which is the Soviet Union, carrying on its fight for peace.

Fränze, who knew these writings by heart, softly read out many of the passages when I had trouble deciphering the tiny letters.

A clanking of keys outside. In a flash we were in our places. "Springtime" unlocked the door and addressed Fränze. "Your husband is waiting for you. You may speak for ten minutes. I'll take you to the visiting room right away."

Fränze's expression was one of utter disbelief. "My husband. Here? Impossible." For a moment she stood motionless. Then, with a happy burst of laughter, she followed the matron.

A quarter of an hour later she returned, sad and tearful. "Oh, how difficult everything is. Gustav was standing there in front of me, separated from me by the bars, tall, blond, powerful, and yet totally broken. He couldn't speak at all at first and was choking back the tears. Of course I had to cry, too. He gave me a bar of chocolate and two apples. But the guard wouldn't allow me to bring perishables back to the cell. So we consumed those treasures together. Then he told me. He had applied for a new job, for twelve marks a week more. The foreman looks over his references, nods with satisfaction, wants to hire Gustav. One last glance at the police identity card. 'What? "Wife is a Communist, an agitator, detained for investigation"? Get out!' Now Gustav continues to work at his same old job, but the shop steward for the Labor Front is threatening to report him: 'You're a decent guy, and politically trustworthy. But a marriage with a Communist is as bad as one with a Jew. Get divorced soon, or else you'll be thrown out of the Labor Front, and then you know you'll never get a job anywhere ever again.' Despite all that, Gustav just said to me: 'Fränze, I will wait for you no matter how long it takes.' But that's easier said than done. I feel so sorry for the poor guy. I just can't allow him to lose his job for ever. Yes, the Catholic Church is absolutely right to forbid its clergy to marry. Anyone who wants to serve a great cause with total dedication must stand alone, without ties to husband and children."

The young woman's misery touched me deeply. "How long a sentence do you expect, in fact?"

"That's hard to say. Just a year or so ago the sentences were lenient, perhaps two to three years in prison. Now they are coming down much harder. For offenses like mine, distributing Communist publications, it's now six to eight years in the penitentiary."

I recoiled in shock: "Six to eight years. Impossible!"

"What's impossible for these fine gentlemen?" laughed Fränze bitterly. "But don't worry. I won't do that much time. The Nazi regime won't survive that long. Russia will see to that. The tension between the two enemies grows with each passing day. Our Russian brothers will not allow us to waste away in prison. But if our liberation is too long in coming—which I don't expect—well, for a courageous person there is always one way left to freedom." Fränze had spoken calmly, deliberately, her words ringing with determination.

"Do not think such terrible, blasphemous thoughts," countered Helene in horror. "Take the words of Solomon to heart: 'Anyone who is among the living has hope—even a live dog is better off than a dead lion!' [Ecclesiastes 9:4]."

"No, no dog, no dog-like resignation, a thousand times rather death!" raged Fränze passionately.

DURING THE NEXT exercise hour a prisoner was hunted down. The silver-haired "White Poplar" was leading us. Down below, at the foot of the main stairs, stood "The Mushroom," her head cocked way back. She pursued the women with her malevolent eyes, which seemed to fuse themselves to each mouth in turn to confirm that it was not defying instructions by opening itself to speak. A young girl became her prey.

The punishment was imposed on the spot: "Three days in solitary with only bread and water."

When we came together again upstairs in our room, Fränze thundered: "Just imagine, Gerda, my comrade, the one they just caught, is totally innocent. Someone else was talking on the stairs. But *she* doesn't have the courage to come forward, and Gerda would be ashamed to betray her. She'd rather suffer a punishment she doesn't deserve."

The strict ban on talking had prevented another woman, apparently a Jew, from addressing me on the way back from exercise. She had approached me, a question on her lips, then turned away from me again with a sorrowful look.

"I saw that," said Fränze. "That was Lisa Goldschmidt, I know her well. She's almost a friend of mine. You see, for a long time my Gustav worked as a chauffeur for her father, a physician in Potsdam. Strange, isn't it? The daughter of our former employer and me, here together in the Alex. After her father's death, Lisa inherited quite a fortune from him, and since she was a trained physician, she also took over his large practice. The Nazis wouldn't stand for that. They accused her of having performed illegal operations on a number of women. The trial proved her completely innocent. There were still impartial judges in

Berlin then. But her enemies kept after her like a pack of wild dogs. They 'discovered' duplicated Communist leaflets allegedly typed on Lisa's typewriter. Lisa denied any part in it. The typewriter was no longer even in her possession; she had given it to a colleague long before. Was he the perpetrator, or perhaps a Nazi informant who used the typewriter to ruin the girl? Such cases are no rarity in today's Germany. Lisa is certainly innocent. But how to prove it? And when it rains, it pours. Lisa, unmarried, charged with performing abortions a year ago, has been pregnant for months."

SUNDAY. THE BREAKERS that the thundering life of the metropolis hurls against the walls of our prison have subsided. Even the din within our giant building has been silenced.

Sunday. An unusual and almost alarming silence enveloped the Alex. There was no clanging of cell doors, the echoing corridors and stairways were deserted, people went about as if on tiptoe, there was no exercise period.

The food, served earlier than usual, was even worse than usual. Apparently the cook regarded even the most modest effort as a desecration of the Sabbath. Atop the foul-smelling soup floated a few slices of half-cooked cabbage. With an expression of disgust, Fränze pushed her tin bowl aside. "Useless, worse than dishwater. Once a week at least, on Sundays, surely they could treat us to a mouthful of meat."

"'Better a meal of vegetables where there is love than a fattened calf with hatred' [Proverbs 15:17]," Helene consoled her friend with a verse from Proverbs.

The only special concession granted on Sundays was permission to use our bunks during the day as well. We made extensive use of this permission, since sitting constantly on the hard stool with no backrest puts a great strain on the body. So we lay stretched out in our resting places and surrendered ourselves to our thoughts. If only we could have had a book to pass the time.

The October sun shone warm and mild through the window. The chiming of church bells filled the room. Helene and Else had fallen asleep. Fränze tossed and turned restlessly in her bed. Then, half turning herself toward me, she lamented: "On beautiful Sundays like this we used to sit in our little summerhouse, enjoying the splendor of the fall flowers, picking apples and tomatoes. The neighbors visited us, we joked and played, we were carefree and happy. But this simple life wasn't enough for me. For the sake of an idea that may be totally unrealistic, I have destroyed our happiness. Without my husband's knowledge or consent, I became a Communist Party journalist. Now I am tortured by doubts. Did I do the right thing or not?"

Helene, her sleep disturbed, sat up. "But at least your Gustav is at liberty, whereas my husband is in mortal danger. The police arrested him along with me. I saw him with a bunch of other prisoners on the way back from my last interrogation. My God, how the poor man looked. Completely dazed, he was obviously in great pain. His arm was in a sling, there were bruises on his face, his mouth was half open, his front teeth were missing. Was this meeting pure chance, or was it deliberately arranged by the Gestapo to soften me up for a confession? I pressed forward close to him and whispered a verse from Matthew: 'But he who stands firm to the end will be saved' [Matthew 24:13]. He didn't recognize me, or didn't want to recognize me—he gazed right past me."

Both women maintained a dejected silence for a while. Helene was the first to regain her composure, and as if in defense against this rare bout of despondency, she recited a verse from Jeremiah: "'The heart is deceitful above all things and beyond cure. Who can understand it?' [Jeremiah 17:9]."

Fränze leapt up, mercurial as ever: "Away with dark thoughts and self-reproach. We want to have fun. Get the 'cards.'"

"Sundays we do not touch cards," replied Helene and Else, as if with one voice.

"But these aren't even proper cards anyway," Fränze urged, "and not even the Lord God would object to an innocent game of 'Old Maid.'"

But the two women stood by their refusal.

"Okay, then, 'Consequences,'" persisted Fränze. "You'll catch on, Frau Herz. Let's go, kids. Helene, you start."

Helene smoothed back her blond hair, thinking. "I was in a small Czech town and getting on pretty well with my recruiting efforts. The brothers and sisters of our community welcomed me warmly. I was to stay with them for several days. One morning I was strolling through the ancient, narrow streets, when I noticed a town crier. He was ringing a large bell to attract attention. Curious, I followed him to the market square, and there, to my great surprise, he read out a warning from the parish priest that was aimed directly at me: 'A foreign woman is in our town making incendiary speeches. Don't believe her. Arrest her and bring her to the town hall.' Suddenly all the church bells were ringing, people were gathering, policemen were popping up. I fled from the town; I hid in a field between bales of straw. The peasants chased me, found me, dragged me to the market square, tied me to a wooden stake, and set it on fire. The fire was already licking at my feet when, in my direst need, when—you continue, Else."

"When," Else proceeded, laughing, "suddenly 'Springtime' emerged from the crowd. 'Children,' she said, 'that's far too big a fire you've lit.' She doused the flames with a fire hose and brought Helene back to us in the Alex."

"Bravo, bravo, well done," Fränze cheered and clapped her hands in approval.

The story had given me pause. "I suspect your tale is based on your own personal experience as well as the fact that you know how Huss was burned in Prague."[15]

"Yes, indeed," answered Helene. "Only the ending when the peasants chase me and the part about the stake are made up. Everything else is true, literally. The venerable men of the cloth are, let us say, not particularly sympathetic toward us. Professional jealousy: we lure too many of their lambs away from them."

"No interruptions, now," pleaded Fränze. "Let's get on with enjoying ourselves."

The game progressed. With wit and humor, the conditions and personalities at the Alex were ridiculed: the prisoners, the interrogators, the director, the cook, the guards—even Hitler and the Nazi elite. The strict observance of the Sabbath protected us from sudden inspections, so the pent-up tension of the week erupted in effervescent gaiety. Helene, above all, was hardly recognizable; I have rarely heard a woman laugh so unselfconsciously. Once the exuberance had abated somewhat, I told her how happy her sudden change of mood had made me.

Immediately she became serious, looking at me in surprise: "'Even in laughter the heart may ache, and joy may end in grief,' so it says in the Proverbs [Proverbs 14:13]."

But this reference to impending grief did not apply to me, at least on this Sunday. Toward evening, "Dear Auntie Anna" appeared and delivered the order for me to prepare myself for transport to Moringen the next morning. "You're lucky to be getting away from here after only a few days. Others have to spend several months here."

THE PARTING FROM my companions was very difficult for me. What brave, proud women! With what dignity they bore their fate! I would have loved to thank them for their friendship in eloquent words, but can one really put one's heart into words? I looked for a gift, but of course I had nothing left. Yes, a small pencil. The precious gift was accepted with great pleasure. I hugged and kissed the three of them. Helene softened: "Dear Frau Herz, may the words of Matthew continue to be realized in you: 'The good man brings good things out of the good stored up in him' [Matthew 12:35]."

"Auf Wiedersehen. Auf Wiedersehen."

Anxiously, I followed the matron.

The waiting room was crowded with shady characters, mostly criminals, street toughs, burglars, second-story men, and a few political prisoners as well. It took many hours to process them and enter their data into files and lists. The guard was not in the slightest hurry, he was conversing with our "Dear Auntie Anna." "No, no," I heard him say, "there's nothing like a government job. The pay may be modest, but you have financial security, even later on for the wife and children." Persuaded, "Auntie Anna" agreed, and the two made a date for an excursion "into the country" the following Sunday.

Downstairs, in one of the inner courts, the prisoners' transport, known because of its color as "the Green Minna [Black Maria]" in the Berliner vernacular, awaited us. It was a quick trip to the train station, where we were led to the platform by a stairway that was closed to the general public, the men bound in pairs, the women taken by the arm and led individually. When my turn came, the policeman studied me carefully, saluted, and let me go first, on my own.

For our transport, a completely windowless car had been coupled to a long train bound for Hanover. In my compartment I found only one rather unpleasant woman. Impassive face, her features hardened and unrefined, her black hair disheveled, with one cheek badly swollen from an infected tooth, at least as far as could be inferred from the cloth wrapped around her head to protect it. Through a constant stream of profanity, she told me her life story. Her name is Rabusky. Her husband is a factory worker, but unemployed most of the time. She's always enjoyed hitting the bottle, and a short time ago, while totally drunk, she yelled out "Heil Moscow!"—that was regarded as a political offense and earned her six months of instructional camp, which she was now to serve in Moringen.

Despite her toothache, the Eternal Feminine was alive in her. In the adjacent compartment sat a man in whose direction she had already cast an affectionate glance in the "Green Minna." Now was the time to resume their acquaintanceship. Breaking the rules, she tried to initiate a conversation by knocking. Unfortunately, that method was far too tiresome. Then she discovered a tiny hole in the wall, which had probably been bored by earlier prisoners with the urge to talk to one another. The opening was just large enough to slip a tiny roll of paper through. She produced some pencil stubs from a secret hiding place, and soon a lively correspondence was underway. They exchanged names and addresses, told of earlier experiences and prison terms. The woman, who until then had been impassive and indifferent, suddenly grew lively.

"Well, can you beat that!" she shouted at me enthusiastically. "He lives right around the corner from me, on the Kottbuserdamm."

And after the next exchange of notes, she added with admiration: "Metal worker, makes tons of money. Name's Georg, real nice name, thirty-two years old. What I wouldn't give to see what he looks like!"

She tried to look through the hole, pressed first her right eye, then her left eye up against it, but the result remained unsatisfactory. "He" had fallen for her as well, and asked for a detailed description. I helped out: fine figure, soulful eyes—but Rabusky refused.

"No way, that's too high-class. I ain't no lady, you know."

Eventually instructions came from the other side: "Go to the john, but walk real slow, so I can see you properly."

She was pleased to hear that. But tough luck about her swollen cheek. She wrote to him that she felt a little "self-conscious" about this. "No big deal," came the sympathetic reply. "I get a lot of toothaches myself."

Now does it look better with or without the cloth? Okay, no cloth. She removed the bandage, rang for the attendant, asked him to let her out to go to the lavatory. After some time she returned, accompanied by the guard, who was about to lock her up in the compartment again. "Oh, nuts," she exclaimed, "I left my hanky in the john." And went back.

The correspondence began anew.

"He's crazy about me. Wants me to marry him. He's only got eight more months left in the clink. By then I'll be out too, and we can make it legal. He's a neat guy, real smart, a lot neater than my old man, that boozer."

After about six hours we reached Hanover, where we were to have a layover. To avoid attracting any unlooked-for attention in the train station, we were not allowed to get off until long after the other passengers were gone. Nevertheless, the news of our arrival had spread, and there were many gawkers waiting for us.

"Look at the fat broad with the bandage. What kinda trouble do you think she got into?"

"Must have coughed the wrong way."

"And look, a lady. Must be a Jew."

Through some set of associations I was reminded of Beer-Hofmann's drama *Jacob's Dream* and its proud affirmation of Jewishness: "As a crown shall you wear it, not as a yoke."[16]

And with head held high, I strode through the gaping crowd.

OUR STAY IN the women's prison in Hanover lasted only three days, but those days were hard to get through. I was locked up in a cramped solitary cell. There was no exercise in the open air: the prisoners were just taken for a "walk" back and forth along the corridor for half an hour. Even trips to the lavatory ceased—you had to use the iron pail in your cell, which I found especially disgusting. In order to avoid the prison psychosis that Fränze had described, I recited monologues from all the plays I knew for hours on end.

Finally, we resumed our transport to Moringen, this time without interruption. Besides Rabusky and me there were now three other women locked up in the compartment as well. Rabusky looked miserable. The medical attention she had sought had been denied, so her tooth abscess had worsened. On top of that, she was deeply distressed that Georg, her newfound admirer, no longer accompanied her on this trip. She eyed her new traveling companions inquisitively and nudged her neighbor, rather rudely, with her elbow: "Hey, you, what kinda trouble did you get yourself into?"

A small, plain woman gazed sullenly and nervously into space. "For the first time ever I stole something and was caught right away. My children with no bread, my husband with no work. At the police station I begged them over and over again to let me go for the sake of the children, but it was no use."

Rabusky nodded deliberately. "Yeah, they got no heart."

Her curiosity was not yet satisfied. "So what's up with you?" she asked the next one, a tall, garishly dressed blonde.

She was silent.

"Oh, come on now, no need to act so shy among us girls. Prostitution, right?"

The prostitute nodded. On the trip to the train station, she had made quite a spectacle of herself. The presence of the policemen had roused her instincts: "I'm horny," she had yelled with a laugh, slapping her thigh. Now, on closer inspection, all I saw was a tired, spent woman with a faded face. From the pocket of her cheap coat her restless hands pulled out a photograph, which she handed to me.

"That's my daughter," she said, her husky voice assuming a tender tone. "I started sending her away from home when she was ten years old, first to a good school in the Harz Mountains, then to a training institute for gardeners. She's been married to a farmer in Westphalia for a year now, and has a baby boy."

I was rapidly developing a sense of respect for this woman, who was now holding forth on the principles of child-rearing.

"'The fear of the Lord is the beginning of knowledge' [Proverbs 1:7]," said the last of our traveling companions, in a deep voice. Word and gesture were the same as those of Helene in the Alex.

"Another Bible Student," I said to myself.

I was right. The woman, Magdalene Mewes by name, had been a Jehovah's Witness for a long time. She comes from the Riesengebirge,[17] where her husband owns a small piece of property. Her clothes, simple but made of good fabric, and her cowhide suitcase indicate a certain level of prosperity. The woman looks ill; her neck reveals a goiter. This affliction has surely only strengthened her religious convictions. She lacks the mental agility of the versatile Helene, as well as the latter's grace and charm, but on the other hand this farmer's wife seems much more straightforward. She most certainly has both feet planted firmly on the ground of her mountainous homeland. She enjoys hearing herself talk even more than Helene, and so it was not long before she was sharing the history of her arrest with us.

"One day the village supervisor summoned me. He's my cousin, a prosperous and decent landowner. 'I have to warn you, Magda, you are taking great risks with your rebelliousness against the Nazis. And people have taken offense that you don't show up at any of our public meetings. You really will have to make some concessions. Next Sunday our group leader [of the NSDAP] will speak on "Germany and Its Neighboring States." The man's bright. Just listen to him once.'

"Yes, 'His speech is smooth as butter, yet war is in his heart; his words are more soothing than oil, yet they are drawn swords [Psalms 55:21],' I answered with the psalmist.

"'Your tongue is going to get you in trouble, Magda,' my cousin replied.

"A fine tongue my own dear cousin has. Sticking to his convictions is hardly his strong suit. He has flown the flags of the Hohenzollern emperors, the Weimar Republic, and now the Third Reich with equal enthusiasm. But, then again, that's how he got to be the village supervisor in the first place.

"Some time later the schoolmaster came to me. We've known each other since we were children. He's a good-hearted man, but spineless. He's another one who goes with the flow, who bends like a straw in the wind. I was supposed to withdraw my objections and permit my Anton to join the Hitler Youth.

"'Impossible,' I replied. 'A twelve-year-old boy ought to be studying and playing. He shouldn't be carrying weapons, going on exhausting night marches, throwing hand grenades and reciting blasphemies.'

"'Consider the consequences, Magda,' said the teacher. 'The school will have to expel Anton, and no other school will be allowed to admit him. His schoolmates will have to reject him. Your stubbornness will be the ruin of your son.'

"I answered him with the psalmist: 'I was young and now I am old, yet I have never seen the righteous forsaken or their children begging bread' [Psalms 37:25]."

THE TRAIN WAS traveling slowly along a little-used branch line and stopping frequently. I did not recognize the names of any of the stops announced by the conductor. But then suddenly it was "Hamelin, ten minutes' stopover."

Hamelin—how well I know this jewel of medieval architecture. How often we would stop here on the way to my husband's hometown [Warburg] in Westphalia, walk engrossed through the narrow streets, stop to admire the great town hall, the guild hall, the gabled Wedding House.

The women in the compartment had sprung to their feet, had stood up onto the benches and were trying to catch a glimpse of the city through a narrow air slot located high up near the ceiling of the car in lieu of a window. But only the gray walls of the train station were to be seen.

"Too bad," said Frau Mewes, "I wish I could have seen the mountain that the Pied Piper lured the rats into, then the children when the city refused to pay his reward. He led them to their deaths with his flute-playing."

I told her about an essay that I had read in an American magazine not long before. "Every people," the argument went, "puts its soul into its legends, reveals its essential character through them. And whatever it cannot express directly, it reveals through the words and deeds of its children. The children in a legend are more than children. They assume all the attributes of adults; they are the true representatives and heralds of the national character. No other country could have brought forth this legend of the Pied Piper. Only the German is so uncritical, so susceptible to every form of influence that he succumbs to all enticements like a child. Today, a new Pied Piper of Hamelin has come to the Germans in the person of Hitler, and again they are captivated by his charms. They are following him with blind faith, heading straight for disaster."

The Bible Student had been listening with great concentration. "Yes, they sacrifice themselves, and they sacrifice their best, their children. But the day of reckoning for this demagogue is near at hand. His glory will soon be at an end."

I was unable to share her optimism. "Every day so far has only brought new triumphs for Hitler. His power is almost limitless."

Frau Mewes shook her head. "You judge too much from the point of view of the present. We Jehovah's Witnesses see everything through the eternal eyes of the Bible. For us, Hitler is just one of the many personifications of eternal evil, of the destroyer of the world, and thus in him will the word of Isaiah be fulfilled":

How you have fallen from heaven, O morning star, son of the dawn!
You have been cast down to the earth, you who once laid low the nations!
You said in your heart, "I will ascend to heaven...."
Those who see you stare at you, they ponder your fate:
"Is this the man who shook the earth and made kingdoms tremble ...?
But you are cast out of your tomb ... you are covered with the slain."

[Isaiah 14:12–13, 16, 19]

The Bible Student had sat herself up straight and spoken emphatically. The drunkard, the thief, and the prostitute all hung anxiously on the words she had spoken with such intensity.

FROM HAMELIN IT was on to Northeim. There we left the train and were packed into automobiles. The drive on the highway was gorgeous. Beautiful rolling hill country, fields left and right covered with stubble, tall silos, the sweet smell of hay wafting from the meadows, woodlands glowing in all the colors of fall. Buzzing and humming, singing and rejoicing in the air. If only this drive would never end. But alas, in half an hour we had already arrived in Moringen. A peaceful little country town. Children played on poorly paved streets, plodding horses pulled heavily laden wagons, low-roofed houses stood in small gardens, curious stares followed us from the windows.

Our car stopped in front of a long building, 32 Lange Strasse. An inconspicuous sign bore the inconspicuous inscription "Workhouse." We had reached our destination.

First of all, the intricate admission formalities ensued once again. Even though our files had accompanied us faithfully throughout our journey and now lay in meticulously ordered piles before the clerk, he seemed to take forever to enter the information into his lists. Does every last pencil-pusher in Germany have to justify his existence like this?

To pass the time while we waited, I scrutinized the bulletin board on the wall. The official staff list, of course, was painstakingly transcribed. First and foremost was the prison director, of course, Mr. Axel Lark [Hugo Krack].[18] An uncommon, Nordic-sounding name. Second of all, Madam Chief Warder [Oberwachtmeisterin] Berns [Frau Rehren].[19] Then the army of matrons: Frau Ebert, Frau Hartmann, Frau Pflugk, and so on. I tried to conjure up a mental image of Madam Chief Warder Berns, who probably commands the regiment here. Undoubtedly an imposing figure, with stern bearing and stern features, about forty years of age. Madam Chief Warder—this odd title made me smile.

But all of a sudden my smile vanished. A newspaper clipping was glued to the opposite wall:

Prayer

Lord, once you sent Moses the Jews to guide,
He saved them, alas, by splitting the tide,
This time, at the sea, once you've led them back down,
Keep their heads under water, O Lord, let them drown.

We were led across a wide courtyard full of sheds and workshops, and came to another spacious building. At the end of a long corridor, a short, heavy-set woman with a peculiar appearance awaited us. About sixty years old, she is wearing a charcoal gray wool dress that reaches almost to the floor and is dated by neither cut nor style. On her short neck sits a spherical head. Her face is covered with wrinkles, but her gray, piercing eyes and her prominent chin announce unbridled, high-powered energy.

The woman's heavy feet set themselves in motion toward us, and in a voice that might have come from a giant she thundered at the two matrons: "These two," and her head indicated the thief and the prostitute, "to the workhouse."

Now the voice bellowed at Frau Mewes: "What are you?"

"A married housewife from Wildach, near Hirschberg, in the Riesengebirge."

"I'm not interested. Why have you been sent here?"

"Because I belong to the Jehovah's Witnesses."

"Good. Great Hall. Step aside."

Rabusky was next. "Ah, yes. 'Heil Moscow.' You bet. Also Great Hall," went the instructions to the matron.

"What are you?" the megaphone blared at me.

"A Jew," I answered.

"What's your offense?"

"I spent several months with relatives in Italy, and wanted ..."

"That's enough. You're a remigrant [*Remigrantin*]."

"So I'm a remigrant," I committed this unfamiliar title to memory.[20]

Her wide eyes rolled first toward me, then toward the matron.

"Jews' Hall [*Judenhalle*]," the voice thundered.

"Jews' Hall," repeated the matron, eagerly. "Yes, ma'am, Madam Chief Warder."

This was my first encounter with Madam Chief Warder Berns.

Moringen, Late October 1936

The "Jews' Hall" to which the command from Madam Chief Warder Berns consigned me nearly two weeks ago is a small space that offers its five occupants only very limited domestic facilities. A long, unfinished table, four stools, one chair, five narrow blue cubbyholes mounted on the wall for soap, toothbrush, and towel compose all of the "furniture." Our few belongings are stored in cartons, cardboard boxes, and suitcases, stacked up under the table for lack of any other storage space. The only window faces the courtyard and is, of course, fitted with iron bars.

Adjoining this room is the "Great Hall," with its approximately eighty women, and beyond that lies the "Bavaria Hall," with its seventeen inmates, and the infirmary. These four rooms, along with a small storage space and a lavatory, take up the second floor of the large building, which had previously served as an orphanage. The attic holds our sleeping quarters. We are considered political prisoners and are kept strictly separate from the criminal prisoners, who occupy the ground floor. Unlike us, these criminals must perform manual labor. They have to wear the black institutional uniform whereas we can keep our own clothes, and any contact with the "blacks" is strictly forbidden.

I have quickly made friends with my four sisters in misfortune in the Jews' Hall. Frau Herta Kronau [Herta Kronheim][21] was the only one to keep a guarded attitude at first; over three years of imprisonment have made her distrustful. But it was well worth the effort to win her over. Herta is one of the most intelligent and most cultured women in the camp, and once you have gained her trust, she reveals herself to be accessible and warm-hearted. Now aged forty-three, she had worked as a commercial artist in her youth, as a nurse during the World War, and later as a social worker in the welfare system, and she had earned qualifications for other careers too. She had joined the communist movement early on and was quickly promoted to a leadership position. She seems to have inherited her restless blood from her father, the descendant of an old Spanish Marrano family, who came from Morocco. After many long and adventurous years of traveling, he had finally settled in Nuremberg, where he set up an art dealership. The olive color of Herta's skin still testifies to this Spanish-Moroccan heritage.

Radical-left convictions are responsible for Ilse Lipinski [Ilse Gostynski][22] being here as well. Endowed with wit, a quick mind, and a good command of several fields of knowledge, she used to work in a public library in Berlin. The gangly movements of her long limbs, her short bobbed hair, her lean body give her a certain boyish appearance. The myopic eyes behind her thick eyeglasses do not exactly improve her looks.

Also not blessed with physical charms is the oldish Fräulein Gertrud Mannheim.[23] A good, devoted soul, she gets on our nerves with her many questions and well-intentioned bits of advice. Like me, she is a "remigrant," a returning émigré. She had spent some time with her brother in Danzig, that thoroughly German city that the Nazis are trying, quite rightly, to get returned to the Reich.[24] Nonetheless, the Gestapo determined that, for a Jew, Danzig counts as abroad, and thus did poor Fräulein Mannheim find herself confronted, upon her return to Berlin, with the surprising fact that she had "emigrated and immigrated back again," an offense whose consequences she is now to ponder here in Moringen.

"Racial disgrace [*Rassenschande*]," that utterly vile mixture of hatred, meanness, and exterminatory intent concocted by the Nazis, was the downfall of the youngest among us, the lovely Anni Reiner. She had been engaged to an Aryan, but the planned wedding was rendered impossible by the Nuremberg Race Laws.[25] But however draconian the law, the groom would not part with his bride-to-be. Entirely understandable: Anni, with her sweet face, her merry blue eyes and her curly blond hair, truly is a feast for the eyes.

DURING THE FEW first days, Moringen seemed like a release to me, given the impact of my most recent experiences.

No more locked cell doors. No humiliating dependency on the matron's keys. I am again permitted—what a relief—to open doors by myself. I am permitted to go alone and unescorted to the lavatory. With certain restrictions, I am permitted to write and receive letters. On specific days I am allowed to borrow books from the institutional library, and I am permitted to do needlework. We are also allowed to use knives and forks again. Instead of the strenuous, half-hour endurance run at the Alex in Berlin, here we walk in the exercise yard twice a day, for an hour each time, during which we may move about freely and confer with our one hundred companions in misfortune.

This courtyard, enclosed by low-roofed structures, is quite neglected, to be sure; when it rains, you sink deep into the gooey yellow loam. Still, the unpleasant impression is softened by green bushes and trees.

The food, though far better here than at the Alex, is still insufficient, but we are allowed to make additional purchases from a communal store and to receive small food parcels from home.

So, then, an undeniable improvement over the Alex. But this improvement seems, perhaps unfairly, increasingly insignificant to me with each passing day. I find the absolute elimination of our personal freedom, the isolation from real life, the constant confinement, the overcrowding, the control, the mental strain harder and harder to take. And it is with ever growing conviction that I agree with Anni's observation: "Alex and Hanover are hell, but that still doesn't mean that Moringen is anything like heaven."

What surprises me the most is the absence of meaningful activity. I asked my companions about this: "Now this is called an 'instructional camp,' but so far I haven't been able to detect the slightest trace of any kind of instruction whatsoever. I know we have to have the *Völkischer Beobachter* (the Nazis' official paper) read aloud to us every day, and we're supposed to pay attention and accept it uncritically. But that's it. In Berlin people were telling the most extraordinary tales about daily lectures, introductions to National Socialist ideology, required reading and memorization of Hitler's *Mein Kampf*—and then physical exercises, marches, ditch-digging and so on. Even paramilitary instruction for the younger ones."

My words provoked general amusement. "They really took you for a ride," said Herta Kronau. "That kind of 'instruction' has never existed here, it would be impossible, given the physical condition of the women. Most of us Communists spent three years at hard labor in prisons and jails before we were transferred here. Take a look at our emaciated figures, our lifeless eyes, our thin arms and legs, our fractures, our paralyzed and broken limbs, the sorry consequences of years of imprisonment and abuse. Since the state apparently does not wish to exterminate us altogether, it must give us an opportunity to 'convalesce.' That's what Moringen is good for."

"Even if physical tasks and physical training are not the point, intellectual instruction would still be possible," I replied. "Why has the state given up trying to win back its opponents? Women are receptive to skillful persuasion."

Herta made a gesture that was dismissive and disdainful at the same time. "The state places absolutely no value whatsoever on winning our support or even persuading us. It avoids all confrontation. It declares that Communists are vermin, sub-human creatures. Discussion is out of the question. Besides, the Nazis know perfectly well that it's useless with us. They can force us to be silent; the silent stillness of the graveyard now lies over all of Germany, but they cannot force us to give up our ideals. We did not fight and subject ourselves to all that suffering only to capitulate in the end. We remain what we are, come what may."

Yes, the Communists here are made of stern stuff. Confronted with the steadfastness of their convictions, external pressures prove completely futile. Even if Hitler piles triumph upon triumph, the women in Moringen are firmly convinced of the ultimate victory of the communist ideal, which they see being fulfilled in the construction of the Soviet state. For all their aspirations to independence and despite their frequent criticisms of the Russian system, they are spiritually dependent on Moscow. Moscow is the sun around which they orbit and from which they receive their light. It is in the light of this vision that they grapple with the great ideological dilemmas: individuality or community, freedom or coercion, democracy or dictatorship. The Russian model remains the standard, not only on questions of working conditions, on wages and the forty-hour week, but also on personal and even intimate matters, on love, marriage, extra-marital affairs, birth control, and child rearing. With consummate vigilance, in fact, the women monitor the successive phases in the development of the relationship between state and family [in the Soviet Union]. They are critical of the [state's] initial indifference to marriage, its facilitation of divorce, the attempts to weaken the status of parents and to strengthen the independence of children often raised in state institutions. They offer their opinions, sometimes approving, sometimes disapproving, on how these attitudes have been changing, gradually returning to the affinities of the past, right up to the recent official declaration that "the family, as the primary social cell, is of supreme value to all structures of the state."[26]

Politically I cannot agree with the Communists, especially their spiritual leaders, the five [former] members of the federal and state parliaments. Their dialectic does not appeal to me, and I disapprove of this egalitarianism, equalization without individual evaluation, the overestimation of reason at the expense of emotion, the whole thoroughly materialistic ideology. But from the human point of view, I have the greatest respect for these strong and principled personalities, for their steadfastness and their moral integrity. I am happy to put up with their various minor faults. Even the simplest of these women, or perhaps especially they, are generally likable people. I seize every opportunity to expand my personal relationships and hence my knowledge of human nature, even if Herta Kronau makes fun of me: "Frau Herz is hunting for people again."

In principle, the Great Hall, which with its nearly eighty inmates houses the overwhelming majority of the women, would be the most productive "hunting ground." But it's difficult to find the leisure and opportunity for a quiet discussion in this huge room, which resembles the lobby of a train station. It surges and swirls, hums and buzzes, with its comings and goings, its endless interruptions. Sewing machines chatter, knitting needles click, sewing needles fly: the women, most of them poor factory workers and sales clerks, are all too eager to earn a few pennies with their needlework.

The Bible Students sit at their special table, unaffected by all this noise. They don't participate in worldly conversations; their work consists of reciting and interpreting passages from the Bible. Magdalene Mewes greets me in a friendly manner whenever she sees me here, but we don't grow any closer to each other. After having made such a strong impression as an individual on our journey together, she is no more than one among many at this table, and I am unable to relate to this collection of unrealistic people, with their air of rapture and their belief in the imminent end of the world.

Alongside the main wall is the table of the "notables," who stand out from the majority by virtue of their former titles and past achievements. This hierarchy was not created by any official directive, of course, but simply established itself according to the "birds of a feather" principle. Assembled here are the parliamentary representatives, among them the solemn Anna Löser, who has to read the *Völkischer Beobachter* out loud to the silent crowd every evening, in deference to her earlier parliamentary activity, to be sure, but also on account of her deep, musical voice. Seated here, too, are the wives of merchants, manufacturers, and engineers, among them a witty and entertaining, but very slovenly, Baltic baroness. She wears a magnificent but unfortunately always dirty Russian lace collar on her black dress. A sculptor by profession, she fashions the most charming miniatures from bread crumbs: a leaping deer, a watchful dog, a charging bull. The place of honor at this table is enjoyed by another, otherwise unremarkable woman, whose distinction lies solely in the fact that she is honoring Moringen with her presence for a second time. She had been released three months ago and, in her joy upon finally seeing her beloved hometown of Erfurt once again, had immediately sent off a food package to a friend here in the camp, an act which resulted in her renewed arrest and reinternment. All contact between released prisoners and those still in custody is strictly forbidden.

Enthroned as the "block leader" [*Stubenälteste*] at the head of the "notables'" table, and, in fact, at the head of the entire hall, is Else Volckmar. This status is conferred by the camp administration irrespective of seniority. It is clear that Else has been appointed to her high office as a result of her unrivaled eloquence. She used to work as a publicist for a recording company and has retained from that job a fondness for loud and impassioned speeches and an emphasis on her own ego. No matter how practical and reasonable existing arrangements may be, whether the seating assignments in the Great Hall, the arrangement of beds in the sleeping quarters, the distribution of laundry, or the regulation of communal purchases, Else has to change them. "It's in the public interest," she maintains so incessantly that mistrustful fellow inmates suspect her, surely unfairly, of looking after her own personal interests instead.

At her workspace stands an unframed photograph of her husband, with the intense, expressive face of an intellectual. Fritz had been an editor for a Communist newspaper. But turn it around, and on the reverse side a playful face with twinkling eyes smiles at the viewer. "Every day I converse with my Fritz," says Else, "and depending on whether my mood is sunny or cloudy, Fritz will either be cheerful or watch me seriously."

She writes to her Fritz as often as she can, each time decorating the stationery with a small illustration, meticulously drawn with colored ink, depicting sometimes a bird, sometimes a bouquet of flowers or a spray of blossoms. Once she had attached a letterhead that was intended to represent, simply yet graphically, her table with the "notables." She was refused permission to send the letter.

Fritz's editorial activities had earned him a nine-year penitentiary sentence. He had served only three. "I still have a whole eternity to wait for him," lamented Else. "I think of my own release with apprehension; what you all long for is only agony for me. I don't want to go back into the world at all. What good is freedom to me without my Fritz?" She stifles her sobbing. I'm beginning to understand that her public display of self-confidence is nothing more than a defense mechanism against fear and insecurity.

CONSTITUTING A KIND of miniature companion piece to the Great Hall is the Bavaria Hall, with its mere seventeen inmates.[27] They all come from Munich, Nuremberg, Würzburg, Augsburg, Regensburg, or their environs, and they are all, with few exceptions, as poor as church mice. They all speak the same unpretentious Bavarian dialect, but in their mouths this dialect is more than a merely superficial manner of speaking; it is the expression of a common spiritual outlook, of an ancient, indigenous, venerable tradition. A pure and unpolluted atmosphere reigns here—mountain air from the inland peaks.

For the most part, these women already know each other from their hometowns. They belonged to the same local Communist groups, were arrested at the same time, and had been held in custody all these years in the same penal institutions. Thus, the fate of each individual was elevated to the higher plane of the community from the very beginning, leading to a sense of solidarity much stronger and far more organic than that of the Great Hall, with its many prisoners brought together from all social classes and provinces.

The absolute ruler of the Bavaria Hall, universally and eagerly recognized as such, is Zenta Baimler [Centa Herker-Beimler], the young wife of the former general secretary of the Communist Party in Munich.[28] Even physically Zenta projects quite a personality. Her proud carriage, her broad, noble features, her high forehead, her firm mouth, her wide shoulders, and her short hair, styled in a men's cut, all accentuate her pronounced masculine nature.

Although Zenta is far more than just her spouse's wife, she continues to be illuminated by the spotlight of his fame. Baimler [Hans Beimler] was taken to the concentration camp at Dachau at the very beginning of 1933. The Nazis took a few months to collect evidence against him and his comrades and then made short work of him. One evening, a revolver was placed on the table for him, and he was given to understand that, should he elect not to commit suicide, he would be shot the following morning. During the night, Baimler managed to escape. While climbing over the dense barbed-wire electric fence, he was critically injured, but was able to drag himself away. Completely exhausted and apparently at death's door, he reached the secluded house of an elderly woman, who, out of compassion, took him in. Baimler recovered and fled across the border.

It seemed inconceivable to me that he could have escaped like this from Dachau without the help of accomplices. The camp is fortified like a citadel—secured by a cordon of sentries, machine guns, and alarm signals. I asked Herta for details, since as a Nuremberger and owing to her own former influential activity she is held in high esteem by the Bavarians.

"I know nothing specific, and even if I knew, I wouldn't say," was Herta's response. "The whole affair is shrouded in darkness. The police discovered the woman with whom Baimler had found refuge and interrogated her intensively. She had taken in the man out of pity for his half-dead condition and swore that she had had no idea who he was. Nothing could be proved against her, and they had to be satisfied with sentencing her to two years in prison. Yes, Baimler is a real man, all right. Not content with saving himself, he had the audacity to return to Germany several months later, in disguise and with a fake passport, to sneak his children across the border."

Since Zenta had never been politically active, she was left unmolested at first. But after her husband's escape, she was apprehended, together with her sister Maxe [Maria Dengler].[29] Her case attracted great attention abroad, with her arrest being interpreted as a return to the brutal medieval practice of exacting revenge on innocent relatives. Members of the English and Swedish parliaments sent a fact-finding commission to her prison, but they could not get anywhere.[30] Still, undoubtedly as a direct result of this vigilance from abroad, Zenta does enjoy a certain degree of preferential treatment. The matrons do not venture too close to this woman, who knows what she owes to her name and holds her head very high.

Moringen, Early November 1936

Evenings drag on interminably, monotonously, exhaustingly. Daytimes are still bearable. The two-hour stroll in the open air is refreshing, but after supper the women collapse. Needlework falls from tired hands, conversation dies down, books demand a level of concentration which is hard to come by. There are yawns, quiet and hidden behind hands at first, then loud and without inhibition, and a common sigh of relief when, shortly before 9 o'clock, the bells signal bedtime. Herta is wont to say, with a deep sigh: "Thank God. Another day gone. Children, we may go to sleep."

From each of the three day rooms, the journey to the attic commences. A matron with a stern expression is stationed at the head of the stairs. She makes the group march past, like a shepherd with his sheep. Mumbling quietly to herself, she counts "93, 94, 95, 96." Oh, woe, if the number is wrong and someone is late.

In the sleeping quarters there is no place to put anything at all—not a chair, not even a hook—so we have to undress downstairs and walk upstairs in our nightclothes. It's the most peculiar procession I have ever seen, a grotesque parade, funny and sad at the same time. "Spirits of the night," I think to myself. Some heave themselves laboriously up the steps, others take them at a run. They shuffle in felt slippers, trudge in heavy wooden clogs, mince in once-elegant patent leather pumps. "Spirits of the night." They are clothed in long, white linen nightshirts dating back to great-grandmother's time, or in provocatively short, pink silk nighties that barely cover their "good reputations." They wear flannel or cambric lingerie, thick chemises, old, patched bed jackets. Some own modern pajamas in loud colors and of every design; others wrap themselves in warm shawls, in blankets, in bathrobes.

Rarely is there a cheerful word, a joking remark. Tired, exhausted, spent, and impassive, they seek out their beds. The electric light is switched off. Soon night spreads its heavy, black wings over all these ghostly figures.

A short time ago, Anni, our little "race defiler," came to me and sat down on the edge of my bed. Her blue pajamas and her blue satin slippers were charming relics of earlier, happier days and nights. Now she was depressed and frightened.

"Tomorrow I'll be called to the local district court, and old wounds will be opened once again. And for what? How happy we once were, Walter and me. My in-laws and Walter's elderly grandmother had come from Stuttgart to Magdeburg to celebrate our engagement with us. 'The boy could not have found a better or more enchanting wife,' said his grandmother, and she hugged me. Even after the Nuremberg Race Laws, Walter remained true to me, and we made preparations to emigrate together. Then came our arrest. That single blow destroyed everything. I've been in custody for almost a year; Walter, the 'full-blooded Aryan,' was released after three months. He has changed radically since then. He wants to become an officer in the air force. His Jewish fiancée has been cast aside, his engagement broken off. But that was somehow not enough. Now—and this is incomprehensible to me—he's taking legal action against me for perjury. At the court hearing, he said the most disgraceful things about me, and his grandmother, who was showering me with tenderness only a short time ago, now can't seem to find enough insulting things to say. Only his father, who expressed his respect for me again in court, remains a man of honor."

I tried to comfort the little one, but I could offer her little solace. I was outraged at this transformation of love into hatred, of loyalty into malevolence. How is it possible that a respectable German man can suddenly turn into a cad and a betrayer? Just because a Hitler has commanded him: "You shall hate, where up to now you have loved"? How can a nation which can boast of such enormous achievements, which has produced a Bach and a Beethoven, a Schiller and a Goethe, a Kant and a Hegel, sink so low and submit without resistance to the commandments of a single person? But Hitler is probably no isolated phenomenon, rather he is the personification, the ultimate manifestation of the German mass instinct. Perhaps German culture is only a thin crust, beneath which rages a volcano of barely suppressed savage drives. I keep looking for a satisfactory explanation for this innate contradiction, for this dramatic and dangerous conflict within the character of a great nation. I do not find one.

It had grown late. The building lay in total darkness. The sound of loud snoring drifted over to me from the neighboring beds. Anni had rested her head on my pillow and had fallen asleep, in a half-sitting, half-reclining position. I woke her gently. She rubbed her eyes in surprise and came to. She kissed me impulsively. "Thank you so much, dear, sweet Mutter Herz," and scurried hurriedly to her bed.

"Mutter Herz—Mother Heart," the name caught on quickly and has stayed with me. The women often come to me and confide in me. They tell me how their children are being neglected, their families threatened with disintegration. They solicit my help in preparing a petition for an early release or for a reduced sentence.

Almost without exception, their husbands have been interned for "subversive activities." As long as they are quartered in concentration camps, their lives are in more or less constant danger. In a single month, three of the women here have lost their husbands. "Shot while attempting to escape," states the official report. We know what such an "escape attempt" looks like in reality. The prisoners are working in the woods or in the marshes. The overseer, a member of the SA or the SS, assigns a few of them a task that takes them away from the work crew, they are told that they are going to hoist a log, dig a ditch, something like that. On the way to their appointed destination, they are then shot from behind, hence "while attempting to escape."

The women whose husbands survive devote all of their energies to keeping their men from sinking into despair. They endeavor to bolster their self-confidence and remind them that their eventual reunion does indeed remain a distant hope. They don't always possess the gift of eloquence, but they possess something far more valuable, an inexhaustible abundance of selflessness and tenderness and generosity. Their letters, though often awkward, compose a singular, moving, almost biblical "Song of Songs."

Their marriages persevere under the most adverse external conditions imaginable, across barriers of space and time, yet with no signs of weakening. All events, the trivial matters of everyday life as well as more serious problems, are reported accurately and vividly. These women, mentally alert and ready for anything, are able to master every situation as it arises.

Robert in Dachau has become crippled as a result of the abuse he has endured. His Trude scrapes together all of her savings and orders a pair of crutches for eighteen marks. "Why else would anyone agonize over needle-work from morning till night?"

Several of Goebel's husband's teeth have "fallen out"—that is, "been knocked out"—dentures cost forty marks. Goebel cannot come up with such a sum herself, of course, so for weeks and weeks her letters work all of her relatives until she finally succeeds in raising the money from an uncle in Augsburg and an aunt in Wiesbaden.

Alois, once an avid mountain climber, now he feels he will surely suffocate in his cramped cell and is pining away for his peaks. His Marerl asks everyone she knows for picture postcards and newspaper clippings of the Bavarian Alps, which she then sends to Alois. He is overjoyed. He copies the mountains, "his mountains," the Wild Kaiser, the Watzmann, the High Goell, quite accurately from the originals and sends his artwork proudly back to Marerl. At the bottom of every sheet she puts a caption with fond memories of their shared climbing trips, stitches all the sketches very carefully into a handmade album, and sends Alois a deeply welcome birthday present.

WRITTEN CORRESPONDENCE IS subject to many constraints. To begin with, there is the dual censorship to get through, both here and at the destination. And then, and this is the greatest obstacle, many prisons and concentration camps permit only one letter to be received in any given two-, four-, even eight-week period. Should several letters arrive during this period, the director determines which is to be handed over. Some directors are kind enough to always deliver the most important piece of correspondence to each prisoner. Others, though, enforce the rule with absolute rigidity. Dachau, surpassing all other institutions in sadism as always, delivers the letter that happens to have arrived first and returns all other mail to the sender. Thus, it is possible for months to pass before spouses hear from each other, simply because two or three friends have interrupted the connection with a few well-intentioned but unimportant lines. In several places, though, the prisoners have devised a secret, closely guarded system that enables communication in cases of emergency anyway.

Of equal concern to the women, besides their husbands, are their children, who are growing up father- and motherless, often in the care of grandparents or other relatives, but for the most part in the custody of the state in orphanages and welfare homes. As much as it is possible to do so from afar, the mothers supervise their children's education: they admonish them, encourage them, demand comprehensive accounts, ask for their report cards, and address many questions to their teachers.

The Bible Students are incensed at the anti-Christian teaching and philosophy of life that is being drummed into their children's heads in the public schools. They try to counteract it with their frequent letters, which resemble religious treatises in form and content. Likewise, representative Dora Doebel [Viktoria Hösl][31] can barely stand it that her son Herbert is being raised in a Bavarian convent. Its emphatic Catholicism is antithetical to her radical-left views. She does not hesitate to express her thoughts, and between this former Communist state representative and the convent's Mother Superior a correspondence has developed that does honor to both parties. "I cannot fundamentally change our educational system," writes the Mother Superior, "but there are many dwellings in our Heavenly Father's house. I promise you that I will arrange our Herbert's little room just as comfortably and agreeably as possible. I shall raise the boy in the love of our God, who has always been a God of the oppressed, and to have respect for you, because you have stood up so courageously and publicly for the rights of the weak."

The letters from the boy himself are a real joy; they always make the rounds through the entire camp. Sometimes lively and cheerful, bubbling over with jokes, humor, and splendid ideas, sometimes innocent, guileless, and pensive, sometimes didactic, they seek to fill "beloved Mommy" with enthusiasm for whatever inspires him at the moment, for the wonders of distant continents, for the life cycle of the insect, for the deeds of great men. Oh, Herbert will work hard so that he may become a famous man himself one day, like Edison, Scott, and Peary. "Then, beloved Mommy, you will be proud of your Herbert, and we'll move away together, and stay together, and never, never part again."

THE DISTRIBUTION OF mail is *the* big event of the day. This event tends to occur quite suddenly and irregularly, one time during the morning exercise, another time around 6 o'clock in the evening, sometimes right before bedtime, depending upon when Madam Chief Warder Berns has found time for her censorship work. You are summoned to her to receive your mail, which she has already opened and carefully read. Madam Berns can get quite nasty if, in her opinion, you write or receive too many letters, or if she considers the compositions too long winded. But a maximum length isn't officially specified anywhere. Entirely in keeping with the spirit of the whole system, everything is left vague and up to the individual discretion of the officials on the spot.

Packages are opened by the recipients themselves, under the supervision of Madam Berns, probably to demonstrate that their contents have not been tampered with. Without a word, Madam Berns hands the addressee a knife to cut the string, and receives each item one at a time, satisfying herself that no forbidden products, such as tobacco and alcohol, are being imported. All original packaging is torn from chocolate, cookies, soap, etc., and examined by her to ensure that no written message is being secretly smuggled in, no medicine, no poison, no dangerous device.

Herta recently received a food parcel from her sister in Berlin. She removed the wrapping in front of Madam Berns, as usual, and then found, to her astonishment, a letter from Munich addressed to Dora Doebel in the ostensibly unopened package. "A harmless accident," observed the Madam Chief Warder, obviously annoyed, biting her lip.

Herta regards the incident as not harmless at all. "I find it suspicious enough," she said to us, "that Berns violated the usual practice by opening my parcel, but even more suspicious that she did not hand it over to me in that condition. Instead, she carefully tied it up again, giving the impression that it had never been inspected in the first place. I feel I'm being spied on, that I'm at risk. The Gestapo was quite embarrassed that they could only charge me with 'subversive opinions' three years ago, that they couldn't find evidence of an actual political crime such as high treason. Perhaps they want to reopen the case against me with new and falsified evidence. This time a letter to Dora was inadvertently enclosed in my parcel, so I don't consider it out of the question that the next time a deliberately planted forged letter, let's say from Fritz Baimler, could turn up. It's easy nowadays to show 'evidence of guilt.'"

Herta's fears disturbed us greatly. The possibility she described could become a reality, not only for her, but for any one of us.

Foreign contacts are most frowned upon. Barbara Fürbringer's sister in New York wrote to inquire about what was going on in the family. She had not been able to understand the latest confusing communication; something out of the ordinary must have happened. Barbara does not know how she is supposed to reply. Her husband, who, like her, had been arrested in 1933, had recently died from injuries inflicted in Dachau, her children have been put into a welfare home, her small piece of property near Lake Tegern was put up for auction. She is now completely destitute. The postage stamps for her letters to her children have to be donated by her companions. Her family's disintegration has bowed her large and stately frame. For days on end she walked around without saying a word. After much deliberation she wrote:

Dear Sister,

Thank you for your inquiry. Unfortunately, we are in a bad way. Theodor, my dear husband, died suddenly in Dachau four months ago. Our three children have been put into the state welfare home in Munich, I am in the women's camp in Moringen. I no longer have a penny to my name, if you could send me a few dollars, I would be very grateful.

Your faithful Barbara

Madam Chief Warder Berns returned this letter with no explanation beyond "undeliverable." With heavy heart Barbara gave in and wrote the letter again. She avoided mention of Dachau and of the sudden death, reporting simply, "Theodor, my dear husband, died four months ago." Still the letter found no favor. The "state welfare home" and the "women's camp" also had to go. An entire week passed before Barbara finally came up with this colorless but unobjectionable version:

Dear Sister,

Thank you for your inquiry. Unfortunately, things are not going exactly as we might wish. Theodor, my dear husband, died four months ago. Our three children live in Munich, 37 Brienner Strasse. I live in Moringen, near Hanover, 32 Breite Strasse.[32] I would be grateful to you if you could send me a small sum of money.

Your faithful sister Barbara

This time the letter was accepted for dispatch without objection.

Moringen, Early November 1936

A genuine dilemma, almost an ordeal, is presented by the handling of nature's physical needs. For the one hundred women here there is only a single lavatory with two seats, side by side. There is a frightening crush early in the morning after we get up and in the evening before we go to bed. The room cannot be locked, and thus the lucky occupants of the two seats at any given time are besieged by the other waiting and impatient women and are goaded to hurry with antagonistic or sarcastic remarks.

"Are you working in slow motion in there, or what? Gretl, my God, do you ever have good digestion!"

"That bean soup seems to have agreed with you pretty well. You've turned the loudspeaker on again. Hey, we can hear you already! Beans, beans, the musical fruit, the more you eat the more you toot."

Personally, I have trained myself to wake up at 5:30 a.m. sharp. With the first sound of the signal bell, I rush down the stairs to be the first to reach the lavatory, where I spend a few minutes of solitude. Then, with a quick "Good morning" to the sleepy matron, I hurry back upstairs to the sleeping quarters, where my companions are slowly rising, and punch my straw mattress into the prescribed shape.

Space in the lavatory, already tight enough to begin with, is restricted even more by the buckets brought here from the sleeping quarters in the early morning hours, further by two huge garbage pails and a cabinet containing cleaning materials and shoe polish. Every object that is so worn out and useless that no one would dare offer it directly to anybody else is brought here. Given the intense and pervasive poverty, however, and behind the veil of anonymity, as it were, these items find their admirers and are put to new uses. Sardine tins are transformed into soap dishes, twine—a much sought-after item—into shoelaces, cloth remnants into neckties, a chemise into warm mittens.

At the same time, the lavatory also serves as a "beauty parlor." Every Monday former federal representative Anna Löser sets up her stool here and attends gratis to anyone who turns up. The scissors are the property of the "hairdresser"; the "customers" must provide their own razor blades, towel, and cream.

The lavatory offers yet another, distinctive attraction. Throughout the entire course of the day, there is not a single minute during which you can be alone with yourself. In the day room, during the exercise period, in the sleeping quarters, you are always together with your comrades in misfortune. But the desire for occasional solitude is overwhelming. From time to time, even if only for a little while, you would like to be able to lose yourself in thought, undisturbed by the others, by their sight, by their talking, by their movements. Forever crowded into this compulsory community, how can you summon the inner peace and composure necessary to think about a difficult letter, to draft a petition? Where can you share an important piece of news with a friend without all ears in the vicinity pricking up? There is only one room for all that—the lavatory. It is visited relatively infrequently in the afternoon hours. To be sure, in addition to the odor the cold is also a nuisance, since the windows are kept open for ventilation even when there is frost on the ground. But you can easily put up with that. And because every woman understands how absolutely necessary a little solitude is, everyone is respectful whenever others, driven by the same desire, visit this place. You simply don't see them. You withdraw discreetly, unless, of course, you are spoken to.[33]

Here I ran into Käte Moser [Katharina Thoenes], depressed and bewildered. As a rule, she's a lively, vivacious person, despite her affiliation with the Jehovah's Witnesses, a wonderful woman, brimming with all the vim and vigor of life. Her sandy hair can barely be tamed in its profusion; she wears it parted in the middle and braided into thick, lustrous rings on both sides. Just that morning she had told me about "home," shown me pictures of her little family, of her husband, who had lost all his own hair when he was buried alive in a trench in the war and who now is wasting listlessly and impotently away, of her eight-year-old son, who writes her such affectionate letters, even if they are somewhat overloaded with biblical quotations. Full of impatience she had awaited her release, but after repeated promises she has just this afternoon received a summons for a new court hearing, which has destroyed all hope for a long time.

Whenever you go to the lavatory, you encounter old Schmitten, a half-crazy little old lady commonly known as "The Bawler." All day long she stands at the open window, despite the cold and the "floral fragrance." Frightened and motionless, she weeps constantly and quietly to herself.

"What is it that makes you so sad?" I asked the unhappy old woman yesterday.

"I don't know, I don't know," she wailed. "Oh, the dreadful life we have here. I wait and wait. What do these people want from me, anyway? Why don't they let me go home? Home is what I want. I want to go home."

I led her back to her place in the Great Hall. Two equally peculiar figures perch next to her there, "The Dwarf," a wizened sixty-year-old, crippled from birth, who nevertheless boasts a third husband and many children and grandchildren, and old Granny Benesch, about the same age, who constantly waggles her head with her mouth wide open, so that one can properly admire her sole but unusually long tooth in all its dirty yellow splendor. When I walked into the Great Hall again barely an hour later, I found the three strange old women happily absorbed in their favorite game, "Mensch ärgere dich nicht [Parcheesi]." "The Bawler" greeted me with a sly grin, but only for a moment.

I tried in vain to find out why these three mentally defective women have been brought here. Presumably, they made derogatory remarks about the government. They basically complain about everything, so why not about the Nazis as well? But in the Third Reich not even the mentally ill have the right to freedom of speech, to say nothing of the healthy, whose fate is decided by a single thoughtless comment.

ONE AFTERNOON IN the lavatory I met Herta Kronau, sad and quite lost to the world. I didn't speak to her, just nodded to her and disappeared. The next morning during the exercise period, Herta took my arm, and as we made our usual rounds, she recounted: "My mother has written me such a sweet, valiant letter again. She preaches courage and hope to me and is doing all she can to get me released as quickly as possible. Soon it will be four years since I was separated from her in her old-fashioned home in Nuremberg, where the high-backed armchairs, the antique wardrobes, the pictures on the walls all convey the peaceful atmosphere of days gone by. My mother was taking her afternoon nap—she's eighty-one, you know—I was standing at the window and looking down at the street below, at the snow flurries that were obscuring the premature March sunshine. A car drove up slowly. It stopped in front of our house, and two gentlemen got out. I felt instinctively that their visit was meant for me and that that was not a good sign. I stubbed out my cigarette and opened the front doors so that they would not ring the doorbell and wake my mother. The gentlemen identified themselves as detectives. I invited them into my room. I calmly accepted the arrest warrant, packed my little suitcase, gently kissed my sleeping mother, and followed the officers. Elderly as she is, I have seen her only once more since then, in the prison at Aichach. The guard did not let us out of his sight for a moment. My mother tried hard to say a few words. Then she gave up. But her wide eyes stared at me intently, peering into my soul, conducting a silent dialogue with me. These eyes accused me: 'Why has your restlessness driven you to this?' And they forgave me: 'I know, you only wanted to do what was right.' I too sat there speechless, motionless, eye to eye with my solemn, silent mother. I felt as naked and bare as Adam and Eve after the Fall. I was ashamed of my past. I was ashamed of the present, of those sad, depressing surroundings, of the tall iron bars that separated me from my mother, of my coarse brown prison dress, of the crude rectangular wooden clogs stuck on my feet.

"It was a relief that the guard's command ensured a swift and unceremonious farewell. But my mother did not wish to part from me so quickly. She arranged to be driven around the prison building in her car five times, and five times the horn sounded for me as a call for renewed courage.

"It is only my longing for my mother that has kept me going so far. Everything in life is insignificant and ephemeral, ideals, passion, success. The loyalty of friends is vain; gold turns them too easily into traitors. Even a husband's love is ephemeral and succumbs to alien temptations. Only one thing remains eternal, through chaos and confusion, in good times and in bad times: a moth- ◦ er's love. Just one more time I would love to hear her voice again, stroke her wrinkled hands and bury my head in her lap like a frightened child."

A photograph of her mother always hangs above Herta's bed, the learned face of a wise old woman, who now leads a life turned fully inward, who is already observing the bewildering game of everyday life from an almost other-worldly perspective.

When I entered the sleeping quarters the evening after our conversation, the picture of her mother was encircled by a small green wreath.

Moringen, Mid-November 1936

According to regulations, we must assemble in the Great Hall to listen to the radio broadcasts of official ministerial addresses. The women see this rule as an oppressive burden and privately rebel against it. The words that shower down upon them from out of the air are no more significant to them than the air itself. They sit silently, bent over their needlework. The Jehovah's Witnesses immerse themselves in their open Bibles, seemingly oblivious to the outside world. The feebleminded trio, "The Dwarf," "The Bawler," and Granny Benesch, silently but passionately play Parcheesi. Underneath the impassive mask of indifference behind which the women hide, however, smolders hatred, loath-ing, contempt. They regard Hitler and his paladins as vile slanderers and they feel a special revulsion toward Goebbels. A rage, repressed only with difficulty, comes over them whenever Reichskulturwart Rosenberg extols the superiority of the "Nordic master race."[34] At that point they like to quote a few powerful observations that Stalin once made. "The Germans," he said, in so many words, "regard themselves as the salt of the earth, and they claim the right to descend upon inferior peoples like the Slavs, in order to raise them up to the cul-tural level of the 'master race.' So also ancient Rome once characterized other peoples, especially the Teutons, as 'barbarians.' But then the subject peoples, the 'barbarians' of old, smashed the Roman Empire. In the end, the Nazis will assuredly be no more successful than the Roman emperors before them."[35]

The length of the speeches is just as annoying as the content, since they usually begin at our normal bedtime, around 9 o'clock, and rarely end before 11 o'clock. The women almost fall over from exhaustion, and a collective sigh of relief travels through the hall when the new national anthem, the "Horst Wessel Song," begins to play at the end of the broadcast. The matron then com-mands: "All rise," and everyone has to stand up. But we are forbidden to sing along or to raise our hands in the German salute.

Not long ago we again had the dubious pleasure of a ministerial address. The Reich minister of justice was announcing a new law. From now on, a judge does not need to rely on statute law such as the civil code; instead, he can base his decision on "the unwritten law, the sound sense of justice of the German people." In other words, he is now completely independent of any normative law. Furthermore, this decree has made any public attack on a prominent figure subject to severe punishment, even if the accusations are factually true.[36] The women were universally indignant at these new regulations. "There is no law and no justice in Germany any more. These deceivers of the people can pile one crime on top of another. They no longer have to worry about public criticism." This law, by the way, though just enacted, is merely the retrospective justification of what has long been going on in practice.

There is a young, good-looking stenographer here, an employee of a large movie studio.

"I was sitting with my colleagues in our cafeteria during lunch hour," she reported. "We were enjoying our meals and exchanging the latest office gossip.

"'Have you heard?' asked one girl. 'The manager of the shipping department was let go all of a sudden. He molested Lizzi and Susi.'

"'What, those two? But they're anybody's,' remarked another.

"'Yes,' I said, 'the little thieves are hanged, the big ones are allowed to get away.'

"'What do you mean by that?' someone asked me.

"'Well, now this little shipping clerk is done for, but Minister Goebbels can force any actress to oblige him with complete impunity. The road to employment and success runs through his bed. He's turning our film studio into his own private harem.'

"People laughed and clapped. We continued eating. One colleague went to the next room to make a telephone call. We had not even finished our lunch when two police officers appeared and arrested me."

THE BROADCAST OF the address by the minister of justice had terrible consequences for us a day later. The radio in the Great Hall is operated by Gerda Loss [Gerda Rose]. She's a sweet, rambunctious little thing, just under twenty years old, a true radio fan. She fiddles and tinkers with the receiver as often as possible, but she's not allowed to do so right after the noon meal, otherwise the women, especially tired at this time, might start to get nasty. But once again Gerda could not resist temptation. She turns the radio on, spins the dial and stumbles unexpectedly upon a recorded rebroadcast of the ministerial address. Only his final words were audible, the "Horst Wessel Song" was already starting up. Gerda, deeply alarmed, did not know what to do, turned it off, turned it on again, moved the dial, but too late.

Frau Hobrecht, the matron on duty, who herself had been dozing till then, awoke to the song's strident and familiar beat and called loudly into the hall: "All rise." The women, roused from their rest, had no idea what this sudden command was supposed to mean. Gerda, completely confused, turned the radio off.

"All rise," yelled Frau Hobrecht into the hall a second time, angrily, since her initial order had not met with compliance. The women told her that it was only a rebroadcast of the address from the day before, that it was over, and besides, the music had already stopped. Frau Hobrecht felt that the dignity of her office had been impugned, that the state, the party had been insulted. "This is sheer insubordination. Open rebellion. I shall report this incident to the director at once." She rushed out the door and ran down the stairs to the director's office.

Frau Hobrecht is the most unpopular of the matrons. She hides her lack of authority behind forceful posturing and loud commands. She pretends to be good natured but is in fact malicious and spiteful. Instead of reporting any real or imaginary irregularity to Madam Berns, as the other matrons do, Frau Hobrecht bypasses that level of authority on principle and immediately calls upon the director, whose special esteem she enjoys.

Toward the end of our free period, Madam Chief Warder Berns appeared in the courtyard and called us all together with her thundering voice: "An outrageous incident has taken place. You all know the details. The administration of this institution takes this to be the result of the insubordinate and rebellious spirit that prevails here. As punishment, a comprehensive mail embargo will therefore be in effect for the next few weeks. All written communication between this place and the outside world will cease. The eventual duration of this measure will be dependent upon your further conduct."

The next day the director reiterated this rule and compounded it by announcing that no releases would be processed during this period of time either, even if the central office in Berlin should authorize them.

Because of an unintentional transgression by a young girl or a few women, the guilty and the innocent alike—the Bavarians and we Jews had learned of the whole affair only much later—were severely punished, without the accused having been heard, without their having been given an opportunity to defend themselves. Gerda Loss cried her eyes out. A delegation of women, with the block leader Else Volckmar at their head, asked for an audience with the director so that they could explain the affair to him. In vain. The director refused to meet with them.

This hit us where it hurts the most. Anyone who is free can scarcely grasp the importance of mail to the prisoner. The letters we receive and send are, for us, our connection not only with the outside world, but with life itself. Without them, this complete loss of our former lives would be an unbearable ordeal. They build the bridge between a pointless present and a better past and to a future that we long for, even though we cannot see it clearly. Without this bridge we would surely break down in despair. Letters establish a link, despite our enforced isolation, to other, larger events. Since they confront us again and again with new problems, they relieve us of the depressing sensation that our lives are a sham, useless and superfluous, that we have been buried alive.

It is difficult to contemplate having to do without this absolutely essential input of spiritual relief for weeks on end, but it is also difficult to think of our loved ones at home, who will have no explanation for this sudden silence and will be worried sick about us. And on top of this is the fear that a thoughtless gesture, a careless word let slip by a companion or by oneself, could mean that this dismal situation will be extended indefinitely.

A mood of desperation hangs over the camp.

Moringen, Mid-November 1936

I tried hard to escape this disquieting mood, the dangers of sloth in general. I don't know how it all began, but one day I started giving English lessons to my dear little Anni Reiner. She had no previous knowledge whatsoever, so I had to start from scratch. Gertrud Mannheim and Ilse Lipinski, our roommates, had taken English many years ago at school, but their vocabulary was very rusty, so they availed themselves of the opportunity to brush up a bit. Herta Kronau, who has an excellent command of English, took amused and mocking notice of this sudden studiousness. "I understand that the energy of dear Frau Herz, unlike us undiminished by a lengthy imprisonment, is looking for an outlet, but I feel sorry for the poor victims of her experiment."

In time, however, she decided that these victims were not so unfortunate after all, that they were rather making quite good progress, and so she brought me her protégées from the Bavaria Hall, Hilde Weber [Hilde Gerber] and Ursula Renner [Hedwig Laufer],[37] as students, too. She feels a sense of maternal responsibility for these two comrades in misfortune, who have traveled with her through all the years along the same trail of tears, and wants very much to see them encouraged. The extension of my "student circle" to include these two young girls, whom I liked a lot, made me happy. As time went on, more women came forward. They seemed to think their companions were already perfect Englishwomen, and they wanted to emulate them. But this prompted the important question of whether these lessons were permissible in the first place.

The fact was that a regulation had recently been issued forbidding the "Aryans" to enter our room and we Jews to enter their quarters, unless there was some exceptional reason. Well, there is no shortage of such reasons. There's always something urgently needed in the one room that is available only in the other, such as yarn, a sewing machine, knitting samples, dress patterns, and the like. Even if this ban has had no practical consequences up to now, still it does exist, and its habitual violation might lead to disagreeable consequences. It seemed to all of us that a clarification of this question was in order. So one day Hilde Weber went to the director to inquire into his position on the matter. He gave her no immediate answer, but did promise a speedy ruling.

Shortly after, I received a summons to appear before the director. He was cool, correct, businesslike. "Fräulein Weber has asked me for permission to receive English instruction from you, along with some other women. Do you possess a sufficient command of that language?"

"Yes, sir."

"Do you have any teaching experience as well as your knowledge of the language?"

"Yes, sir. I've passed the English and French language examinations and have given many lessons."

The director assumes an official air. "I believe you. Your conduct here and your spouse's good name afford me every confidence. All the same, I must inform you that members of the Jewish race have recently been forbidden to give instruction to Aryans."

I had to restrain myself from showing my outrage. The director coughed slightly.

"Look, instruction cannot officially take place, but still, in the event that you might wish to converse in the English language with your two Aryan friends during the exercise period, in that event, you see, in that event—well, let's just say I would have no objection."

Thoughtfully, I made my way back up the stairs to the Jews' Hall, my heart becoming heavier with each step.

"No Aryan may be taught by a Jew." But then have the creators of the Bible, the teachers of all mankind lived in vain, the lawgivers, the poets and philosophers, the judges and the kings, the seers and the prophets, Amos, Isaiah, Jeremiah, and the greatest of them all, Jesus of Nazareth? How dare these narrow-minded fanatics misrepresent historical truth in order to deny the influence of the Jewish intellect on German culture! They resort to the most petty-minded measures, they remove the paintings of Jewish artists from the museums and galleries, the works of the great scientists from the libraries, even Spinoza's immortal principles, which provided Goethe with the building blocks of his beliefs. Wherever the German tongue is heard, Heine's song reverberates—"Ich weiss nicht, was soll es bedeuten ... [What it means, I do not know ...]"[38]—but these blasphemers of culture lie brazenly: "Author unknown." They banish the operas of Offenbach and Felix Mendelssohn, the symphonies of Mahler from the stage and the concert hall. They take full advantage of the inventions of Wassermann, Haber, Ehrlich, but they conceal the names of the inventors.[39] They have burned the books of contemporary Jewish authors, and they have used hammer and chisel to hack away the names of the Jewish war dead from public monuments. Oh, these vandals.

Word of the director's ban got around at once and precipitated a storm of indignation. "We don't need an official directive to know how to behave to our Jewish countrymen," said Dora Doebel to me. "They're simply part of us, no better and no worse than we are. But while the world assesses other peoples on the basis of their great men, the Jews are judged according to their most contemptible elements. That's how the tragic caricature emerges."

For the Bible Students, this amounted to an assault on their personal sense of honor. Nearly every one of them approached me and squeezed my hand. "Our Lord and Savior was, in His earthly form, a Jew," said Magdalene Mewes. "The Gospel according to Matthew, and thus the New Testament, begins with the explicit statement, 'A record of the genealogy of Jesus Christ the son of David, the son of Abraham' [Matthew 1:1]."

Another Bible Student added, "Paul says in his first Epistle to the Romans: 'Did God reject his people? By no means! I am an Israelite myself, a descendant of Abraham, from the tribe of Benjamin' [Romans 11:1]."

Finally, the beautiful Käte Moser said: "Frau Herz, not long ago you consoled me as I shared my burden with you. Today let me say to you: 'To be a Jew is nothing, and to be an Aryan is nothing—to be a good person, that is everything,' or as Paul puts it, 'Circumcision is nothing and uncircumcision is nothing. Keeping God's commandments is what counts' [I Corinthians 7:19]." She kissed me affectionately, and I gratefully returned her kiss.

That afternoon, the director summoned all of the prisoners except the Jews to the Great Hall. "A desire for instruction in English has been expressed in several quarters, and I am happy to accept this proposition. At my request, one of your companions, Fräulein Laburke of Insterburg, will be offering such a course. I strongly recommend that you make the best use of this opportunity." He was barely out of the hall before some eighty women had added their names to the registration list. This high rate of participation could be attributed partly to a genuine desire for learning, partly to naive delight at any diversion, but mostly to well-considered calculation. You want to be on the director's good side. The conduct report he sends to Berlin every quarter carries the greatest significance to every prisoner.

The following day, the director convened a second meeting. "I am truly delighted by the extent of your interest. Unfortunately, however, it is not possible to accommodate so many applications at this time. For the time being, we will make choices based on age and ability."

There was widespread speculation as to who the lucky ones would be. The suspense was further heightened by the director's departure for Berlin. This was thought to be linked to recent events here. The opinion was that he would confer with the higher authorities and return lavishly laden with textbooks, dictionaries, and similar materials.

Fräulein Laburke of Insterburg enjoys no great popularity. Although her pacifism is responsible for her being here, her behavior is, well, anything but peaceful. She is always scheming and stirring things up. Now she was buttering me up and begging for information about my teaching methods. A number of her questions baffled me. They betrayed an astounding lack of linguistic expertise. All of a sudden, Fräulein Laburke became hoarse, completely hoarse. She went around wearing a thick woolen scarf with a handkerchief to her mouth, and silently dismissed any inquiry about her condition from the deeply sympathetic women. She remains hoarse to this day and has apparently given up all hope of a speedy recovery.

The camp reverberates with jeers and laughter.

Moringen, Late November 1936

We resume our English lessons with increased enthusiasm. I teach my three Jewish students in our room and the two Bavarians, Hilde Weber and Ursula Lenner, during the exercise period, as the director had suggested. This is not exactly easy: to be limited to the spoken language alone presents considerable difficulties. I have to constantly repeat and have them constantly repeat back to me every word, every regular and irregular verb before it sinks in. Only very slowly am I able to expand their vocabulary and thus proceed to construct simple sentences. A primer and reader would be a great help, of course, but procuring them would probably lead to new questions and further debate and therefore can't be done. But the two Bavarians make a virtue of necessity. They find the verbal method forced upon us quite effective; they memorize tirelessly and with genuine enjoyment. Ambition has seized them.

Of the two friends, Hilde is dearer to me, perhaps because she is much younger, because she is looking for something to hold on to, looking for protection. She is just under twenty-one years old, and across her beautiful, childishly sweet features lies a shadow of melancholy and grief. She is blond, lanky, but fragile and pale. The four years in prison have destroyed her youth; she's wilting without ever having flowered. Her father, a lithographer, a quiet, refined man and an active Communist, had fled abroad with his two grown sons as soon as Hitler had seized power, while the youngest son, not yet of age, was taken to Dachau by the Gestapo. Hilde, then just under seventeen years old, barely a grown-up herself, had been serving as a Communist youth leader, supervising ten- and twelve-year-old boys and girls, organizing afternoon meetings and outings with them, until she met her fate.

"It was a Sunday in the springtime," she told me. "The beautiful weather had lured me out of doors. I was wandering alongside a stream through fields blanketed with flowers, happy and more at peace with myself than I had been in a long time. Radiant spring sunshine bathed the vast Franconian landscape, and the reflection of this radiance, jubilation, and Sunday contentment bathed the faces of the people I met as well. A group of kids had overtaken me, one with a guitar decorated with fluttering ribbons. Their singing still echoed from far away. Suddenly I shivered. I became sad, sadder and sadder. An abandoned soul, I stood by the wayside. An inner voice spoke to me: 'Say goodbye to mountain and valley, to light and joy, absorb this splendor once more with all of your senses, so that you may preserve the memory as long as possible.' In a strange mood, full of apprehension, I went back. When I got home, two men were waiting for me in the hallway, showed me their badges, and arrested me."

This sweet, contemplative creature is always agonizing about the unalterable rules of this world. Countering her idealistic dreams of the coming universal brotherhood of mankind, I tried to persuade her that wars are as old as mankind and will probably never be preventable. These observations disturbed her so deeply that, in guarded language, she sent questions to her older sister, who lives in Munich. The sister answered: "Leave the great issues of world affairs to those who have been appointed to resolve them. Be content to perform the little duties of everyday life conscientiously."

Hilde is as cuddly, soft, talkative, and affectionate as her friend Ursula Renner, six years her senior, is serious, withdrawn, and taciturn. Her stocky figure, her broad face with its prominent cheekbones, her straight, black hair, suggest a Slavic ancestry. Until her arrest in 1933, Ursel had worked as an unskilled laborer in a shoe factory in Augsburg, and it still pleases her greatly to demonstrate on occasion her expertise at making slippers. At home, poverty had been the rule: her father drank away his wages, and it was hard for her mother to support herself and her children. But her mother was one of those exceptional women who prevail over all the hardships of life, owing to an abundance of heart and strength of character. Her mother's letters, written in a pure Bavarian dialect with no inhibitions of spelling or grammar, are couched in extraordinarily expressive language. Even our stern and usually surly Chief Warder cannot suppress a sympathetic smile, occasionally even an appreciative comment. You can feel the humor, joie de vivre, tenacity in every line. Her mother is a home worker, making dolls and simple toys, but the pay is low, and she can send only small sums of money to her daughter.

So Ursel lives here in the sorriest of states. All she owns is the most basic clothing. In spite of the inclement weather—heavy rain has turned our yard into one deep puddle—she wears only worn-out sandals and a threadbare woolen overcoat. When it is very cold, she gets her dark blanket from the dormitory and throws it over her head and shoulders, which gives her the appearance of a peasant woman. Whenever I see her like that I am reminded of the wood carvings of Barlach, their austerity and intensity.[40] The precisely formulated, simplified lines do not convey poverty but rather an intensive inner richness.

It's difficult to say which of the two friends is the better student. Hilde, always inquisitive, almost pushy, comprehends more readily and faster, but also forgets quickly. Ursel, on the other hand, catches on slowly, but once she has grasped something, her mind is like a steel trap. Her command of Esperanto gives her a certain edge. This artificial language relies heavily on English for the structure of its ingeniously developed grammar and for the foundation of its vocabulary. The remarkable spread of Esperanto was surprising to me. The language is easy to learn and is especially useful among workers for communicating with foreign comrades. The Nazis have banned it, of course, partly to discourage international communication, partly because its inventor was a Jewish physician.[41] But this ban is not strictly enforced, and so the women always carry their Esperanto workbooks around with them and memorize from them studiously during the exercise period.

It was during one of these exercise periods—I was coaching my students "teach, taught, taught; think, thought, thought"—that a matron appeared and proclaimed loudly: "Frau Volckmar, mail call."

We could hardly believe our ears, but after only a few minutes Else Volck-mar reappeared. Her face radiant, she was waving two letters around triumphantly. Then another of us, and another, and a fourth, a fifth, and then me. I received a whole stack of letters.

The camp had certainly not seen so many happy people for a long time. At every tree, along the walls of the buildings that enclose the courtyard, in every corner, on the stairs, the women stood and laughed softly and happily, suppressed a gentle sigh, and read and read. The buildings could have collapsed, and they would not even have noticed it.

Moringen, Late November 1936

Great as the joy was at first over the repeal of the mail embargo, a certain disillusionment began to set in during the next few days. The director had announced at the same time that none of the prospective releases authorized by the central office in Berlin would take place. Now it turns out that Berlin had not issued any such orders in the first place. The release process had been at a complete standstill for months. No prisoner knows whether she'll be spending weeks, months, or even years here.

The Gestapo determines the sentence on its own authority, arbitrarily and regardless of whether or not a decision is pending before a regular court, and it refuses on principle to give prisoners a release date. That is part of the system and is one more link in its long chain of psychological abuses.

This uncertainty about the length of imprisonment ruins the prisoners' health, upsets their emotional balance, gives rise to chronic irritability and frequently to serious psychological problems. Aware of these dangers, the women attempt to fight them on their own.

A nervous breakdown or other illness brings transfer to the "infirmary." This somewhat pretentious name is a poor fit for an unpretentious room that is completely unsuited to proper medical treatment. It contains six beds, but that's it. Nursing staff is no more in evidence than are hygienic facilities. Relegation to this unfriendly, foul-smelling room is regarded almost as punishment.

A widowed estate owner from the Rhineland has been a resident here for weeks now. She doesn't bathe, she doesn't comb her hair, she only complains about the mismanagement of her farm. She's not of sound mind; misfortune has clouded her soul. "The Nazis arrested me because I laughed about the many splendid uniforms of General Göring. Then they arrested my son, and now our beautiful old estate is going to rack and ruin. If only I could get out of this hole and set everything to rights." And then follows invective hurled at the manager of the estate and at herself and all of her ancestors and descendants.

Things are going even worse for the woman in the neighboring bed. Her screams resound throughout the building and resemble the howling of a dog. The doctor pays her no attention.[42]

He pays just as little attention to seventy-year-old "Grandma." She was brought here several months ago in such critical condition that the director didn't want to admit her, and he appealed, albeit unsuccessfully, to Berlin. She's crippled and often lies for hours and hours in a state of deep unconsciousness. When she's awake, however, "Grandma" is infused with humor and good cheer. On Sunday afternoons, the old woman hobbles on two crutches into the Great Hall and assembles an audience, which attends gleefully to her hilarious stories. Not long ago her husband had sent her two packs of cigarettes, carefully concealed in a pair of slippers. But Madam Chief Warder had discovered the forbidden cargo, and instead of her cigarettes, our good "Grandma" received only bread and water for two days.

Barbara Fürbringer, the one who had conducted the difficult correspondence with her sister in New York, was brought to the infirmary with an advanced case of tonsillitis. Despite the totally inadequate hygiene, she actually recovered quite quickly. I visited her several times and learned with what kind of inventive dirty tricks her court case had been conducted. "My husband and I were arrested in 1933. He was taken to Dachau, where those monsters slowly tortured him to death. I was sentenced to a year in prison, which I served in Aichach. It was a terrible time. But I was released on schedule, to the day. Anxious to finally see my children again, I went to the train station and was about to board the train to Munich, already waiting at the platform. Then two police officers approached me, served me with a new arrest warrant, and I was taken to the prison in Landshut 'for the protection of the people and the state.'[43] I was held there for a year and a half, and now I've been in Moringen for ten months, with no end in sight. The 'blacks' have it so much better. Once they have served their court sentences, they are set free. But they are only 'criminal prisoners'—thieves, fences, prostitutes. They enjoy the protection of the law, while we 'political prisoners' are outside the rule of law altogether."

The stay in the "infirmary" would be unbearable if not for one of our companions, Grete Uhland, who, with no mandate from the administration of the institution, takes care of the patients with selfless devotion. A strange person, this thirty-something, unmarried Grete. Whenever she's not keeping herself busy with her voluntary Good Samaritan activities, she sits quietly, almost indifferently, in the Great Hall, usually bent over her needlework. She exchanges scarcely a word with her companions, keeping mostly to herself, even during the exercise period. Nobody knows anything about her personal fate, which must be very sad. In her care of the sick, she's looking for diversion, perhaps solace and a new purpose to life. She cleans bedpans and overnight pails, makes the beds, procures hot-water bottles and medications, sits down on the beds of the patients, and, in a deep voice almost unaccustomed to speech, says a few comforting words to them, which she then always repeats softly: "Don't worry. Don't cry. Things will get better. Stretch out. Close your eyes and sleep, sleep."

Whenever she is at a loss how to help, she certainly does not turn to the unfriendly doctor, who's indifferent to physical and emotional suffering, but to Herta Kronau, a trained nurse and an experienced massage therapist. Although ailing herself and often quite frail, Herta knows how to ease the pain of the sick with gentle massage and skillful touch.

Moringen, Late November 1936

For several days there was an unusual amount of activity here. Trucks drove up with a rumble, loud commands rang out, bales and crates were unloaded and dragged through the corridors on the ground floor into the basement. The racket reverberated as far up as our second floor.

Suddenly, the thickset, hulking figure of Frau Hobrecht trudged into the Great Hall with a pile of old, worn-out clothes. Without saying a word, she threw the whole load onto the "notables'" table, right in front of block leader Else Volckmar's place. A cloud of dust and dirt rose up from the bundles.

"What's that supposed to be?" asked Else indignantly.

"That's work for the Winter Relief Campaign," responded the matron, hoarse and out of breath.[44]

"But this dirty, stinking stuff has no business on the table where we have to eat."

One word led to another. Finally, Else threw the bundles angrily down from the table. Frau Hobrecht's frizzy, unkempt, reddish hair stood up in all directions. "Defamation of a public official while on duty, that's what this is," she yelled, and rushed out of the hall, down the stairs.

A quarter of an hour later, Else was summoned to appear before the director. He had assumed an air of authority, ready to interrogate the offender. But Else did not feel the least bit guilty, and she made her point of view eloquently clear. All she had wanted was not to have the dubious material piled up on the table right before lunchtime. In any case, neither she nor any of her companions could be accused of being shirkers. For once the director was lenient and let the matter go with a warning, perhaps because Frau Hobrecht got on his nerves with her insistent agitation.

Well, we're in for it now. The Winter Relief Campaign. So even we are to be made to work for this enormous agency. Since early fall, a massive propaganda campaign has used every technique—appeals from leading personalities, newspaper articles, posters, advertisements, speeches, radio announcements—to hammer the slogan into the heads of sixty million Germans: Remember your needy fellow citizens, help them through the hardships of winter. Give—give money, give food, give clothing. Almost every family has taken part, mostly with donations of clothing. A hundred thousand industrious workers were busy transporting the unexpected flood of goods from farms, villages, and cities to official distribution centers.

And the outcome, as far as I am able to see it from here? A substantial portion of the materials collected from the province of Hanover is being stored in a huge room in our basement. And what a grotesque hodgepodge, what a hopeless mess!

There are piles of silk evening gowns, fur jackets, tuxedos, threadbare blouses, gray work trousers, windbreakers, riding outfits—but in filthy, unusable condition, often moth-eaten. To the extent that any principles of sorting could be discerned, they had been limited to a mechanical lumping together of trousers with trousers, coats with coats, skirts with skirts, so that complete two-piece outfits, even men's suits, had been mercilessly uncoupled. When you look at these hundreds and thousands of bundles, it makes you furious. So much goodwill, so much effort wasted so senselessly. This relief action had begun as a great gesture, with genuine idealistic enthusiasm, but then the bureaucrats, more out of inability than apathy or indifference, had allowed this momentum to wane. And this indifference persists here.

Something like a hundred thousand articles of old clothing are being stored here. Cleaned, repaired, refurbished, they could offer welcome comfort to tens of thousands of needy people. It is a worthwhile but difficult task, which would require good judgment and organizational skills to master. But to whom is it being entrusted? Frau Hobrecht, of all people—the most incompetent of all the matrons. She claims to have been employed as a seamstress at one time, and now she is driven by a desire to show off her skills. And a meager set of skills it is, consisting primarily of the capacity to fashion short pants for boys and mittens for road workers out of men's heavy overcoats.

This matron has not the slightest sense how to plan a large-scale project so that it can be carried out coherently and systematically. To begin with, of course, the dirtiest articles ought to be washed. But there is a shortage of soap, even of hot water. Soap and coal are allegedly too expensive. For the necessary repair work, each table, naturally not each prisoner, is given one spool of white thread and one of black. Also available at each table are one pair of scissors, a few dull kitchen knives for ripping seams and, for all one hundred women, a grand total of *two* sewing machines.

We are annoyed by this persistent incompetence and cannot throw ourselves into our work. Only occasionally does the pure pleasure of good work and our need for creativity prevail. Some of my companions are quite gifted at handicrafts, and so they cannot resist making the children's clothing, cut out by Frau Hobrecht to resemble little widows' weeds, more attractive with lots of embroidery, colorful trimmings, bright collars, and belts. But they get little thanks and soon give up their special efforts. Unfortunately, I myself am no expert with a needle. I specialize in boys' trousers, where the experience I had gained with my own unruly scamps helped. I fear only that these trousers made of heavy overcoat material, which I sewed together by hand, since neither of the two machines was ever free, will come apart at the seams with the first boisterous movement of their youthful future owners.

Frau Hobrecht aside, the Winter Relief means absolutely nothing to most of the matrons; even their inspection of our work is only rudimentary. If an attempt at repair proves unsuccessful, or if the hopeless patchworking of a tattered article would be just too ridiculous, the unfortunate article of clothing is smuggled into one of the sacks placed in the corridors for the collection of garbage and material scraps—and eternal oblivion provides protection against investigation and punishment.

Before we can undertake the alterations, we find we first have to beat the dirt out of numerous articles of clothing that have not been washed. Instead of establishing an orderly rotation for this activity, Frau Hobrecht strides self-importantly through our rooms calling excitedly for "volunteers." A few women in each hall reluctantly come forward, and I join them.

It's not exactly a pleasure to stand for hours outside in the rain-drenched courtyard at this time of year, to be jarred by the cutting east wind while going at thick coats and capes with thin willow rods.

"If they'd only give us proper, heavy carpet-beaters, like the ones you'd find in every home," says the spirited young woman next to me heatedly. "We can't get anywhere with these pitiful willow switches. We're just rubbing our skin raw with them. A few pennies is all a carpet-beater costs, but that's beyond the means of the bosses here. Hundreds of thousands of marks are collected every week by the Winter Relief—allegedly for the poor, but really for rearmament. This whole thing is a shameless national con game. Look up there, there flies the Winter Relief." She pointed to some airplanes high in the air, their engines roaring, proudly and confidently making their way to Hanover.

Zenta Baimler had also joined the "Volunteer Beater Corps." "I can't stand it in our room upstairs with all that old stuff," she said to me. "The brisk air and physical activity give me some relief from all the worry. I've heard nothing from my husband in months, either directly or indirectly. I don't know if he went to the Comintern in Moscow after he escaped from Dachau, or whether, more likely, he's fighting against the Fascists in the Spanish Civil War."[45] She beat the jackets and trousers with such force, as if her attack were intended for an invisible enemy, that the dust swirled high and enveloped her in a gray cloud.

Despite all the obstacles and obstructions, the Winter Relief Campaign moves slowly forward. Our rooms gradually begin to resemble tailors' shops, or rather second-hand stores. Before us, beside us, behind us, in our rooms, in the hallways, on the landings, everywhere nothing but old clothes. A foul, musty odor emanates from them, covers everything with a dark crust, burns our eyes, permeates our skin, corrodes our lungs. The hopelessness exhaled by these bundles covers us like a thick black cloth, threatening to suffocate us.

We try hard to think about other things. Ilse Lipinski resurrects the now-faded glory of these clothes. She speculates about their previous owners, about beautiful women, wealthy gentlemen, loud parties. But none of her stories have happy endings. You climb up on the ladder of life only to fall down it again, that's the sad story told by these shabby remnants of once-splendid garments, now in the hands of poor prisoners in a German women's concentration camp.

"All due respect for your imagination, but paint us some happier pictures," admonishes Herta Kronau.

Ilse shrugs her shoulders.

THE BIBLE STUDENTS have refused to accept any role in the Winter Relief Campaign. For them the state is fundamentally a creation of Satan; consequently, any order from the state derives from Satan, too. Their refusal was extremely awkward for the director. He had to take a stand on the matter but was apparently reluctant to administer severe reprisals. He's surprisingly well versed in the Holy Scriptures himself, and it has often given him considerable pleasure to put the biblical knowledge of the Jehovah's Witnesses to the test with little-known quotations. So now he tried to win the devout women over with biblical references. "Your conduct places you in flagrant contradiction to divine law. Charity, relief of the poor is the duty of each and every one of the faithful. Isaiah preaches 'Is it not [your duty] when you see the naked, to clothe him, and not to turn away from your own flesh and blood?' [Isaiah 58:7]."

"But it is also written in the Gospel according to Matthew: 'Watch out for false prophets. They come to you in sheep's clothing, but inwardly they are ferocious wolves' [Matthew 7:15]," Magdalene Mewes, serving as spokeswoman for the Bible Students, responded bluntly.

It was hard for the director to restrain himself. "Winter Relief is required by the state. Paul commands explicitly in his Epistle to the Romans: 'Everyone must submit himself to the governing authorities' [Romans 13:1]."

"And Paul continues in the same sentence: 'There is no authority except that which God has established' [Romans 13:1]," objected Magdalene Mewes. "But God cannot have promoted this new state, for Paul says in a different passage, in his Epistle to the Corinthians: 'For God is not a God of disorder but of peace' [I Corinthians 14:33]. In today's Germany, where exactly does peace prevail?"

The director abandoned the theological realm and gave worldly inducements a try. "Everyone who contributes to the Winter Relief can request one article of clothing from the inventory for herself and one for her children."

"'What good will it be for a man if he gains the whole world, yet forfeits his soul?' [Matthew 16:26]," Magdalene Mewes, citing Matthew, declined indignantly.

The director finally lost his patience. He fumed at the women: "I could easily break this foolish resistance with the right kind of measures, such as reducing the daily food rations, or corporal punishment or confinement.[46] But I'm reluctant to turn fools into martyrs. Nevertheless, I'm not prepared to allow this resistance to proceed without reprisal. I am therefore ordering your complete physical isolation. You will be removed from the Great Hall, from all contact with any other prisoners, and you will be housed in a separate cell."

"Luke says: 'Blessed are you when men hate you, when they exclude you and insult you and reject your name as evil' [Luke 6:22]," Magdalene Mewes encouraged her companions.

"Since this punishment apparently makes so little impression on you," the director continued, "I hereby strengthen it with a renewal of the mail embargo. This time it applies to you and you alone and will be in effect for six weeks in the first instance."

That was a heavy blow. The women knew only too well, from previous sad experience, what this mail embargo means. For a moment, even Magdalene Mewes was speechless. Then she pulled herself together, and her voice, at first a little shaky, became resonant, joyfully triumphant, buoyed by inner strength: "Who cares about letters? Thus speaks Paul to all of the righteous: 'You yourselves are our letter, written on our hearts, known and read by everybody. You show that you are a letter from Christ … written not with ink but with the Spirit of the living God, not on tablets of stone but on tablets of human hearts' [II Corinthians 3:2–3]."

The director held no power over these zealots. Far from hurting them with his punishment, he had actually fulfilled their most secret wishes. Their isolation, which even excluded them from communal exercise with us, was seen by them, quite seriously, as preferential treatment, as a reward for lives lived in service to God. Now completely together among themselves, with no diversion from any other activities, with no need to worry about those with different views, they dedicated themselves from dawn to dusk to the study of the Holy Scriptures and indulged in the most esoteric of interpretations, comparisons, and allegories. Undisturbed, they could now imagine the horror of the imminent end of the world, the details of Armageddon, the impending final battle between the righteous and the unrighteous. They could fantasize about the miracle of the Last Judgment and the splendor of the kingdom of righteousness, newly established by Jesus himself. The mail embargo was not too high a price to pay for this freedom to organize their lives completely around their religious desires and needs. In any case, the few letters that they had exchanged with their relatives up to then were less the expression of their personal experiences than an accumulation of impersonal biblical quotations.

The Jehovah's Witnesses had lost little and gained much. Whenever we happened to meet up with them, they would whisper to us, with joy and conviction: "God does not forsake his own."

Moringen, Early December 1936

The vagrant Pauline Langner, in one of her sudden fits of rage, has gone after her companions with clenched fists, a brandished stool, and a mighty scream, and finally had to be locked up in solitary confinement, for safety's sake. From time to time, the old irrepressible passion for the road is aroused in her; she needs space, motion, she has to travel, to "tramp." Even if she's hungry and cold, she feels compelled to carry her insatiable restlessness from place to place. Whenever this desire seizes her here in the camp, she lashes out wildly and desperately and bursts into a long-drawn-out howl like a wounded animal. It's dangerous to approach her when she's in this state. During her normal periods, she behaves calmly and reasonably and likes to talk about her "voyages." Despite her dreadful dialect, the whole romance of the carefree journey, the spirit of the great outdoors, and the beauty of the German landscape are alive in her simple but vivid narrative. We understand her better than she does us; it's incomprehensible to her that people could spend the best years of their lives behind the stone walls of a house, in the narrow confines of an office or the din of a factory. She is skilled, is Pauline. She had once worked from home as a seamstress, and she now sometimes takes on a rush job from a companion here in the camp in return for a few pennies or a morsel of sausage. She speaks with surprising tenderness of her two daughters and with equally unbridled hatred of her husband, who is having an affair with another woman. "My old man's slut is wearin' my Sunday best now, but am I ever gonna get even with her when I get ahold of her," she yells, furious.

In addition to this untamed vagabond, some of the other women gathered in the Great Hall are also beyond the pale of polite society. First of all, there's the "boarding-house proprietor" from Hamburg. At her arrival, we were showered with a torrent of words: "I've grown gray with integrity and honor, I've been running my boarding-house business for more than twenty years, no one's ever seen me do anything illegal. Then all of a sudden the police come—apparently I've said something to offend the SA. Wouldn't have dreamt of it. I've never cared about politics, only about payment on the nail."

We take her word for it about the "gray hair," although it has been dyed a fiery red, but are less ready to concede that it has turned gray "with honor." Because on closer inspection, her so-called boarding-house business turned out to be a bordello. To know we have a "madam" in our midst is odd, to say the least. If only she were at least entertaining. But with her frizzy hair, her flattened red nose, and the stained leather jacket over her imposing mass of flesh, she comes across as merely lewd and vulgar.

Her friend, on the other hand, presents a picture of elegance. She refers to herself cockily as a "woman of independent means," and even if she is too heavily made up, she's a strikingly beautiful and shapely woman. Her life of "independent means" appears to have brought her a lot of money, since she wears conspicuously fine clothing and lingerie. When the weather is good and she struts about the courtyard on the high heels of her dainty patent-leather pumps, dressed in silk stockings, a short, tight-fitting skirt, a chic little hat atop her blond curls, swinging her hips and casting come-hither looks in all directions, then in her thoughts she is obviously not in the narrow confines of the concentration camp, but rather "walking the street" down the wide promenades of the big city. She loves to wear low-cut blouses, which display her charms for all to see, and she behaves so shamelessly in word and in manner that the director has admonished her sternly. The Bible Students have applied one of the Proverbs to her: "'Like a gold ring in a pig's snout is a beautiful woman who shows no discretion' [Proverbs 11:22]."

The prostitute Margot, on the other hand, is so inadequately blessed with physical charms that we are always asking ourselves incredulously how, with her short, stocky build, her heavy legs, her homely face with its thick, protruding lips, she could ever have found so many admirers, and paying admirers at that. She is evil, she *loves* evil, not always for the sake of any specific objective, but out of an innate, unadulterated delight in evil. Admittedly, she occasionally shows signs of goodness; she can be pleasant at times, or shower a newfound friend with gifts she has made with some patience and skill. But then her true nature suddenly breaks through again. She had become extremely close with a fellow prisoner, a simple, good-natured person; but no sooner had the woman been released than Margot pressed charges against her for illicitly taking away one of the Winter Relief dresses.

Prostitutes and suchlike women are in fact assigned to our section only if they have committed a "political" offense, if, say, they have vilified one of the [Nazi] Party bosses. For "non-political" offenses, such as a breach of the regulations [on prostitution],[47] they are sent downstairs to the "blacks." Down there they have it worse than we do, save for the one, priceless benefit of a fixed date of release. They have to perform forced labor, to do the laundry for the entire camp, including the men's section of the workhouse. They are not permitted to improve their diet by buying extra food, are not permitted to receive food parcels, and may write only a single letter per week. Their daily exercise is limited to one hour.

Curiously, the matrons behave much more charitably toward the "blacks" than they do toward us; with them, now and then, they will let fall a friendly word, a sympathetic remark. For the matrons, the "blacks" are still people you can feel sorry for, after all. But we, whether we are Communists, Bible Students, or Jews, are regarded as enemies of the state, to be partly despised, partly feared. We are hated, shunned, treated with icy reserve by these junior agents of the government. They don't utter a single word to us that isn't work related; no bridge of human understanding extends to us.

Margot the prostitute was hauled off to Berlin for a court hearing not long ago. We breathed a sigh of relief. After she denounced her friend, she had been shunned like a leper, and we were happy not to see her in our midst any longer. Our happiness did not last long. After only two weeks Margot turned up in the camp again. On the return trip she had committed an act of gross insubordination, with the result that the director blasted her immediately with a very strong reprimand and imposed ten days of strict confinement.

We all know that Margot's moral inferiority is due in large part to her physical inferiority. She is afflicted by frequent epileptic seizures, during which she throws herself to the ground, muttering incoherently and foaming at the mouth.

Hilde Weber [Hilde Gerber]

On the occasion of her arrest in 1933 (top), and in a later, undated photograph (above).

She is just under twenty-one years old, and across her beautiful, childishly sweet features lies a shadow of melancholy and grief. She is blond, lanky, but fragile and pale. The four years in prison have destroyed her youth; she's wilting without ever having flowered.

Both images reprinted with the permission of the Studienkreis Deutscher Widerstand 1933–1945, Frankfurt am Main, Germany.

Gerda Loss [Gerda Rose]

In an undated photograph.

The radio in the Great Hall is operated by Gerda Loss.... She's a sweet, rambunctious little thing, just under twenty years old, a true radio fan.

Reprinted with the permission of the Studienkreis Deutscher Widerstand 1933–1945, Frankfurt am Main, Germany.

Zenta Baimler [Centa Herker-Beimler]

In an undated photograph.

Even physically Zenta projects quite a personality. Her proud carriage, her broad, noble features, her high forehead, her firm mouth, her wide shoulders, and her short hair, styled in a men's cut, all accentuate her pronounced masculine nature.

Reprinted with the permission of the Studienkreis Deutscher Widerstand 1933–1945, Frankfurt am Main, Germany.

Dora Doebel [Viktoria Hösl]

With her son Herbert (above) in 1929, and in a 1937 portrait (left) sketched in Moringen by Vera List [Gerda Lissack].

Dora Doebel sent the drawing to her son Herbert. The boy thanked her effusively: "I recognized you right away, dearest Mommy, even though I haven't seen you for four years. You really look terrific. The Mother Superior of our convent said: 'That is the portrait of an intelligent and kindhearted woman.' I'm so proud of you. I kiss your picture every morning and every evening."

Käte Moser [Katharina Thoenes]

In an undated photograph (left), and with her husband Heinrich and son Hans in 1935 (below).

Just that morning she had told me about "home," shown me pictures of her little family, of her husband, who had lost all his own hair when he was buried alive in a trench in the war and who now is wasting listlessly and impotently away, of her eight-year-old son, who writes her such affectionate letters, even if they are somewhat overloaded with biblical quotations. [Note that young Hans Thoenes was actually born in 1925.]

Both images reprinted with the permission of the Jehovah's Witnesses, History Archives Department, Germany.

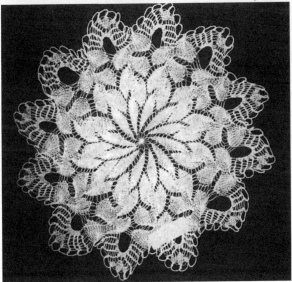

Needlework and Handicrafts

Evenings drag on interminably, monotonously, exhaustingly. Daytimes are still bearable. The two-hour stroll in the open air is refreshing, but after supper the women collapse. Needlework falls from tired hands, conversation dies down, books demand a level of concentration which is hard to come by.... My two students, Hilde and Ursel, surprised me with handmade gifts, a beautifully woven bast basket and a skillfully knitted little coverlet.

Berlin and Moringen

Gabriele Herz's Griegstrasse home in Berlin (top), photographed in 1997, and the prison yard at Moringen (bottom), photographed in 2003.

Barely two weeks have passed since my arrest in Berlin, and only a few days since my incarceration here in Moringen. And yet this brief period seems like an eternity to me. What a difference between the old security of my protected home in Berlin and the insecurity of the present; such a profusion of events and individuals, so many strange destinies.

Berlin photograph by Ellen Kracauer Hartig; Moringen photograph by Thomas Meredith.

Hanukkah in Rochester

Gabriele Herz (right) celebrating Hanukkah with her husband Emil (center), daughter-in-law
Hildegard (left), and several grandchildren in Rochester, New York, ca. 1955.

I was asked to tell the women about previous Hanukkah celebrations that we had observed at
home in the company of our children and our friends and which we had endowed with solemn
and joyful meaning in those earlier happy times.

Photograph by Arthur Herz.

A NEW RULE prohibits us from keeping articles of clothing in our day rooms; they may be stored only in the wardrobe room.

The incompetent and malicious Frau Hobrecht has decided once again that she must exercise exceptional strictness to prove her proficiency as a matron. She inspected the Great Hall and searched each one of the small lockers to see that they didn't contain, say, a pair of stockings. And so she approached the little locker of the feeble-minded Granny Benesch. The poor old woman, who assumed that someone wanted to steal her few belongings, became extremely agitated and screamed: "No one goes near my things."

Former federal representative Löser, who had observed the proceedings from close at hand, approached Frau Hobrecht and said quietly to her: "Granny Benesch, as you know, is not all there. She doesn't understand the first thing about this new ruling. Please show a little consideration."

"I don't have to show any consideration here. I just have to do my job," Frau Hobrecht rebuffed her angrily.

She opened the little locker. Granny Benesch, furious, grabbed her arm, shoved her back. "Get out of there. Don't touch my things."

For a moment Frau Hobrecht was speechless. Then she erupted, her breathless voice breaking: "Violent resistance against the state, that's what this is. I shall report this incident to the director immediately. You, Frau Löser, come with me at once as a witness."

Frau Löser tried to convince our all-powerful director that the whole affair was harmless, but to no avail. The director, otherwise always cool and detached in word and bearing, always projecting the image of a man of the world, chewed her out: "Oh, shut up! Parliamentary speeches are out of order here."

He knows Granny Benesch well enough. Together, she, "The Bawler," and "The Dwarf" form "The Feeble-Minded Trio." Contrary to the rules, she never rises when he enters the room. She smiles at him constantly with her stupid grin whenever he makes a speech. But it had never previously occurred to him to hold her accountable. Now somehow peeved, perhaps by the resistance of the Bible Students to the Winter Relief Campaign, he imposes three days in the punishment cell [*Arrest*][48] on this mentally defective woman.

That dreaded penalty appears to be coming into fashion here.

"Three days in the punishment cell. Very tough for a seventy-year-old. I spent an entire month in solitary confinement myself when I was barely eighteen years old," Gusti Folander informed me.

"How could that be? What had you done?" I asked.

"Just a childish prank. At that time I *was* still partly a child, you know, a Young Communist. I had thrown a note into the cell of Hilde Weber, your English student, in the prison in Landshut. 'This poison-gas war against the defenseless Ethiopians is unbelievably terrible, don't you think?' Hilde, who was completely innocent, got ten days of solitary, and like I said, I got a whole month."[49]

"How can one stand that kind of punishment for so long?"

"It's really hard. If it had lasted any longer, I'm sure I would have lost my mind. I suffered terribly; I don't know if I will ever get over it completely. My hair fell out. It took a year for it to start to grow back in again, even thinly. I was kept in total darkness. The wooden platform that made a bed at night was tied up flush against the wall during the day, so I sat hunched over on a little stool. I wasn't allowed to bring anything with me into the cell, not even a brush or a comb; I had to wear the same dress and underwear for the entire time. I was freezing. There was no blanket, not even at night. Hunger gnawed at my innards. For three days there would be only water and a little bread. Every fourth day I got the regular daily food rations, a hot dish of sauerkraut, lentils, or beans. But my stomach was so weak that often it could not tolerate this heavy fare and threw it back up again. You just have to chew very carefully and slowly, and only swallow very small bites. One of our comrades who was ravenously hungry had wolfed down his whole meal. He died in terrible pain a few hours later. Every day I was escorted to the courtyard for ten minutes. Out in the open, unaccustomed to the light and the air, I staggered around like a drunkard. Every third day they lifted a flap on the cell door so that I would not go blind. Soon after I had completed my sentence, I was taken to Munich for interrogation. The police officer simply didn't recognize me: "'Girl, they really gave it to you,' he said."

A FEW DAYS later I saw for myself just how accurate Gusti's description had been. I happened to see Margot as two matrons brought her into the courtyard. She was ashen, completely bent over, her disheveled hair hanging over her face. Her hands groped unsteadily in the air or moved to her eyes, in order to protect them from the sudden brightness. She could scarcely stay on her feet and kept collapsing.

Granny Benesch had to be transferred to the infirmary after her release from the punishment cell. She lay for days in a state of unconsciousness. When she came to again, she could remember nothing.

Moringen, Mid-December 1936

It is Hanukkah, the eight-day Festival of Lights, the feast of the Maccabees, of the rebuilding of the temple, dear to us Jews as a reminder of heroic resistance, as a symbol of impending renewal.

On behalf of my fellow believers I appealed to the Madam Chief Warder and received her permission to observe the holiday in the traditional manner. She was even generous enough to grant us a two-day leave from the unpleasant Winter Relief work. From Berlin, Ehm sent us a big package of apples, nuts, gingerbread, and chocolate, along with the words and music for the songs. Using an old cardboard box, Anni Reiner had skillfully crafted a gold-painted menorah, which was positioned on a sheet of cardboard, also gilded, in the middle of the table. We made grand preparations too: we cleaned our room so that it was absolutely sparkling, we scrubbed the table until every last speck of dust from the Winter Relief had disappeared. Throughout the previous week we had only sparingly fed our stove, known as the "handsome Adolar,"[50] so that we could now spend the holidays in cozy warmth. We laid out small gifts that we had long been saving up for this evening, and for the holiday meal we all collaborated to prepare a marvelous chocolate dessert. We filled empty "vases," that is, jam jars, with richly scented sprigs of fir, which we had procured at our joint expense, and over the table we spread a tablecloth on which Anni had been working for months.

A strange feeling enveloped us as the hour of celebration drew near. Hanukkah, always celebrated within the family circle, was now being observed in the concentration camp, in an atmosphere of distrust and open hostility, in a transformed Germany, which refused any longer to be our homeland.

We stood thoughtfully before the menorah for a long time.

My colleagues invited me, as the oldest, to be the one to begin. Profoundly moved, feeling no longer like an individual but like the representative and spokeswoman for an entire community, I recited the ancient blessings and lit the first candle. Devoutly and reverently we sang, in German and in Hebrew, the beautiful song of defense and defiance that begins so solemnly only to build to sheer jubilation: "Ma-oz tsur ye-shu-o-si—Rock of Ages, let our song praise Thy saving power; Thou, amidst the raging foes, wast our sheltering tower."

Afterwards, we chose passages to read from the Bible, notably from the Books of the Maccabees, from the Prophets, from Job. Before us arose the great figures of Jewish religious history, and we, we who had been expelled from the German "national community," felt within us that ancient Jewish solidarity, a community with neither spatial nor temporal boundaries, with no focus other than the Bible and the hope for the fulfillment of that ancient prophetic dream of justice, peace, humanity, brotherhood.

I was asked to tell the women about previous Hanukkah celebrations that we had observed at home in the company of our children and our friends and which we had endowed with solemn and joyful meaning in those earlier happy times. I also remembered last year's very solemn Hanukkah and my husband Ehm's address, in which he had applied the metaphor of the Flood to the current situation [in Germany]. All the forces of destruction have been set loose, they are destroying the ancient values, the creations of a fertile culture. The waters rise ever higher. When will this flood of hatred finally subside, when will the first mountaintops become visible again, when will the voices of free German people speak to us again? We know that from this long darkness a brilliant new morning will dawn someday.

Yesterday, a high government official, Heydrich, suddenly appeared among us to conduct a thorough inspection of the entire camp.[51] "This is the Jews' Hall," the director explained to him. "The women here are celebrating their

Festival of Lights at the moment. They are free to observe their religious customs. Otherwise they are expected to work on the Winter Relief Campaign." The distinguished gentleman did not offer so much as a greeting, a salutation, a question; he left the room wordlessly.

On the other hand, there was an atmosphere of keen interest among our Aryan companions. They were curious. They had us explain the meaning of the holiday to them, and were generous with their praise: "You've prepared everything so beautifully."

My two students, Hilde and Ursel, surprised me with handmade gifts, a beautifully woven bast basket and a skillfully knitted little coverlet. On behalf of the Bible Students, Magda Mewes greeted us with this verse from Peter: "'And we have the word of the prophets made more certain, and you will do well to pay attention to it, as to a light shining in a dark place, until the day dawns and the morning star rises in your hearts' [II Peter 1:19]." Later, as she left, she honored us with these flattering words from Thessalonians: "'You are all children of the light and children of the day' [1 Thessalonians 5:5]."

OF ALL THE letters that had arrived, I was particularly pleased by one from a young friend. "This year I shall be celebrating Hanukkah not in your home, but in Palestine. I've been a farm worker here for almost a year. We've drained broad areas of the Jordan River lowlands, and now we're cultivating parts of the desert of Judea with our hatchets and our shovels. It's difficult to make this land arable again, after it's been parched for so many centuries. The Arabs give us a hard time as well. We have to ward off their attacks constantly. But we're going to make it."

This young optimist's letter did all of our hearts good. It takes a great deal of courage and self-confidence to resurrect a process that has been dormant and apparently abandoned for two millennia, and under such difficult conditions to start building a new state on top of the ruins of the past. Naturally, this tiny country can offer only a partial solution at best, but it can become a center for physical and spiritual rebirth. How remarkable that all the suffering, persecution, exile have not succeeded in extinguishing our will to live. Quite the contrary, they have given it new impetus and infused it with new purpose. Still, we feel within us untapped sources of energy, an ardent longing to find a happier fate; we ourselves feel young, although our blood has become so old, thick, and sluggish. Other peoples, our contemporaries of old, have long since exited the theater of human events. We have remained. We are still active on the great world stage, not as mute, detached spectators but as untiring actors in usually tragic roles. We face the fact of this immortality with bewilderment. The law of growth and decay has not applied to us; we do not know if we should consider this to be good fortune or ill.

Perhaps Providence has spared us for new missions that we are unable to foresee, missions that we will have no choice but to accept with both humility and pride.

Moringen, Mid-December 1936

The first releases have finally arrived. Twelve of our companions can prepare for the journey home. The entire camp was in a state of absolute exhilaration; happy, shining faces were everywhere. The women to be released were showered with hugs, kisses, token gifts, and grand words. We felt no jealousy toward our privileged colleagues. Perhaps tomorrow we will be among the lucky ones ourselves. After all, last year more than half of the prisoners were set free right at Christmastime. In any case, at least the sense of stagnancy has been disturbed. Apparently, the Gestapo is again recognizing political prisoners as living people and not merely as dossiers gathering dust unnoticed in file cabinets.

Among those released, to our great delight, were the "veterans" Toni Fleck and Barbara Fürbringer of the Bavaria Hall. Toni Fleck, "the cold maid," who used to work preparing cold cuts and salads for a large restaurant, was returning to Munich. Her neighbors there, simple, unassuming people, have been taking care of her little girl as if she were their own. What's more, they have continued to pay the rent on Toni's one-room apartment all these years, so that the home she knew would always be available. Toni visualized the reunion with her child and her steadfast friends in living color.

Barbara Fürbringer, on the other hand, was less happy. She walked around silent and depressed. "The whole camp is delighted about your release, but you seem to be the least pleased of anyone," former representative Dora Doebel took her to task.

"But I have no idea if I'm even really and finally free," Barbara answered. "Maybe I'll just be arrested at the train station and brought to another camp, like with my last 'release.'"

"That won't happen twice. This time you're certain to make it home."

"Make it home? Where to? My husband is dead, my children are in a welfare home, our property in the hands of strangers."

"But at least you're free now."

Barbara's stooped figure slumped even further.

"Okay, I'm free. I most certainly wouldn't be if my husband were still alive. The monsters who tortured him to death probably just wanted to ease their consciences a bit by letting me go."

"Maybe. But it would be better if you could focus on the present instead of the past. You need to think what you owe your young ones," cautioned Dora.

"For three years I have been forcibly prevented from meeting those obligations; they have been delegated to the welfare home instead. I know so little about my own children. My two eldest daughters write strange letters, they've joined the League of German Girls [Bund deutscher Mädel],[52] they rave about their 'Messiah, the Führer,' about 'Germany's special calling,' about women's duty to preserve the German nation, and nonsense like that."

Barbara raised her hands slightly in a weary gesture of doubt and uncertainty. "The Nazis have taken my husband from me, and, I fear, my children as well."

Barbara does not have a penny to her name. The money that she requested from her sister in New York has not yet arrived. We collected the money for her traveling expenses. Her wardrobe is extremely shabby.

"We won't let you travel without at least one warm thing to wear," Zenta Baimler said to her. "In this cold you'd be sick by the time you got there. I'll give you my heavy winter coat to take along, but unfortunately I can't do without it altogether, so I'll have to ask you to send it back to me once you get there."

The coat was returned promptly. Barbara had placed a letter in the side pocket: "This time my journey went without incident. In Munich I visited my children, they're tall and healthy. But otherwise it's as I had expected. The big farmer in my village has persuaded me that he doesn't want me to go off somewhere else, that he and his wife will take me in. So I plan to give it a go as their housekeeper. Maybe later I can have one of my children join me. I often think about all of you and about Moringen. Last Sunday I went out for a walk by myself. Along the river. Straight ahead. I can't believe that you can just walk like that for hours and hours, straight ahead, straight ahead. And then suddenly I knew, I'm free again, free again."

Her reference to the joy of walking "straight ahead," in implicit contrast, of course, to the constant walking in circles in the prison yards, served to remind the camp administration of the ban on any kind of contact between former and current prisoners. Only in deference to the approaching Christmas holiday were the writer and recipient allowed to get off without punishment this time.

A few more women were released over the next few days, among them Friedel Günter, a pretty nineteen-year-old girl. "And now there'll be wedding bells right away. Hannes, my fiancé, wants to take me straight from the train station to the registry office," Friedel told me, as she cheerily bade me farewell.

"Wonderful," I answered. "Congratulations. But why the big hurry?"

"Well, I wouldn't want to get into the same trouble twice, you know."

I looked surprised.

"If my Hannes had been better at keeping his mouth shut, I would have been spared these three months here. You see, before we were engaged, my long-time boyfriend was a nice young Jewish businessman. Siegfried was his name. The Nuremberg Laws put an end to our relationship. He emigrated, established a business in Naples, and besieged me with letters asking me to join him there. Well, you don't want to keep such a nice boyfriend in Italy waiting for long. We had a marvelous time. Naples, the sea, smoldering Vesuvius, the Blue Grotto of Capri, and on and on. But in the end I felt drawn back to Germany after all. Your homeland is your homeland. I separated from my Siegfried with nothing but the sincerest love and friendship. A week later I met Hannes in Berlin. He's a foreman for Siemens and Halske.[53] A terrific job. We became engaged. I told him about Naples, too. 'Who cares,' he said, 'I've had a few girls myself. All that matters is that you'll be faithful to me in marriage.' 'Absolutely. It's a deal. Understood,' I answered. The wedding was set for a Sunday. On the Wednesday before, Hannes was celebrating his farewell to bachelorhood with his workmates.

Well, and then he drank a little too much and began to brag about me and my excursion to Italy. One of his friends could not stop congratulating him on his charming bride, proposing toast after toast and inquiring about the details until there were no longer any secrets. Then this fine fellow went to the police and pressed charges against me for racial defilement [*Rassenschande*]."[54]

How privileged Friedel is, though, as an Aryan. Her imprisonment had ended after exactly three months, while our little Anni Reiner, as a Jew, has been detained for almost a year now for exactly the same offense. Her beauty, once so radiant, has suffered badly; every day that passes ravages it further.

Also set free was our housekeeper, a woman of imposing stature, the loyal wife to a bricklayer. Actually, she could have gone home to her beloved in East Prussia three months ago, but this selfish man had refused to send her the twenty-seven marks she needed for the trip. "Where do you think I can lay my hands on so much cash in these hard times?" he had written. "Them that took you away from here, it's them that should bring you back again. I ain't paying a penny." But the township refused to pay either, and so the poor woman would have been stuck here even longer if her relatives had not shown some compassion and collected the fare.

Moringen, Mid-December 1936

Our excessively ambitious hopes have not been fulfilled. There were no more releases, and those that did take place have been completely offset by the number of newcomers. About twenty prisoners have just been brought here. They are all leading Communists, former legislators, party officials, local party leaders. All of them come from prisons in which they had served four long years' penance for their past activity.

It breaks my heart whenever I see the sad procession of these feeble beings, this collection of every kind of affliction. There is no one in even marginally tolerable condition, no one who can walk straight and move easily. Their heads are bowed, their backs bent, their joints swollen. Some of the women limp with canes, still others wear supports, many spit blood.

We don't know what decided their transfer here; perhaps Moringen is supposed to prepare these women for eventual freedom. In any case, it wouldn't be possible for them to be restored to the "German nation" straight from the penitentiary, given their current state. Without saying a word and by their appearance alone they would serve as mute yet all the more eloquent critics of a system that dares to abuse people so cruelly for their beliefs.

The attitude of the Moringen "veterans" toward these comrades is remarkable. Penitentiary, once the essence of dishonor and moral degradation, has been transformed into a title of honor. Only the greats, the leaders are accorded the honor of the penitentiary. The foot soldiers of the party, who have made it only as far as jail, pay them respect and obedience.

The influx of so many "notables" unquestionably elevates the life of the community to a higher plane. Now, far more than before, intellectual questions, mainly politics, are the central topic of interest. Little news of the ominous changes in the European situation had penetrated the isolation of the penitentiary, so first of all the new arrivals are informed of these developments. Images from the great world theater scroll before them like a newsreel: the successes of the rebels in the Spanish Civil War, supported by Hitler and Mussolini; the domestic and foreign affairs crises in France, which has lost one ally after another since the reoccupation of the Rhineland; the unsteady political situation in England; the encircling of Czechoslovakia. What provokes the greatest anxiety and fear is the enigmatic picture of Russia with its "purge trials," which are claiming the best and brightest of that country as their victims. The women, bitterly disappointed, find the whole situation incomprehensible. They express grave doubts about the dangerous course that Stalin is navigating, about his personal and professional opposition to Trotsky, about the achievements of the workers, and about the ultimate goals of the Russian Revolution.[55]

Among the newcomers, Matilde Urban,[56] a former federal representative, about forty years old, particularly impressed me with her quiet, thoughtful manner. All these years, from the beginning of 1933, she has been serving time in the dreaded Jauer penitentiary,[57] and the effects of this imprisonment are manifest in her frequent shortness of breath and the trembling of her hands. She is gripped by a ravenous intellectual hunger and reads every good book she can find here; even during the exercise period, she is absorbed in her reading. Recently, I heard her repeating to herself, with great fervor, the famous oration of Mark Antony from Shakespeare's *Julius Caesar*.

"Still so fond of public meetings and speeches?" I joked.

"Not for a long time, and I'm not sure I ever felt like that anyway. But I'm struck again and again by this magnificent mastery of the masses' instincts, this art of demagogy, which slowly turns the will of the people around to the opposite of its original purposes."

I loaned her some books that Ehm had sent me recently, but she tends to judge the merit of each and every work altogether too one-sidedly, strictly according to the author's position on social issues. Still, it's nice to chat with her; often state representative Dora Doebel, who is also an avid reader and always keen to discuss serious topics, joins us while we exercise.

Matilde is gradually regaining her confidence, and even though she's constrained by a gag order and under the threat of severe penalties, she occasionally discusses her penitentiary experiences anyway. "It's hard to say exactly what made these years in Jauer so terrible for me. Perhaps it was not any particular experience but the cumulative effect—that and the need to adjust to a total regime which tries not only to abolish all individuality, but to destroy the will and the capacity to live at all. They make it a deliberate strategy to limit speech to the absolute minimum. Our communal work—mostly sewing buttonholes, embroidering cushions, or weaving straw mats—was conducted in total silence. It was the same with the exercise hour. We had to keep a distance of one meter from one another. We were not allowed to bow our heads but had to hold them upright, so that the matron could always be sure that our lips were tightly closed. Because of the millions of unemployed, there was sometimes no work to be assigned to us. Then the administration allowed us to kill time with board games, but not a word could be spoken. Our hall felt like a deaf-mute convention. Also cruel was how little they let us sleep and how they kept interrupting it. Our beds, if you can call a wooden plank with a straw mattress and a blanket on top of it a 'bed,' were set up in locked compartments like cages. Every two hours the guard made her rounds and woke us up with the blinding light of her lantern. Often there was a special inspection in the middle of the night, where we had to get up, spread our arms and legs and submit to a humiliating body search."

"I never heard of night-time inspections," Dora Doebel commented. "We didn't have them in Aichach or Landshut. Was it just harassment, or did it have a real purpose?"

"I don't know. Maybe they were looking for illicit slips of paper, secret messages. Oddly enough, the administration was in constant fear of a revolt. They saw even the most innocuous act as dangerous, if it was committed by several people at the same time. At one Sunday meal, the haddock was spoiled, and the prisoners left it untouched. An investigation was conducted immediately, not of the kitchen, mind you, but of us, for collusion. One of our comrades saved the dangerous situation—she had eaten the fish because she was absolutely starving. This was the evidence that there was no 'conspiracy'—though it gave her enteritis."

"All prison food is practically inedible," said Dora Doebel. "Unbelievable, really, that anyone can stand it year after year."

"In Jauer," [responded Matilde,] "a group of women felt that they could bear their treatment no longer. They decided to begin a hunger strike. I had the greatest difficulty talking them out of it. I told them that a hunger strike had no chance of succeeding except in a democratic country like France, England, or America, where the press is always on the watch and would be eager to publicize it and press for an end to the abuses. In Germany, however, there is neither open debate nor an independent press. Your self-sacrifice would proceed in utter silence. Not a sound would escape beyond the prison walls to the outside world. You would only be doing your tormentors a favor."

MATILDE URBAN KEPT her silence about the use of corporal punishment in Jauer. Her comrades, intimidated by the strict gag order, were also afraid to talk about it.

One recent incident, however, broke that silence.

The male workhouse inmates—vagrants, drunkards, and petty criminals—are quartered in a complex of buildings on the other side of the courtyard, completely separate from us. Recently, two of these inmates attempted to escape under cover of darkness. They were caught, dragged back, and brutally beaten with nightsticks by the guards. Their cries of pain echoed across the courtyard to us. The women became very upset. The matron reassured them: "Come on, it's only a couple of bums." Suddenly, one of the women recently arrived from Jauer fell off her stool onto the floor, clutching at her heart. In her desperate cries we heard a harrowing recollection of her own suffering: "Help! Help! Don't hit me again! I can't stand it any more. I'll tell you anything you want me to. Let me live, for the sake of my children."

Moringen, Christmas 1936

Christmas. "Peace on earth and goodwill toward men." Peace and goodwill here in the concentration camp as well? Well, maybe, within certain limits at least.

The women are enjoying the two-day holiday break. Dressed in their Sunday best, their spirits are up. They are kind, endearing. They link arms fondly, talk about their husbands and children, read the letters they have received out loud to one another, and will not rest until their neighbor has tasted a slice of the sausage or the cake from back home.

Packages have been pouring into the camp. Besides foodstuffs, they contain for the most part practical gifts, gifts well suited for the stay here: warm clothes, wool stockings, underwear, shoes. Often, though, people have sent presents which are totally useless here or anywhere else, for that matter: tall, thin glass vases, huge fruit ornaments and flower bowls, silver tea strainers and pastry servers. The women have arranged their gifts at their places and can't seem to get enough of looking them over. A piece will be taken out again and again, inspected in its most minute detail, and proudly displayed to an admiring friend. The more questionable the usefulness of an item, the higher the collective esteem in which it will be held.

No one has come away empty-handed. For days, collections had been taken for the needy, who could expect no contribution from home. Zenta Baimler and Else Volckmar competed in this labor of love, and to that end, with a merry wink, made good use of a quotation from Paul that they had picked up from the Bible Students: "'God loves a cheerful giver' [II Corinthians 9:7]."

For each prisoner, the camp administration has contributed a *Klöben*, a raisin bread that tastes wonderful and that manages at least to mute our anger over the Christmas Eve menu a little. For some reason they served, of all things, "pea soup," a thin, lukewarm broth that was indignantly, though wordlessly, left untouched. On the first day of Christmas, on the other hand, a roast pork and red cabbage dinner was served that lived up to the most eager of expectations. This festive meal, served only twice a year, at Christmas and at Easter, had been discussed for days beforehand, complete with earnest debates about which dish deserved to be considered the epitome of gourmet delights: Moringen's roast pork or the veal cutlet with mountain cranberries in the Landshut jail.

In the middle of the Great Hall stands the enormous Christmas tree, supplied by the camp administration. It extends from floor to ceiling, and when its candles are aglow, it is a gorgeous sight to behold.

I was very much looking forward to the Christmas Eve celebration itself, with its ancient, beautiful Christmas carols, but, unfortunately, my hopes were dashed. To begin with, an address by Minister Goebbels was broadcast that was perfunctory and meaningless. But that alone was not responsible for the absence of a reverent mood. This was precluded by the women themselves: they utterly refused not only any kind of religious ritual but also any religious feeling. It's simply not consistent with their Communist ideology. True, old Granny Mehlert, a shriveled-up ancient with disheveled hair hanging down over her forehead, swung herself up onto the sewing machine table and broke into "Silent Night." But no one joined in. On the contrary, an awkward silence prevailed. However, that did not deter the singer from reeling off every last verse of the song in her brittle monotone.

I was watching the women around me closely. You could see the stubborn defiance in their faces, on their tightly pursed lips. And yet, and yet. I could feel that some of them would have liked to sing along, would have liked to relax for once and to give themselves over to spiritual exaltation, perhaps also to long-suppressed childhood memories. But apprehension about doing so in front of the others remained stronger than this urge. Anything but publicly renounce the principle of freethinking, which everyone is so proud of, and which now, like a tyrant, robs this one beautiful and rare moment of its true meaning.

How much better the criminals, "the blacks," have it, at least as I see it. In their full black skirts, to which white aprons have been pinned in honor of the occasion, they walk in a long, festive procession to the chapel. Yes, they are able to submit to their simple, spiritual urges without inhibition; they may pray and be devout. Surely, they endure their fate more easily these days than their Communist sisters in misfortune, who consider themselves so superior to them.

As a holiday present from her son, state representative Dora Doebel received a handmade album with pictures of some fifty famous inventors and explorers glued inside. Under each picture, in longhand, was a brief but vivid summary of these heroes' accomplishments and fates. The boy had also included in his package a letter overflowing with Christmas spirit, which at the same time expressed, in touchingly affectionate words, his longing for his "dear Mommy." The Mother Superior congratulated Dora on her son, who was a joy for the entire community, and added a holiday greeting in such tactful, sensitive words that not even a Communist legislator could take offense at them.

"As much as I appreciate the love and care that the convent is showing to my Herbert," said Dora, "I'm still depressed whenever I think of him growing up in an atmosphere so alien to me. But the fact that these true believers are so convinced that they have found true happiness makes it easier for me to come to terms with the situation."

"Why," I asked her, "do you refuse to look for any happiness for yourself? Why do you repress the natural desires of the human heart?"

Dora became very serious. "My own fate, and the fact that I know how so many millions of people are suffering, stands like an insurmountable wall between my intellect and what you call 'the natural desires of the human heart.' Perhaps I would be less vehement in my rejection of all religious sentiments if my antipathy toward the church were not part of the equation as well. The church has used its enormous power not to advance its allegedly divine mission, but, quite the contrary, to eliminate true religion from the workings of the heart. It has been content to push off its huge social obligations onto the narrow track of poor relief, as if the grave illnesses of the body politic could be cured with alms. It has prevented neither bloodshed nor war, not even the cruelest devastations of the human body or the human spirit. It has spread the halo of heaven over the thrones of princes and has degraded itself to the status of a servant, often enough a mere lackey of the state. That's been the same attitude right up to the present day. The crimes of the Nazis would have been impossible if the distinguished clergy had set an example for the German people and had shown that they were determined to guarantee the courage of their convictions with their freedom and, if it came to that, with their lives. But the good men of the cloth soothed their Christian consciences with lame paper protests, and instead of calling for resistance against Hitler they united with him in a ridiculous crusade against the heterodoxy of Moscow. In contrast to the tiptoeing of the German clergy, the Russian priests behaved like heroes. They refused any reconciliation with the new state. They whipped up the masses, excommunicated the leaders of the Revolution, and they did not blink, even at the bitter end: the fathers were incarcerated and shot by the hundreds and by the thousands. They were our adversaries, but they were men."

"And yet," I objected, "even though the Soviets were aware of the enormous spiritual power demonstrated by such heroism, it didn't stop them from declaring war not only on the church but on religion itself. They are not content to have transformed the churches into museums, granaries, movie theaters, and music halls; their state-sponsored 'godless movement'[58] is trying to eradicate the last vestiges of religion among the people. What they fail to appreciate is that religion as such is as old as human society itself, and that without religion, without its moral idealism and its ethical influence, there would probably be no state to begin with."

Dora's delicate, ethereal face assumed an expression of profound piety, in peculiar contrast to the words she spoke. "That is exactly the kind of opinion we are fighting against. Communism rejects this idealism, which views reality only through rose-tinted spectacles and builds up castles in the air. Communism recognizes only established and identifiable facts; it dismisses all otherworldly interpretations. We believe only in the miracle of human reason and the human spirit. We strive to harness all creative energies, to promote technical and industrial development, to expand production. All these increased efficiencies translate to art and science, to the simple pleasures and the pure joy of life—in short, to human happiness. And 'the greatest possible good for the greatest possible number'—that is our platform. But we always have both feet firmly on the ground. We don't recognize any other dependence. We are the masters of our own fate. In our ideology there is no place for 'a Father in Heaven.'"

"Yes, Dora, I understand. You've put lifeless matter, lifeless machinery in His place! Once God was imagined and even represented as a person. Now, out of the doctrines of the traditional religions, with their alternations between flexibility and rigidity, and through a process of infinite steps and stages, an impersonal concept of the divine has emerged. It's inspired by all the miracles in and around us; it expands to fill the infinity of space and time. Doesn't some bridge of yearning lead you to that other shore?"

Dora shook her head and held out her hand to me: "Each must find his own salvation."

Moringen, Early January 1937

The year 1936, with its horrors, sorrows, and fears, has disappeared into the abyss of time. We do not mourn its passing. But we have also lost all immediate hope for any improvement in our fortunes, and so we enter the year 1937 without eagerness and without confidence, seeing no path that could lead us out of this chaos.

As on every evening, we had to go to bed at 9 o'clock, even on the last day of the old year. I couldn't get to sleep—the present and the future were haunting me with bleak images. Hour after hour went by. The clock struck twelve. Midnight. The New Year. The echo of the chimes had barely faded away when a solemn hymn began to waft down from the top of the church tower. Slowly and reverently, a brass ensemble played the "Dutch Prayer of Thanksgiving" [Nederländisches Dankgebet].[59] The high trumpet blasts and the deep, sustained tones of the tuba echoed oddly, in an almost dreamlike and surreal manner, through the cold winter night, through the expansive snowy landscape in which the little town lay embedded and slept.

It's remarkable how startlingly opposites are juxtaposed in Germany. Pious observation of old customs, affectionate obsession with the past, and the wild, headlong rush into the future. Quiet, comfortable bourgeois life, and the riotous delight in violence. Peaceful idyll, and ultimate, inconceivable brutality.

New Year's Eve held a special surprise for me. I was summoned to the central administrative office. The official, a young man, was somewhat impatient at having to deal with bureaucratic tasks so late in the day, but all the same was in a friendly mood in anticipation of the coming New Year's Eve festivities. He informed me: "Two remittances have been received from your husband. The one sent to the camp administration is for 14.80 marks and is labeled 'As directed by the police precinct Berlin-Dahlem. Train ticket Moringen-Berlin for Frau Herz.' The second is addressed to you with the postscript: '12.00 marks advance for the trip.' Both sums were transmitted by telegraph."

He drew out the word "telegraph" slowly. There was a discernible tone of reproach in his voice about this waste of money. A regular transfer, he thought, would have been far less expensive and would have served the purpose just as well.

I was completely taken aback. My mind was racing. Hopes that until now had had to be forcibly repressed slowly took shape, and I thought I could clearly see a hand reaching out and opening the gates of Moringen for me.

"Perhaps," I said softly, "the transfer by telegraph has special meaning. The three-month sentence imposed upon me by the Gestapo ends today. Perhaps—it would not be totally out of the question—perhaps …"

"I have to disappoint you," explained the official. "It's just a coincidence that your husband was instructed to make these payments just now. It can often happen that the money for the eventual journey home arrives here earlier than the prisoner himself, if he has been held in pre-trial detention for any length of time. The money then sits here for months and months. Of course, we do hope things will go more quickly in your case."

My companions were amazed that I had allowed myself to indulge in false hopes, even for a moment. "But you can see for yourself here every day," said Herta Kronau, "how the Gestapo doesn't tie itself to any deadline or commitment. Did you think that you would be an exception? For these distinguished gentlemen we're no more than objects of blind hatred. Even at best, they play with us as they please."

A few days later a letter from Ehm provided more detailed information. "The police captain in charge of your case in Berlin thought that prompt payment would secure your immediate release. I did not leave our house for a second the entire time. I waited day and night for your return. This is a terrible disappointment. Now our attorney and I have submitted a petition to the Gestapo pointing out that the three-month term has expired. We have to wait and see what happens next."

With this letter Ehm had enclosed, on a separate page, a copy of a poem by Goethe to Frau von Stein:

Seit du von mir bist	Since you've been away
Scheint mir des schnellsten Lebens	Even the tumultuous bustle
Lärmende Bewegung	Of life at its busiest
Nur wir ein Flor,	Is like a veil
Durch den ich deine Gestalt	Through which I discern your image,
Immerfort wie durch Wolken erblicke.	Ever as if through clouds.
Sie leuchtet mir freundlich und treu	Kind and true, it lights the way for me
Wie durch des Nordlichts	The way the eternal stars glimmer
bewegliche Strahlen	Through the shifting rays of the
Die ewigen Sterne schimmern.	Northern Lights.[60]

I placed the page carefully in my drawer. The poem is right on top. I open that drawer every day.

THE CAMP HAS received more newcomers, even our room has been favored with four new inmates. They come from Vienna, Madrid, Jerusalem, and Moscow. Through their presence we feel ourselves temporarily transported to these hubs of historic world events.

Vienna, under the leadership of Chancellor Schuschnigg, is playing a high-stakes game to hold onto its independence in the face of Hitler's constant threats that alternate occasionally with seductive bribes. Spain is presenting the final or penultimate act of their tragedy, a ghastly civil war. Onlookers watch heroes and martyrs, soldiers and priests, citizens and workers in bloody battle or in silent, enduring resignation. They see the country ravaged by foreign military forces and the ancient, glorious culture of their cities destroyed by bombs. Palestine, unnoticed for two millennia, has suddenly acquired an important role, at the nexus of three continents, in the struggle between England and Italy to dominate the Mediterranean. Russia, for the time being, still remains slightly aloof, and yet it stands at the forefront of current events, willingly or unwillingly, whether driving or driven, but always threatening and dangerous. This giant carries in its mighty hands the key to the fate of our world: curse or blessing, the torch of destruction or the olive branch of peace.[61]

In part, the experiences of our new arrivals reflect life in the different countries from which chance or force has taken them and brought them here. In part, they illustrate the typical fates of returning emigrants.

Ilse[62] had studied mathematics for several semesters in Vienna, could no longer support herself there, and had to return to Germany. This resulted in her arrest here, even though her stay "abroad" in Vienna had been expressly approved by the German authorities.

Sophie[63] had gone to Barcelona as a German governess for the children of a distinguished Spanish physician. She had to flee with the family and wandered the country for a while, until a German warship picked her up and brought her to Hamburg. But while the Aryan German refugees found warm receptions in private homes, hospitals, and sanatoriums, Sophie was deported to Moringen.

Lilo, the Palestinian farmhand, had tried to make a new life for herself in a co-operative settlement near Jerusalem. The struggle between the Jews and the Arabs flares up in her vivid descriptions. But the wonders of the Holy Land also appear: the beautiful, sweeping line of the Galilean Hills, the salt deposits of the Dead Sea, orange groves in blossom, the sand dunes in the lonely desert; Jerusalem, the city on the hill with its shimmering Mosque of Omar, its white Church of the Holy Sepulcher, and its Wailing Wall; Tel Aviv, practically conjured up from the earth, and its Great Synagogue with the eight-branched menorah atop its enormous dome. Lilo was able to spend only a single, happy year in Palestine; she couldn't tolerate the climate and so, with heavy heart, had to return to Germany. With her chronic heart failure and asthma she belongs in a hospital, not in a concentration camp.

Frau Schloss has been hit even harder. She and her husband had been visiting their married daughter in Moscow. Their return trip, for which a deadline of three months from departure had been imposed by the German police, was postponed for a month because her husband fell seriously ill in Moscow. Result: Despite his seventy years and his incurable heart condition, the husband was brought to the dreaded concentration camp at Oranienburg-Sachsenhausen, and his 65-year-old wife to Moringen, by way of those standard stations of the cross, [the prisons of] Berlin-Alexanderplatz and Hanover, where she had almost lost her mind in her solitary cell. The sad fate of this tiny, fearful old lady affects us all deeply. Totally consumed with worry about her spouse, she sits impassively among us, practically oblivious, her empty, dead stare fixed in space. We make every effort to oblige this fastidious woman, accustomed as she is to a well-kept household; we relieve her of all chores, attempt to sustain her with words of consolation. Herta Kronau, the only one among us permitted to use a chair with a backrest instead of a stool, owing to her delicate condition, immediately surrendered this much-coveted piece of furniture to Frau Schloss. Even our uncompromising Chief Warder shows touches of compassion.

But we are all surpassed in practical benevolence by Addy, a simple furrier's assistant. She had met the old woman at Berlin-Alexanderplatz, one of the seventeen inmates in the large communal cell, and had developed a genuine liking for her. She had taken care of the helpless old lady, spent entire nights awake at her bedside, and intervened to comfort and help her whenever Frau Schloss experienced bouts of hysteria and crying fits. Addy continues her charitable work here in the camp as well. A daughter could not care for her ailing mother more selflessly than she.

Moringen, Mid-January 1937

Following Frau Schloss, several other returning emigrants have arrived from Moscow and Leningrad. Spirited and talkative, they've seen a lot, experienced a lot, and don't grow tired of telling us about it. Thus does the Russian problem, which always commands a great deal of attention here, achieve a new, almost topical significance. Wherever you go, you catch snatches of political conversations. Especially popular for these debates is the Bavaria Hall, since, with its seventeen inmates (compared with the Great Hall's eighty or more), it is not watched over by a matron.

As a member of the "bourgeoisie," I do not seek out these discussions, nor am I called upon to participate in them. My relationships to my Communist companions are purely personal, not political in nature. I admire their decency, their courage, their steadfastness, and their intelligence, at least as far as this last attribute applies to purely human matters. But as soon as ideology, the Communist Weltanschauung, comes into question, I cannot go along with them. I am too much a captive of the great, free democratic tradition, and hence see no benefit in the sacrifice of personality, of individual values, for the benefit of the homogeneous, totalitarian claim to authority that communism places at the heart of its doctrine.

Those of my companions who think otherwise have long since given up their initial efforts to convert me. Beyond any political differences, we are bound by mutual respect, sincere friendship, and the identical, or at least shared, fate of the concentration camp. So it doesn't bother them in the slightest if, given my frequent presence in the Bavaria Hall, chance makes me a witness to their political conversations. They consider themselves safe from any breach of confidence. And I am grateful in turn for the fact that these discussions keep me reasonably well informed about the events taking place on the great world stage.

Hitler recently gave official recognition to the ultra-right revolutionary government of General Franco, which seeks to eradicate the existence of the liberal People's Republic of Spain. The sympathies of the women here, of course, lie with the endangered leftist government. They are sharply critical of the "non-intervention pact" mandated by the League of Nations in Geneva and supported by England and France.[64]

Former federal representative Anna Löser is their self-appointed spokeswoman. In her own way, steady, often didactic but nonetheless effective, she argues: "Unfortunately, this pact will only one-sidedly benefit the insurgent Spanish military, Germany and Italy are dismissing it with contempt. It's clear from his public speeches that Hitler sees the spread of nationalism and fascism to another country as a welcome affirmation of his own ascendancy. German troops, German weapons, tanks, and airplanes are now flowing steadily into Spain. Italy is supplying even greater quantities. Mussolini is proud of his successes in Ethiopia, and he wants to secure his predominance in the Mediterranean through an association with Franco. He has now established the 'Rome-Berlin Axis' with Hitler, around which all of Europe is supposed to revolve.[65] So France is now beset by a fascist front at three of its borders, but narrow-minded partisan disarray is crippling its resolve, and England, as always, is withholding its assistance. No doubt they are anxious in London about these dangerous developments, but they don't wish to intervene. In the final analysis, they would rather see the leftist Spanish government toppled than concede a new sphere of influence to Moscow. Russia is the only major power supporting the Spanish People's Republic with arms. But the great distance is almost impossible to overcome, and so the Soviets have appealed to international conscience and established the 'International Brigade.' We all know what miracles of valor it has performed on the battlefields of Spain."[66]

Her comrades' faces are radiant. It had recently leaked out that Fritz Baimler, after his escape from Dachau, had made his way to Spain and is now fighting in the ranks of this "International Brigade." Zenta Baimler, who is adored, almost worshiped, by the women here in the Bavaria Hall, doesn't talk about it; of course, officially, she doesn't even know anything for sure. But her spirits are high, her carriage even straighter and taller than usual, a smile suggestive of secret triumph plays at her lips.

"As tragic as this Civil War is," Anna Löser continues, "it seems to me that Spain is only a proving ground. All the speeches and official declarations, all the commitments not made in good faith and not honored, even the bloody battles themselves may be interpreted as nothing more than advance skirmishes, in my opinion. At its core, this is about something infinitely larger, more decisive, about the ultimate conflict between our international communism and national fascism. This antithesis is personified by their public representatives, by the giants Stalin and Hitler. Each is committed to his own point of view. But while Stalin remains cautious and reserved, always keeping doors open somehow, Hitler counters with insults, harangues, and provocations that make it impossible to bridge the abyss. As you know, I have the dubious honor of having to read the latest edition of the *Völkischer Beobachter* aloud to you every evening, by command of the camp administration. You'll surely remember some of the points it harps on, for Hitler sees Russia and Bolshevism as a deadly enemy who appeals to the scum of the earth, hoping to use them to turn the world upside down. This false doctrine promises heaven to the faithful masses, but leads them into hell. In the country that was once the breadbasket of Europe, constant famine prevails, millions of people are starving. Hitler rejects any compromise with this savage 'Asiatic' ideology, and believes it is his duty to destroy it. This is not to be taken as idle talk, but as a sacred oath that he will honor at all costs. He would sooner hang himself than enter into a pact with Bolshevik Russia. [In his view] there is more at stake here than Germany alone. All of Europe is endangered, its glorious past, its magnificent culture, the foundation of all governmental and social order. He trembles for Europe. By keeping communism at bay, Germany, as it has done so often throughout its history, is fulfilling—in the words of Hitler—its 'European mission.'"

Herta Kronau has sprung to her feet. Whenever political matters are being discussed, her new sense of weariness and apathy disappears. "To fulfill this 'European mission,' Hitler employs the strangest of means," she scoffs. "He removes Germany from the supranational community of the League of Nations, allies himself with Japan, tramples on the most elementary concepts of justice, freedom, and human dignity in his own country, strives in every way possible to weaken the great democracies of England and France, is building up massive armaments against them, in violation of existing treaties, and simultaneously seeks their support against Russia, a country he despises even more, by means of his theatrical reconciliation with Poland.

"For years and years we have been inundated with legitimate complaints about the 'Polish Corridor,' with depictions of the alleged 'Emergency in the East' [*Ostnot*] afflicting the German populations of the lost provinces.[67] Hitler has made these complaints his own and he has demanded the return of those territories. For him, the corridor was a thorn in Germany's side, an eternal source of ethnic hatred. Now all of a sudden, to the utter amazement of us Germans and of the entire world, he signs a friendship pact with an enemy that's been ostracized for a century. He's recognized the despised corridor and the borders it created, which up till now, we were told, were intolerable. Suddenly, our newspapers, magazines, books, and films are overflowing with hymns of praise for our neighbor Poland, for the home of a great, patriotic people, with whom it is Germany's only desire to live in peace from now on. What hypocrisy! What an outrageous farce!"

"It's all true," Anna Löser agrees with Herta Kronau's observations. "I would just like to add that, as far as we can tell, many of our fellow citizens are for the first time no longer on Hitler's side, at least in private. They cannot change their views so abruptly from one day to the next, but they have become suspicious of this complete reversal of German foreign policy. Up to now they have done nothing but cheer for the Führer. He has given them one success after another, especially when he reclaimed the Rhineland and the Saar region for Germany.[68] So now they are all the more disappointed by the way the eastern provinces have been sacrificed, by this unnatural fraternization with the long-despised 'Pollack.'

"For Hitler, this reaction is extremely troubling. He hopes to counteract it by pointing to the realities of the situation. We should understand [he says] that he feels compelled to alleviate international tensions, including those with Poland, in the interests of a lasting peace in Europe. For him, the World War remains a terrible warning; he is convinced that a second world war would inevitably lead to the total collapse of Europe.

"Stalin, for obvious reasons, has little patience with this line of reasoning and its conspicuously lopsided declaration of peace. He is warning his Polish neighbor not to try to erect a barrier between East and West or to offer itself to whoever might want it as a vanguard for their own aggressive plans against Russia. He demands candor. What are Hitler's intentions? Some kind of understanding or co-operation with Russia, in the spirit of earlier German pacts, or an open breach, with a greedy eye on Russia's natural resources?[69]

"In his speech before the Party Congress in Nuremberg, Hitler has now given an answer that removes all doubt about his intentions—a fight to the finish against Russia and communism and, as a reward for the victory of which he is so confident, the annexation of valuable territories. 'If we could take control,' so his argument goes, 'of the unimaginable mineral riches stored up in the mountains of the Urals, and of the infinitely vast and fertile plains of the Ukraine, if we National Socialists could exploit all this, then there would be no limit to our production, and our German nation would be wallowing in plenty.'[70]

"In earlier times, a speech like this would have led to an immediate declaration of war, but now it rolls innocuously off the Russian Bear's back. I don't understand Stalin. The disquieting question remains: is his reserve a sign of weakness or of the equanimity of the powerful?"

This question troubles their minds constantly, leading to new, heated discussions every day. Many of the women attribute Stalin's indecision to an insecurity stemming from his domestic political problems, which the "purge trials" have thrust into the open, shocking the world with their bizarre spectacle.

"We're completely in the dark here," complains Else Volckmar, the block leader of the Great Hall. "The accounts in the German newspapers are misleading, especially those in the *Völkischer Beobachter*. One thing that *is* clear, however, is that Stalin is systematically ridding himself of all of the great men who secured the victory of the Revolution after Lenin's death. Kamenev and Zinoviev, once members of the ruling triumvirate with Stalin, are among the numerous executions, as is Radek, the long-time editor of *Izvestia*, a newspaper known to be the official mouthpiece of the government. And now they have begun proceedings against leading army officers and generals.[71]

"Even more unbelievable than the accusations themselves are the full confessions made in open court. The defendants admit to having committed acts of high treason while in the employ of foreign powers—meaning Germany and Japan. Their alleged plot, planned down to the most minute detail, was to assassinate Stalin and his closest confederates and supporters. Then, through deliberate and widespread sabotage, work in the fields and factories would be brought to a standstill and the government overthrown. It is striking that all of the many accused always confess their guilt along identical lines, often in the same words. What's missing is any hint of the personal, any reference to individual experiences. They have obviously memorized their testimony word for word in anticipation of the expected cross-examination, and they quote it back mechanically and dispassionately. It's clear that these are coerced confessions. Exactly how this coercion is applied, we don't know. There are a number of possibilities: torture, if not physical, then surely psychological; the erosion of resolve by means of lengthy solitary confinement, darkened cells, little sleep, and little nourishment; perhaps the use of special drugs that cause a paralysis of the will by inducing a hypnosis that is long lasting but not obvious. It seems particularly effective to promise prisoners that if they confess, the lives and limbs of their wives and children will be spared."

Much to my surprise, my student Ursula Renner joins in the debate. I know her only as quiet, introspective, almost taciturn. Now her inner turmoil has loosened her tongue, giving her words an unfamiliar tone as well, her eyes are aglow, and the cheekbones defining her broad face seem sharper and more severe than before. "All these years," she exclaims bitterly, "these men have been held up to us as shining examples of perfect allegiance to duty. Now we're supposed to curse them as traitors, only because Stalin says so. But perhaps *he* is the sole culprit, the one who is guilty of treason. Perhaps—I hardly dare finish these thoughts—our blind faith has led us astray and we have sacrificed the best years of our lives, our freedom, and our health to a mere phantom." A pensive, dispirited silence follows her words.

Slowly Dora Doebel rises to her feet and slowly she walks around the table that occupies the middle of the Bavaria Hall. As she walks, she drags her shorter leg more than usual. But that's really the only sign of her agitation, and it is perceptible only to a few. Her delicate, thin face remains composed, her voice is calm: "Every revolution consumes people on a massive scale, destroys their lives, often breaks their spirits as well. The current struggles, however, are confined to the narrow realm of the highest echelons of power; they are not affecting the general population. At its core, this conflict can be traced back to the old antithesis between the two overpowering personalities of Trotsky and Stalin. From the very beginning, and especially since his exile, Trotsky has had an international perspective. He sees the ultimate victory of communism in the expansion of the Russian Revolution into a worldwide revolution. Stalin, on the other hand, firmly rooted in his native soil, wants first to secure everything that has already been achieved within Russia itself. For him, the goal, first and foremost, is 'Communism in *one* country.' Up to now, developments have proved *him* right, not Trotsky."

"That's your personal opinion, Dora, and I don't agree with it," replies Ursula Renner. "Perhaps Russia would be better off if Stalin had not seized power, against the express wishes of Lenin in his testament, and if Trotsky had become the leader instead.[72] Stalin is tough but he's slow-witted. Trotsky is more fiery and animated. He's not all caught up in workaday matters; with his brilliant intuition, he can see the bigger picture."

Dora does not let up. "No," she persists, "Stalin is doing the right thing. He's a pragmatist [*Realpolitiker*] with no interest in vast visions. Instead, he first wants to make Russia strong. I don't agree with all of his measures, but he has done miracles. In twenty years he has transformed a backward agrarian state into one of the most advanced industrial countries. Already Russia ranks third in world production now."

"The price of this success is certainly high enough," interrupts Auguste Lampert, a former Communist Party official. A tall, blond woman with severe features, she arrived here recently. "I've been working these last three years in Russian factories, offices, and retail shops, and I'm telling you, Stalin does not deserve your praise. He has betrayed the Revolution."

"How can you say such a thing?" exploded Dora indignantly. "It's an established fact, the capitalist exploiter class has been eliminated. The worker is free."

"Free? That makes me laugh. He has simply swapped his chains. Now he's a slave of the state. The old capitalist techniques are again being put to use. Piece-work, piece wages, longer working hours—it's an insidious system that gives the workers only a tiny part in the production process and reduces them to cogs in the machine. Their low wages are barely enough to live on, but civil servants, bureaucrats, and plant managers earn many times more. They accumulate property, even hereditary property. They can buy houses and cars, keep servants and elegant mistresses."

"That's a deeply discouraging report," interrupts Anna Löser in a tone of bitter disappointment, above the increasing restlessness of the women. "We thought things would develop differently. We were too optimistic. In the end, it's not possible to stamp out a thousand years of corrupt czarist dysfunction in a short time. But I'm sure we'll live to see the ultimate victory of the Revolution."

Auguste shakes her head dismissively. "I regret that I'm not able to share such hopes. The Revolution is long since in decline; it's been superseded by Stalin's counter-revolution. No more steps forward, only steps backward. Everything that the bitter, bloody struggles achieved has been abandoned. The forty-hour week is now only on paper. The same is true of communal child-rearing. Divorce has become harder to get. Abortion used to be entirely the woman's own choice; now it's permitted only in exceptional cases and with the special approval of the authorities. Personal freedoms, even the right to move freely from one place to another, have been completely revoked. Equality, once our highest goal, is now held to be an absurd, ascetic ideal. The old dream is at an end."

Auguste has stuck her neck way out and she hit some extremely sore spots. And yet it is not so much the substance of her remarks that provokes the women as it is her embittered, unyielding, defiant tone.

"We refuse to let you rob us of our faith," retorted one of the working-class women from the Great Hall. "We think your description is inaccurate, or at least highly exaggerated. Perhaps, even if you didn't mean to, you've allowed your view to be colored by your own disappointment with your marriage." Auguste, as we all knew, had found brief success in love in Russia. Her husband, to whom she clung with almost slavish devotion, had soon left her, while she had been unable to free herself from her emotional attachment. Now, stung by this hurtful reproach, she stood there pale, almost motionless. Her words came softly and haltingly: "If you believe that my political convictions are influenced by love and marriage, then I certainly have nothing further to say to you."

Dora Doebel tried to salvage the painful situation with friendly and conciliatory explanations and with renewed questioning. Auguste did not answer.

A DIFFERENT AUTHORITY, in the shape of our esteemed German Propaganda Ministry, saw to it that these political confrontations would continue, however. One day, the matron deposited some albums on the table with the instruction that each inmate was to look through them carefully. These albums contained a collection of large-size and high-quality prints depicting conditions in Spain and Russia. A diabolically masterful compilation. Gruesome, repulsive, but inflammatory and provocative. "The Triumph of Evil," that's the title you could give these prints. They record precisely and in the most minute detail the atrocities of the radical left—while the Fascists and Nazis, of course, are portrayed exclusively as saviors and agents of Christian charity. In the pictures from Spain you can see mass executions of leading citizens and members of the bourgeoisie and atrocities committed against their wives. You see how priests are rounded up and lined up against the wall, while a bishop in his ceremonial robes administers last rites. Stretched out on the pavement, or leaned up against burned-out houses, are the bodies of nuns, often with obscene epitaphs pinned on them.

The images from Russia also highlight the hostility toward religion. In one church, teen aged boys and girls with cocky expressions dance the fox trot in front of the altar, in another, the legend beneath a statue of Christ proclaims: "Mythical Figure Who Never Lived." Other photographs depict economic and social abuses. Freezing women line up in front of a pitiful shop with half-empty shelves. Inside the factories, notices posted above work stations announce "Good Performance," "Average," "Poor Performance," "Attempted Sabotage." Living conditions are desperate, dilapidated wooden huts serve as communal dormitories, workers lie on the floor or on benches. No pillows, no blankets, occasionally straw. For comparison purposes, there are images of luxury hotels for the "privileged," with wide balconies and a marvelous view of the sea. The gangs of ragged children are painfully affecting. Ten- to fifteen-year-old boys and girls, barefoot, in tatters, wander around in amusement parks and sleep under bridges, on public park benches, in stables next to cattle. In their faces there is hunger and need, but great depravity as well.

We would love to throw these albums to the floor with a gesture of disgust, or to leaf through them with our eyes closed, but the matron does not avert her gaze for a moment. We must absorb print after print, we are forced to run this emotional gauntlet whether we want to or not.

These pictures plague us day and night, even though we recognize that many of them are doctored. They provoke repeated and often vehement debates. Lotte Albers, in particular, is bombarded with questions, even though she is no Communist. Her husband, an engineer, had been visiting and reorganizing Russian factories since 1933, first as an agent of German business concerns, then on behalf of the Moscow government. Lotte, who had accompanied him on all of his trips, can thus speak from the most intimate experience.

"I certainly don't need to say anything more about how biased these albums are. Soviet propaganda could show you different scenes, real scenes as well as true images of them: pleasant three-room working-class apartments, kindergartens with delightful toys, libraries, movie houses, theaters, crowded cafes and restaurants. You could see the eight-story school buildings, in which thousands of pupils are taught in two shifts, see the enormous number of newspapers that bring enlightenment in a hundred different languages to even the remotest of villages. You could admire the comprehensive social welfare system with its paid vacations and its health, accident, and life insurance, with the freedom to choose your own doctor, and with government subsidies for childbirth. You could visit cities constructed and perfectly maintained by former gangsters, burglars, and murderers, tour newly opened factories with the best machinery, the mightiest power plants in the world."

"In a word," rejoiced Herta Kronau, "the albums they have shown us are a big fat lie."

"That's not what I said," Lotte Albers emphasized. "They give the other side of the picture and focus entirely on the mistakes and weaknesses of the Soviets, in order to persuade us that the regime has totally failed."

"I see nothing but forgeries," persisted Herta, "especially the photos of what look like well-known figures. The Nazis have used technical tricks; they've enlarged, reduced, cropped the photographs, so as to reduce men like Dimitrov, Litvinov, and Molotov, even Trotsky and Stalin, to common criminal types, to scoundrels and rogues."[73]

"True," conceded Lotte Albers. "But on the other hand, I think many of the pictures are absolutely authentic. There's much more misery in Russia than you can imagine. The spacious apartments for the working class do exist all right, but they are rare and are usually a reward for special services. More often than not, a family of six has to make do with a single room with no closet and no table. There's a lot of construction underway because of the rapid growth of the population, but while the design is always grand, the workmanship is almost always inferior. Houses are built as quickly as possible with substandard materials, and they usually fall apart after four or five years. It's the same with the machinery; it doesn't perform well and it falls apart fast. Ford trains Russian machinists in Detroit and sends its newest machinery to the Kirov and Stalin plants, but Russian productivity is a mere fraction of American levels."

"That can change," objected Dora Doebel. "Russia is in the first stage of a new evolution that's unprecedented in the entire history of mankind. Of course the initial costs are going to be extraordinarily high."

"Yes," agreed Lotte Albers, "we ought to be patient and avoid hasty generalizations. I disagree with the followers of Trotsky, who speak of 'progress at a snail's pace,' who maintain that 'only want, need, and misery have been socialized in Russia.' But I can't agree either with Stalin's sycophants, who proclaim the ultimate victory of socialism and the Revolution on a daily basis and extol Russia as a heaven on earth. There's no doubt that a lot has been accomplished, but there is still an immeasurable amount of work left to be done."

Moringen, Late January 1937

Lotte Albers, who had taken such a reasonable and moderating position in the Russian dispute, continues to gain prestige. Upset by the new purge trials, which have again exacted fresh sacrifices, the women turn to her almost daily, hoping she can lift the veil of secrecy a little from the Russian sphinx. As far as she has any to give, Lotte shares information most willingly. She doesn't offer just her personal opinions but disburses light and shadow evenly in all directions.

"Don't be disturbed by my critical approach," she said. "For all of my misgivings, I love Russia. I gave birth to two children there and led a pleasant and carefree life. I would have been all too happy to stay in Russia, but my husband suddenly began to feel such primal homesickness that he was powerless to fight it. We Germans really have a peculiar disposition—always this obsession with foreign lands, the urge to travel, but then all of a sudden, at the height of our success, comes mushiness, sentimentality, homesickness. The German consul in Odessa examined my husband's many supportive references. 'I can only encourage you in your decision,' he said. 'Germany needs men of your caliber and will receive you with open arms.'

"But this friendly reception was strangely transformed at the border. My husband was taken to the concentration camp at Oranienburg, I was brought here, and our children were placed in my father's custody. Since we knew that bringing cash across the border was not allowed, we had invested our savings in valuable Siberian furs, which are now moldering in a warehouse in Cologne."

Her father's disappointment about all of these hardships was vividly expressed in a letter that Lotte received a few days ago. Owing to its contents, of course, this letter was not delivered to her; instead the director sent for Lotte and read the message aloud to her. "You know, my child," it read, in so many words, "I admire Hitler. He wants to make Germany great and he believes in his mission. But the people around him—God help me, I despise them. They crowd around the public trough and squander the German nest egg. If the Führer knew what they are perpetrating in his name, he would have thrown these puppets and profiteers out of the temple long ago."

It took courage to send such a message to a German concentration camp. It won't exactly be easy for Lotte's father to defend himself for this. But he doesn't have to fear excessively harsh punishment, since he's an "Old Guard" and has been a distinguished member of the Nazi Party since its foundation.[74]

Lotte was congratulated by her companions on the old man's principled position. Even the Bible Students appeared on the scene again for the first time in a while: "'A word aptly spoken is like apples of gold in settings of silver' [Proverbs 25:11]," they rejoiced with a verse from the Book of Proverbs.

THE "PUPPETS AND PROFITEERS" continue to rule Germany and appear to be establishing a reign of terror. Judging by the undiminishing influx of new admissions, they would like to turn half of Germany into a concentration camp.

Among the new constituents is a former city councilor from Weimar. Even though Herta Kronau makes fun of me for the way I chase after everyone's life story, I took steps to make contact with this new sister in misfortune. In fact, she was very talkative; she spoke about the latest measures to suppress all freedom of speech and about the increased pressures on courts, schools, universities, and newspapers. But she also reported on people's inner resistance, which unexpectedly surfaced every now and again.

One incident that occurred in Weimar itself gave me particular satisfaction. Schiller's *Don Carlos* was being performed at the National Theater. In the pivotal scene of the play, during the great, programmatic confrontation between tyranny and human dignity, when Marquis Posa shouts the famous line at King Phillip: "Grant us freedom of thought, Sire," the audience rose to its feet with a pointed and sustained ovation. This sequence of events repeated itself at each subsequent performance, assuming such extreme proportions that this Schiller drama was removed from the repertoire.

Weimar. What a pleasant diversion, to escape momentarily in spirit into this broad homeland of German genius, away from the narrow confines of the concentration camp, that perversion of the German national spirit. I had often accompanied my husband on his business trips to Weimar and had visited, always with a sense of uplift, those sites filled with memories of the poet princes: the National Library, the Wittumspalais, Tiefurt, the charming country estate of Duchess Amalie, Goethe's gloriously elegant house on the Frauenplan, and Schiller's modest, almost shabby dwelling. And yet it was precisely Schiller's home, outwardly so inconspicuous, that became the spiritual focus of a cultural ideal that broke through the barriers of nationalism and called for a universal and free humanity instead of rigid national loyalties. This movement unchained the greatest strengths of the nation, led to spiritual development of unprecedented proportions, and transformed Germany into the homeland of poets and philosophers.[75]

Characteristic of this glorious tradition, it always seemed to me, were the three books with which Schiller was preoccupied at the end of his life, which were piously preserved on his work table exactly as he had left them the day before he died. The three are Cervantes' *Don Quixote*, Shakespeare's historical dramas, and volume 6 of Moses Mendelssohn's writings on aesthetics.[76] The greatest Spanish author, the greatest English author, and the outstanding German Jewish philosopher of the Enlightenment. Human universalism condensed into three individual personalities.

"Are those books still on display in the room where Schiller died, like they used to be?" I asked the woman from Weimar.

She laughed: "A short time ago Hitler paid an official visit to our city. He saw all the sights. Including, of course, Schiller's house and deathbed.

"'How did this book by a Jew get here?' he shouted in outrage.

"A comment about the respect due the memory of the great author intensified his rage further.

"'That's not respect, that's sabotage. Get this book out of here!' he screamed, and he threw the book against the wall."

Hitler in Weimar. An altogether unimaginable thought. The upending of all values. The desecrator of the temple in the temple of humanity.

OUR CAMP IS filled to capacity. While the Great Hall and the Bavaria Hall have received newcomers from Germany alone, other than the few women returning from Russia, the involuntary occupants of the Jews' Hall come from Holland and Belgium, from France and Italy, from Czechoslovakia and from Yugoslavia. Everywhere they had tried to make a go of it as German governesses and domestics, as dressmakers and shorthand typists, but they were unable to keep it up for long. Work permits were soon taken away from them or were never granted in the first place. The pressures of unemployment weigh too heavily on all of Europe. Domestic markets have to be protected from foreign competition. Nations are isolating themselves from one another as if with barbed-wire entanglements. Even the large countries overseas have either banned immigration altogether, like Canada and Australia, or, like Brazil and Argentina, are allowing it only in special cases and only in exchange for large sums of money. "A colonist without capital is like a soldier without arms," as the South American saying goes.

Some kind of emigration process [from Germany] could have been devised without difficulty. In the past few decades, many nations have implemented such policies humanely and without coercion. They planned them properly, designated the destinations in advance, and paid for them out of public funds.[77] Nazi Germany, on the other hand, robs its Jewish emigrants of even the clothes off their backs, leaves them standing naked and bare at the border. If they cannot get any farther, if they have to come back, what awaits them in their "homeland" is the concentration camp.

The mood in our Jews' Hall is not just gloomy, it's utterly desperate. No prospects for a better future. No path to freedom. The situation is made more difficult by the unbearable overcrowding. When I came here nearly four months ago, the space was barely sufficient for the five of us. Now there are sixteen women packed in here like sardines. We literally cannot move our elbows without poking someone on the right or the left; we cannot stretch out our legs without rudely bumping into the knees of the person across from us. The air is foul and stale, but it's almost impossible to refresh it. Whenever the window is opened, the women sitting in the immediate vicinity lodge an angry protest against the draft and the penetrating, icy cold. In such close quarters, things are always in the way, and that goes for people as well. Every word, no matter how harmless, elicits a sharp response. It takes a great deal of goodwill to avert the ever-imminent outbursts.

Herta Kronau is the one who suffers the most under this adversity. Four years of prison and concentration camp, and the anguish of not knowing whether this imprisonment will ever end, eat at her strength more and more each day. But she maintains her self-control and her strength of will. No word of complaint ever passes her lips. It's a different story with the elderly Frau Schloss. She laments incessantly: "My God, if only we had stayed with our children in Moscow. We had everything we could possibly want. If only it hadn't been for my stupid homesickness. How easily I could have spared my husband and myself all this misery."

When conditions in our room became too bad, I went to the Madam Chief Warder, at the request of my companions, and begged for relief. She was quite receptive. We would just have to make do for the moment; a proposed new building would be providing additional rooms soon. She offered the use of an extra cell, suitable for four women, and recommended that I relocate there myself.

I conferred with Herta Kronau. "I would take it immediately, if you were to come with me."

Herta resolutely declined. "I would very much welcome a closer relationship with you, not to mention the greater peace and quiet and the better air. But no power on earth can get me to voluntarily submit to a locked basement cell ever again."

In the end, we agreed that the four young girls, Anni Reiner, Lilo the Palestinian, Ilse from Vienna, and the Spaniard Sophie, should move into the cell. They made the move with considerable pleasure.

But their delight didn't last long. One evening, shortly before bedtime, Anni rushed up to us: "Help! Help! Lilo's dying! She's suffocating. Frau Kronau, please, come quickly."

Lilo had been stricken by one of her frequent asthma attacks, which this time became severe enough to be life threatening. Her desperate companions knocked in vain on the locked door, in the end pounding on it with their fists and the heels of their shoes until the matron finally appeared.

"Oh, come on, now, she's hardly going to die," she barked angrily, and slammed the door shut again. But a short time later she returned after all, recognized the danger, tried to reach the camp doctor, without success, and sent for Herta Kronau, who is a trained nurse. Only slowly was Herta able to give Lilo some relief.

Herta's efforts met with a peculiar reward. The following morning, the doctor decreed that she was to take on formal night duty for the patient for the time being. Despite her own fragile condition, Herta endured this ordeal for several nights, then Lilo had to be transferred to the infirmary.

Also recently admitted to the infirmary is Addy, who had been coming over to us from the Great Hall every day to pick up her Frau Schloss for the exercise period. A strange individual, this Addy. Loving, loyal, and devoted in her relationship with this old woman, who was a perfect stranger to her, but inexplicably cold and hard-hearted toward her own. For years she had gone out with Gustav, who had fallen in love with her sharp and restless manner. She was skilled at sidestepping his proposals of marriage and kept putting off her decision, but in the end she declined. Her persistent suitor would not be deterred, however, and continued to court her. Addy had neither enough courage for marriage nor enough resolve for a final break-up. This suspense lasted for several years, until, tiring of her own resistance, she finally gave her consent. The wedding date was set and the couple, dressed up to the nines, went to the registry office. But before they could be married, the police intervened and arrested the bride as a result of one of her many thoughtless anti-Nazi comments. Gustav's love did not falter. In passionate letters he lamented the postponed wedding. Addy, vacillating again between yes and no, did not answer for a long time. Finally, she broke off the engagement from here in Moringen, citing the eloquent adage about fate: "That which God has put asunder let no man join together." The other day she received word from the police that her Gustav had hanged himself. On his table lay her rejection letter. Addy went into shock, refusing all nourishment. Only the constant pleas and encouragement of the elderly Frau Schloss succeeded in gradually bringing her back to life.

Moringen, Early February 1937

Our room has acquired a powerful new attraction in the person of Vera List [Gerda Lissack],[78] a graphic artist and designer. A gifted portraitist, she succeeds brilliantly in capturing not only the physical appearance but also the inner essence of the women she portrays. She depicts Dora Doebel bent over a book, and the strength of Dora's will and her powers of concentration find breathtaking expression in the tension on her face and in the firm grip of her hands, which grasp the book as if it were her most prized possession. In a charming double portrait, two friends are contrasted: the older, weary Herta Kronau, firmly committed to the life of the mind, and the younger, robust Ursel Renner, ever eager for new experiences. The picture elevates the personal to the archetypal; you perceive the pair not only as separate individuals, but as representatives of two different races as well. A charcoal sketch features Anna Löser, always solemn and melancholy. You would think that her thin, firmly closed mouth was about to give voice to her perpetually unspoken plea: "Children, just leave me alone with my fate."

Dora Doebel sent the drawing to her son Herbert. The boy thanked her effusively: "I recognized you right away, dearest Mommy, even though I haven't seen you for four years. You really look terrific. The Mother Superior of our convent said: 'That is the portrait of an intelligent and kindhearted woman.' I'm so proud of you. I kiss your picture every morning and every evening."

Vera List had received her training at the Academy of Arts in Antwerp. She had been pursuing her career in Germany until the authorities used her stay abroad, now two years in the past, as an excuse to send her here.

She's disabled, has an artificial leg and walks with a limp. The universal approval with which her achievements are met boosts her self-confidence, which had suffered as a result of her physical handicap. The women crowd around her, flattering her, until she interrupts their overtures with the question: "Okay, okay, so tell me, when is his birthday, anyway?" In order not to attract the attention of the matrons, the sittings are held in secret, mostly with the co-operation of several friends. Often the lavatory has to serve as a rather unappealing studio. The cardboard tubes that make the solid core of toilet paper rolls are used for shipping the pictures. Every shipment must pass censorship, of course, but this is administered rather benevolently by the Madam Chief Warder. She critiques each drawing in detail and she is generous with words of approval. "I happen to know something about sketching," she says, a bit smugly. "I used to love to do it myself in my younger days."

The portrait drawing continued without problems for quite a while. Suddenly things changed. At first we were at a loss to explain why all at once it seemed that our doors would be flung open at any moment, until one day Frau Hobrecht appeared and snapped at us in her accustomed manner: "Who's making drawings of the women in here?"

"I am," replied Vera List. "I don't think I'm breaking any rules."

"Whether rules are being broken or not is up to us to decide, not you. How were these drawings done? At the very least it's violating the regulation that the Jews may not visit the Aryan halls without special permission, or the Aryans the Jews' Hall."

Vera remained calm. "I've been drawing the women outside, during exercise."

"I don't believe you. I hardly ever see you during the free period, and besides, you can't walk properly because of your leg."

This reference to her disability hit Vera where it hurt the most. "There's a bench in the courtyard," she countered abruptly.

The matron, exasperated and angry, left us without saying another word. By the following day, the bench had been removed.

A melancholy mood blankets the courtyard. The weather is awful. A leaden, dark gray sky hangs over the barren earth. A piercing wind sweeps down from the mountains across the plains, bringing snow flurries and lots of rain. The women are freezing. During the exercise period, the many who lack warm clothing wrap themselves up in the black woolen blankets that they take from their beds, which give them the appearance of dark, drifting tents. The courtyard is swamped by a pool of yellowish, muddy water.

I recently observed former federal representative Anna Löser as she very deliberately waded through the deepest puddles in the new shoes that her sister had given her for Christmas. "What are you doing that for?" I asked her. "Too bad for those nice shoes."

"They're too tight for me. Moisture is supposed to stretch them out."

"The shoemaker can do a better job of that. For ten pfennigs he can stretch them on his lasts."

"Maybe. But I don't have ten pfennigs to my name."

IN A SIDE ROOM of the washhouse, which borders the courtyard to the north, an empty coffin always stood, intended perhaps as some kind of symbol. At any event, the women, not overly sensitive to begin with, poked fun at it, calling it "the nose crusher." One day there was a dead man in the coffin, an old workhouse inmate. The cloth that was supposed to cover him left his stiff, emaciated legs and feet visible. "'What is man that you are mindful of him, the son of man that you care for him?' [Psalms 8:4]." The dead man lay there for two days. The noise of the courtyard during the free period was silenced.

DEATH HAS CONFRONTED us once again. A rumor had been circulating in the camp for some time that Fritz Baimler had been killed in action in the battle for Madrid. A number of German newspapers were said to have reported this news. Several unsettling days passed, yet we refused to give credence to these unsubstantiated rumors. War reports have never had a reputation for reliability. Zenta Baimler walked around more dead than alive. In truth, she looked like a living corpse. Terrible, this uncertainty.

Then one day the director sent for Zenta. "Frau Baimler, yesterday Russian radio reported that your husband met his death in one of the recent big battles. Moscow dedicated a laudatory obituary to him, to his achievements, and his personal valor. I consider myself obliged to inform you of this."

Zenta rose to her feet, stood upright before the director. No sound, no movement betrayed her inner turmoil. "Thank you, sir. Would it be possible to procure me a more detailed official account?"

"I don't think so, but perhaps you could appeal yourself to the Spanish envoy in Berlin, or directly to the Spanish government."

Shortly thereafter Zenta learned she was to be released. She had been made to pay for her husband's escape with three years of incarceration, and his death was now restoring her freedom.

As much as the inmates in the Bavaria Hall were saddened by the demise of Fritz Baimler, whom they revered as one of the great personalities of the [Communist] Party, they were delighted about the release of their friend.

Zenta's request to be permitted to make the journey alone and at her own expense was denied. The Gestapo, probably assuming that it had already shown sufficient generosity, insisted on group transport with many other prisoners who would be collected along the way.

The day of departure came. There was a wordless but very moving farewell. The Bavarians were keenly aware that this meant the end of a community which a difficult fate had so firmly bonded together through shared pain and suffering.

The first news from Zenta arrived some time later. "The trip was very trying. We passed again through all of the stations where we had stopped back then on our way to Moringen, and I already knew some of the prisons in which we spent the night this time. Finally one evening the train pulled into Munich. At the train station I thought my heart would burst, I was so excited. I walked slowly through the familiar streets until I reached our house. Upstairs, the light was on in my mother's living room. I felt that I didn't dare go up, and yet suddenly there I was in front of our doorway in the entrance hall, helpless and confused. It took me a long time to bring myself to ring the bell. How will I come back to my mother after so many years? But then I pulled myself together and rang furiously until the door was flung open and my mother took me in her arms. The dear old woman has hardly changed at all, thank God, and now I remember what homeland, home and freedom all means."

Zenta had addressed this letter to her sister Maxe, who had been brought to Moringen at the same time as she, but who, surprisingly, has not yet been released.[79] Since all contact between a freed prisoner and one still in custody is forbidden, it was only with great difficulty that Maxe was able to secure the delivery of this letter. Zenta has now submitted a request to the Gestapo for permission to enter into written correspondence with her sister. The request is still pending.

Moringen, Mid-February 1937

Undisturbed by all these events, I had continued throughout to give my usual English lessons to my two students, Hilde Weber and Ursula Renner. The distresses of our situation notwithstanding, it gave me satisfaction to visualize a goal and to carry out an assignment, even of limited proportions. The morning exercise period was completely devoted to grammatical exercises, vocabulary, and conversation. In the evenings, the two wrote down what they had learned in their exercise books, which they then handed over to me for revision. This method, which confined the instruction to the exercise period in accordance with the director's instructions, proved to be quite successful. Gradually, we were able to converse in English with reasonable fluency, not just about the trivial events of the day, but about political and social issues as well. It gave me particular pleasure to begin to introduce these two studious and receptive young girls to English literature, first and foremost to Shakespeare's plays. For them, this was a brand new world, full of pathos and majesty, which inspired them and gave them a chance to forget the wretchedness of their immediate surroundings for a while. Whenever the new concepts and problems were too much for them, they liked to talk things over with Herta Kronau, who had initiated these lessons months ago and is following their progress and their results with approval. Even the other women have long since abandoned their original skepticism and mockery. They respectfully make way whenever "Frau Herz and the two English girls" are pacing back and forth across the courtyard, enthusiastically reciting English poetry.

Unfortunately, both Ursel and Herta have been in very poor health lately. Ursel has developed an acute kidney and gall bladder condition, which appeared most painfully and is threatening to lead to serious complications. Herta suffers from hypertrophy of the heart, associated with a general loss of strength. The camp doctor thinks it would be dangerous for either of them to remain in prison. He has advised them both to immediately petition the Gestapo for a speedy release and says he is willing to endorse their requests.

This led to tense confrontations in the Bavaria Hall. The extreme radical-left faction expressed serious misgivings: "A step like that, whether or not it is successful, is not consistent with [Communist] Party principles. It signifies a recognition of the Nazi regime, which it is our duty to resist to our dying breath."

In response to this uncompromising rigidity, Dora Doebel set out the moderate position: "Self-sacrifice is senseless if it is simply to uphold a theoretical principle to the bitter end. When your life is at stake, you have to be able to compromise with your adversary."

Temperate, reasoned thought ultimately prevailed. The appeals were drawn up and submitted. We were on pins and needles as we awaited the decision. Will the Gestapo be reasonable and restore the freedom of these women who have been physically destroyed by their four years of incarceration?

Ursel has by far the better chance. She is endowed with the enormous advantage of "pure Aryan descent," and she has a tireless and able assistant in the person of her mother. We know her mother, "Old Frau Renner," only from her letters, but they have brought an unusually lovable, inherently warm person to life for us with their vitality and originality. When she describes a winter stroll with her dog Rolf, who bolts off with long bounds, ventures hesitantly onto the cracking ice, and then sniffs at the earth beneath the thawing blanket of snow, you can virtually feel and smell the coming of spring. When she describes buying knitting yarn for her Ursel, you visualize along with her the large store, the tasteful displays, the pretty salesgirls, the bewildering profusion of colorful woolen strands, and you wait impatiently for the promised shipment of the balls of yarn "in a green that's like the color of the newly opened leaf of a young birch in the springtime."

"Old Frau Renner" had been an ardent radical leftist in the past and had endured a six-month prison term as a sacrifice to her convictions. The story of her release and immediate rearrest is still good for a laugh here. Two days after her release, she was crossing the street to go shopping, heard someone calling to her from a second-floor window, and recognized a former fellow prisoner. She cheerfully and immediately accepts this woman's invitation to come upstairs for a chat. The friend puts out some cake and makes coffee. The reunion is being appropriately celebrated, when suddenly a policeman appears, having observed the entire sequence of events, and immediately takes both of the women away. They each get another three months in prison for violating the regulation that prohibits contact between former prisoners.

Frightened by Ursel's illness, her mother has gotten it into her head that no price would be too high to pay for her daughter's release. She has pursued this with amazing energy. She knocked on every door, worked her way up from one government office to the next, refusing to be turned away, until one day she finally stood before Streicher, the dreaded Gauleiter of Franconia.[80] He gave her to understand, in no uncertain terms, that before she could make a case for her daughter, she would first have to provide proof of her own National Socialist convictions. For her mother, Ursel's freedom warranted a political change of faith. She converted to the Nazis, became a member of the German Labor Front, and participated in all of the "club nights" it sponsored. In her earthy manner and in the spiciest of Bavarian dialects, her letters described these social events. You are transported, as you read, into this howling, half-drunken assembly. You hear the crowd roar with laughter as the chairman, in the lofty, pretentious language of the Third Reich, describes the exodus of the children of Israel from Egypt, taking those sacred biblical tales of divine intervention in time of human need, of release from the most brutal oppression, and blasphemously relegating them to the realm of vulgar sacrilege.

Ursel was honest enough not to withhold these letters from Herta. Herta was deeply distressed: "You'll be in the same boat as your mother someday, too. Once you become free, you too will be unable to escape this onslaught of distortion, lies, and crudeness for very long."

"Have you transformed me," replies Ursel, "have you molded the ignorant little worker that I was into the informed, discriminating person I have become only to now distrust my judgment, my sense of decency and gratitude? Why do you hold me in such low esteem?"

"It's not that I hold you in low esteem, my dear Ursel. It's just that people far more accomplished than you, than both of us, men at the pinnacle of great achievement and success, representatives of the best of German culture, role models for the entire nation have all, in the end, had to bend beneath the power of reality."

"Don't forget, Herta, they did not give in freely, but under the threat of dishonor and property confiscation, of prison and concentration camp."

"That's only true up to a point. Men like Gerhart Hauptmann, Richard Strauss, Furtwängler, Sauerbruch, Blomberg, and Fritsch did not have to give in without a fight.[81] They had an obligation to speak out publicly and loudly against barbarity. But they have remained silent. As brave as the Germans are on the field of battle, in civilian life they lack any sense of responsibility and personal courage. Bismarck's old complaint about the Germans' 'lack of civil courage' is more fitting today than ever before."

"Hitler would certainly have made short work of such people. What do a few hundred or thousand human lives mean to him?"

"Hitler does not even have to resort to violence. He has only had to wait and to make his propaganda more seductive, and all of these leading figures either already have or will come over to him, maybe hesitantly and inconspicuously at first, but then openly and triumphantly. That ancient Teutonic ferocity and brutality is still ineradicably in the Germans' blood, this joy in annihilation, oppression, tyranny, the Nibelung-like joy of wanton destruction, to the point of self-destruction, if need be. These barely repressed primitive instincts have just been waiting for an opportunity to break through again in all their glory. Hitler has now created this opportunity. In this orgy of destruction, the Jews have become the first defenseless victims. Others will follow."

"No, Herta, you know yourself that the German workers reject this call to hatred at any rate. They see the Jews as an integral part of the German people, so they fear that to get rid of this group would be terribly dangerous to the nation as a whole."

Herta shook her head. Her words were full of hopelessness: "The workers have lost all influence over the future shape of Germany. The strength of their ideology has been shattered. And so the program of dishonor and destruction of rights, the merciless annihilation of hundreds of thousands of lives, will continue uninterrupted."

Ursel embraced her troubled and doubting friend as if she was trying to give fresh heart to her. "I am convinced that it will not be long before Germany will be convulsed by shame."

"May you be proved right, my child. You must keep your inner resistance going against the pressures from outside. Don't give up too soon. I couldn't bear to lose you too."

Throughout the time that her fate was being decided, Herta was in a very unstable frame of mind. She fluctuated between fear and hope, between strength of will and weakness of spirit. Her mother had sent her a few twigs [of forsythia], carefully packed in moss. Caring for these apparently dried-up plants became Herta's favorite pastime. She carefully measured out a mixture of lukewarm water and sugar, to which she added a weak copper solution in the shape of a copper coin, and treated the forsythia branches with it with such care and skill that they produced their full complement of flowers and, with their bright, luminous yellow, suddenly gave our dreary room a most cheerful appearance. Or she sat dead to the world at the window, to which she had affixed a tiny handmade feeding dish, tempting the birds with dainty little morsels. She was now living in the past much of the time and, more spontaneous and communicative than ever before, she talked occasionally about her own personal history. For the first time, she spoke with me about the tragedy of her marriage.

"A young student showed up at our art dealership, inquiring about drawings and etchings by Old German masters. Before long we fell into lively conversation. He came back the following day, and the day after that as well, and so it went over the course of several weeks. We fell in love with one another, but I had second thoughts about accepting his proposal, since he was twenty-one and I was twenty-seven years old. Yet it was precisely his carefree exuberant youth that so appealed to me. Eventually I yielded to his urging. We moved to Berlin and had a few good years. But I began to feel the age difference ever more powerfully and painfully. My husband was making a name for himself as an art critic; buoyed by his successes, he grew steadily happier and more secure. But I was held back by various physical ailments. I couldn't keep up with him. My first son died three weeks after he was born, my second son at six months. I felt like an innocent unjustly condemned by fate. I clung passionately to my husband. The thought that I might not be able to give him children drove me to despair. But then my pride rebelled. Anything but to chain him down, be a burden to him, stand in the way of his happiness. I drove him into the arms of other women. He protested, he stood by me, but his love felt oppressive. I interpreted it as generosity or in difficult times as charity. I refused to sleep with him. I pushed him away from me.

"After six years, our divorce brought release and at the same time a sorrow from which I'll never recover. My life was destroyed. In order to regain my balance, I went back to the ideas of socialism, which I'd been interested in earlier. I deepened my knowledge through years of intensive study, until finally I began to be active in the movement."

"In other words," I suggested, "you broadened the unfulfilled love of your husband into a fulfilling love for suffering humanity."

"I wouldn't go that far. But in any case, my activity gave me satisfaction, I discovered I had abilities within me that I'd never recognized before, organizational and rhetorical skills. Soon I became the leader of the Berlin party group."

A WEEK LATER Herta was ordered to appear before the director. Barely even looking up from his document-covered desk, he said, in the cold, aloof voice of the civil servant: "Frau Kronau, the Gestapo has denied your request for release, and at the same time states that any further appeal would be pointless."

Herta leaned heavily on the desktop. "I've heard you, and I shall act accordingly." She turned to leave.

The tone of voice with which she had spoken these few words caught the director's attention. He sensed the woman's hopeless desperation, knew that in similar situations people like her easily choose the last remaining path to freedom—suicide. He knew that these cases entailed quantities of unwanted paperwork for the authorities. This had to be avoided. Herta had already closed the door behind her, but he called her to return. "Frau Kronau, I hope that you will face the facts here, that you won't get carried away and do something rash, that you will spare me and my staff any inconvenience."

Herta stood up straight. "The director may rest assured that I shall not cause any inconvenience to him and his staff," she said, icily and contemptuously.

Pale and silent, she returned to us. She refused to give us any information, listened to our anxious conversation without taking any part in it, sat among us speechless, immobile, without response. Suddenly, with a soft moan, she slid to the floor and slipped into a state of complete unconsciousness.

SHORTLY THEREAFTER, URSEL was summoned by the director. Anxiety reigned in the Bavaria Hall. What kind of news will she bring? Ursel reappeared, collapsed on her stool, covered her face with both hands, and wept.

"Was your request denied?" her companions asked. No answer.

"Have you been released?" No answer.

"Did something else happen to you?" No answer.

It was quite a while before she recovered enough to explain to her friends what had happened. "Yes, I've been released. I'm so ashamed. I feel like a criminal. For me freedom, for Herta and for you more of the concentration camp. I'm one of you. I don't want preferential treatment. I won't go. I won't desert Herta."

She was completely serious; in particular, she could not bear the possibility of separation from Herta. It was very difficult for her companions to console her.

In tears, she finally packed her little suitcase. Dora Doebel gave her the final rules of conduct. "The Nazis will be watching you like a hawk. Be extremely cautious. You have suffered enough these past four years. You deserve a rest. So rest up and wait for the day when our German brothers will call you."

It took Ursel a long time to find the words when she took her leave of me. "I'll always be in your debt. I'll never forget your love and kindness."

I took her in my arms. My heart was very heavy.

Ursel reached out her hand to Herta in a final farewell. The two women gazed silently into each other's eyes. Neither had the strength to say a word.

Ursel had arranged for Herta to receive, on the day after her departure, her most prized possession as a farewell present: her fur-lined boots.

Moringen, Late February 1937

Our situation here is becoming ever more hopeless and unbearable. Almost every day brings new burdens and new deprivations. Lately, an acute food shortage has even set in. As recently as two months ago, bread was available in such abundance that we asked for reduced rations, so that it would not go to waste or be thrown into the pig troughs. Now there is a palpable shortage, and we are happy if by chance a companion with no appetite lets us have her slice. We are no longer given margarine for our bread, and the turnip jam is unpalatable. The mushy soups that make up our noon and evening meals every day consist almost exclusively of water now; they contain minuscule quantities of fat and meat, even of cabbage and potato. Only the black, lukewarm swill that the matrons imaginatively and blasphemously call "coffee" is available in the same enormous quantities as before, three times a day. We use this dark-colored fluid as a detergent, to scrub the floors and clean the toilets.

They are also drastically cutting back on coal. We're often cold. On less chilly days we sometimes succeed in saving two or three briquettes, but the matrons pursue every lump of coal like the devil pursues a lost soul. Just as grandma once hid her fancy cakes in the linen closet, away from her sweet-toothed children, we conceal the precious fuel between the linens and articles of clothing in our suitcases.

The wholesale cutbacks apply even to toilet paper. From now on we are doled out a weekly allotment of sheets by the smirking steward, along with his not very subtle comments.

Up to now we had been allowed to bring a blanket from the sleeping quarters into the day room and cover our hard stool with it. Suddenly, the director forbade even that modest relief: "The blanket supply must be conserved. New supplies are out of the question, owing to a shortage of fabric. The concentration camp is no sanatorium. I regret that I am unable to supply you with leather easy chairs."

Most painful for us is the control of the mail. Previously we had been allowed to send two letters a week and to receive two letters in return. Things have now changed. The notepaper that we must use from now on—at a cost of two pfennigs per sheet—bears the official imprint:

Moringen. Protective Custody Camp for Women.
Each prisoner may write and receive only one letter per week.

The page at our disposal is wide ruled and offers no space for lengthy messages.

After an extended hiatus, the Winter Relief Campaign is again making increased demands on us. A sizable new shipment has arrived. A matron distributes the work and, in the course of doing so, observes: "You've not exactly distinguished yourselves up to this point, you know. At the Hanover headquarters they are not very satisfied with your efforts. Don't make trouble for yourselves and for us. Please work more slowly, but more carefully."

We conscientiously comply with the first part of her instructions.

The relatively hopeful mood that had prevailed at Christmas evaporated long ago. At that time we were under the spell of the numerous releases and were anticipating that there was to be a general amnesty.

With not the faintest ray of hope, with no motivation from within, with no faith in a brighter future, you trudge along, exhausted and resigned. Everything makes you sick. The overcrowding and the wretchedness of your surroundings, the monotony of the food, the loathsome "clinkclank," as the tin dishware is known here, the pitchers and mugs of damaged enamel. You find the stupid, hostile matrons disgusting. Often, you find even your friends disgusting: you know them too well, their mannerisms, their whole attitude. Mostly, you find yourself disgusting: you don't want to look at yourself any longer, always in the same dress that you have to wear constantly, day in, day out. You don't want to think the same thoughts any longer, they keep slamming, dazed and confused, into the same brick walls. The whole pointlessness and meaninglessness of the camp is disgusting. When will this misery finally end? Will we be buried alive here forever?

Our existence in Moringen is like artificial life in a vacuum under a bell jar. We have been removed from the circulation of real life. The principles of meaningful existence do not apply to us. By order of the state, we have been denied any responsibility, any real participation. We can no longer care for our families, for husband and child, can no longer earn money to meet our own needs, no matter how modest, cannot give any advice, cannot be of any use. We are no longer the subject of events, merely their object. At this time of momentous upheaval we sit helplessly in the background, at the mercy of the enemy; we have to put our hands in our laps and do what we're told.

We are always fully conscious of the gravity of the situation we are in. Yet it would be unbearable in the long run if the organism's healthy defense mechanisms did not in fact prevail. As strange as it may seem, the women have never laughed as much as they do here in the concentration camp. It's just that this laughter has a different psychological basis; it's a forced laughter, a deliberate oblivion.

Only rarely do we enjoy an atmosphere of measured tranquility, and it never lasts. Joy and sorrow are exaggerated to extreme degrees, often vacillating kaleidoscopically, suddenly and abruptly. The tears flow as you take your leave of a companion, but she is barely out the door before you are doubled over with laughter over some remark or other or over some ungainly mannerism of hers.

There's a dead man in the ever-open coffin again. Their normal rounds take the women past the morgue a good twenty times during the free period. At first they are downcast and distracted, walk on tiptoe, don't raise their voices; then suddenly, they lose all inhibitions and squeal with pleasure. A young girl whose sweetheart has broken up with her is crying her eyes out. Suddenly she's running after the prison cats and trying to catch them, as if possessed.

The three cats are a constant source of diversion. They have adopted us and now feel at home with us. The black tomcat, Murkel [Shrimp], is idolized by all the women. With that slight spring in his step and his sleek fur, he's quite a fellow. Also he's useful in the battle against the mice, who gnaw at our personal belongings and whose tracks we find among our food supplies and our sewing utensils. The single mousetrap we were given can only do so much about these many unwelcome guests. Not long ago, Murkel caused us grave anxiety. He climbed onto the roof of the barn, couldn't find his way back down, and meowed pitifully for help down from the skylight. The women in the courtyard spread their aprons out as jumping blankets and enticed him with the most affectionate pet names, but the intrepid tomcat had lost his nerve. For two days and two nights, Murkel wailed so pitifully it could have melted a heart of stone. Finally the women discovered a slat long enough to reach to the roof, and after several attempts on the wobbly plank, the runaway carefully made his way down, received by his loyal followers with shouts of joy and a saucer of milk.

A few days ago we organized, in all secrecy, of course, a regular Mardi Gras. From 9 o'clock in the evening on, we posted sentries on the steps leading to the sleeping quarters, to give us timely warning in case one of the matrons approached. Then the real masquerade began. There are, in fact, some outstanding dressmakers among us, who had managed to create the most remarkable costumes out of bed sheets and out of some of the formal apparel borrowed from the Winter Relief. A most peculiar procession marched solemnly through the sleeping quarters. Out in front tripped "Baby," our youngest, skinniest little girl laced up in a bed sheet, a milk bottle in her hand, whining "Mama, Mama," in a thin, high-pitched voice. Behind her strutted the "Queen of the Night," an elderly parsonage cook in a purple velvet dressing gown and with a tinfoil tiara on her head. Then came a ghost, skulking around in artistically knotted bed sheets. Her eyes, outlined with thick rings of coal, shone with an eerie luminescence from her face, which had been powdered white with flour. There followed tramps, Gypsies, *vivandières*, and Spanish dons.

A suspicious noise outside—and in a flash, the ghostly apparitions had vanished, or rather crawled under the beds. The light was switched off and complete silence reigned in the sleeping quarters. Fortunately, it was a false alarm; a gust of wind had rattled the shutters. The women could safely re-emerge and even risk a cautious dance between the rows of beds.

The varied program concluded with a humorous cabaret act. Dora Doebel, to my surprise, proved to be blessed with wit and style as a stand-up performer. She presented a "Russian salad," a mixture of anecdotes, original humorous sketches, amusing speeches, songs and Alpine ditties. We had a hard time keeping our thunderous applause from growing too loud. Our memories [of the evening] gave us pleasure for many days.

Moringen, Early March 1937

Dora Doebel has received devastating news from the Mother Superior of the convent. "I am deeply distressed to have to inform you that your son Herbert has fallen seriously ill. The medical diagnosis is pulmonary tuberculosis, already advanced to a critical stage. It is not immediately life threatening, but it would be sinful to conceal the severity of the situation from you. Herbert is devout and resigned to the will of the Lord. He bears his suffering with admirable patience; he is a hero in spite of his youth. He has a great longing for his mother."

For days on end Dora was in a state of physical and emotional paralysis. She did not eat, she did not speak, she did not sleep. After much private debate, she submitted a petition to the Gestapo. She did not gloss anything over, did not minimize anything, did not complain, was not defensive. In the kind of insistent language that only a desperate mother could muster she asked for her release or, if this could not be granted, for several weeks of parole, which would allow her to care for her critically ill child.

She awaited the response in a feverish state. Every day she found an excuse to call on the Madam Chief Warder right at the time the mail was about to be distributed. She waited and waited.

"My son is my life's achievement. But I should probably never have been allowed to have a child," Dora lamented to me as I accompanied her in the exercise period, as so often. "My father was a poor laborer in one of the poorest villages in Bavaria, always sick, always drunk. He abused my mother, my brother, and me. After his death, my mother followed her lover to Munich, abandoning us children in the village, in dire need. The community had to provide for us, and since they had to pinch every penny, they organized a kind of auction. We were to be placed, 'for rearing,' in the custody of whoever would make the least demands on public funds. A destitute elderly couple bought us. We were exploited terribly. We were badly fed and had to perform the most exhausting physical labor. I had been sickly from my earliest childhood on; I had inherited the old family illness, tuberculosis of the bones. I've limped a little for as long as I can remember. Our 'foster parents' wanted to squeeze money out of us. They sent me out to work, washing dishes and waiting tables for the guests at the village inn, working in the fields for the farmers. From time to time, I would herd the cattle, and then our neighbors' son would keep me company. We became friends, pals. Later we 'dated' for many years. After we came home from a fair late one night, I finally yielded to his desire and let him into my bedroom. I became pregnant. When I told him about it, he turned crimson with rage. 'That's all we needed. You'll have to get rid of it,' he yelled, and kicked me in the stomach as hard as he could.

"I fainted and was seriously ill for a long time. But I recovered. Herbert came into the world. My stingy, ill-tempered old foster parents threw me and my child out of their house. We moved to Munich. I never saw the child's so-called father again."

"Didn't he want to marry you?" I asked.

"Oh, sure. But I was afraid of him. I couldn't forget his brutality. He would like to have avoided paying child support. I had to take him to court to collect. What a gentleman he was, every step of the way."

"All the more remarkable that you have been able to do so well by your son."

"Want remained my constant companion. I was a milkmaid, a washerwoman, a cleaning woman in a third-class hotel, a domestic, and last of all a cigarette factory worker. After I succeeded in mediating a wage dispute between the factory administration and the workers, my workmates turned to me as their spokeswoman for all work disputes. I was able to get some improvements for them, and so later on, with the encouragement of Fritz Baimler, they urged me to represent their interests as a member of the Bavarian state legislature. I became one of Fritz Baimler's closest associates and his top adviser on issues relating to the legal status and economic circumstances of women factory workers. I convened meetings, gave lectures, wrote articles for newspapers and magazines. But there was not much money to be made from these activities. I held onto my old job in the cigarette factory and took a leave of absence whenever the parliament was in session. My son was already ill by then. I never had enough resources to provide him with nursing care or medical attention, to say nothing of a sanatorium. His illness could probably have been successfully treated in its early stages. Now I'm afraid it's too late. I just have to see my Herbert again, hear his voice, be truly close to him. I have to give him the opportunity to feel all the love and tenderness of his mother again."

BAD NEWS RARELY travels alone.

Frau Schloss was ordered to report to the office. She was in there for a long time. Then a matron appeared and brought me to the director as well. He was pacing back and forth in a state of agitation, Frau Schloss sat collapsed in a chair next to his desk, whimpering softly.

This time the director's voice was neither thunderous nor commanding: "The Gestapo has informed me of the sudden demise of Herr Schloss in the concentration camp at Sachsenhausen. I have arranged a fourteen-day leave for Frau Schloss and have already notified her family by wire of her impending arrival. The train for Berlin leaves in two hours. Frau Schloss asked me to call for you. Perhaps you can be of assistance to her."

The Madam Chief Warder led us into the doctor's empty waiting room. "There are no office hours today. You may wait here until the train leaves. I'll make sure there's plenty of heat." She said a few sympathetic words and left the room, shaking her head.

Frau Schloss continued to weep softly to herself, moaning occasionally: "Oh, those dogs, those barbarians. I'm certain they tortured my poor husband to death. A seventy-year-old man with a heart condition. If only I had not come back to Germany with him, then he could have died in peace in Moscow. For forty long years we were hardly separated from each other for even a single day, and now he has to come to such a horrible end, far from his wife and children."

Carefully, I steered the poor woman back to the demands of the moment. There was still a lot to be taken care of. First and foremost there was a bag to be packed.

"I can't do it," she whimpered. "I want to stay here, downstairs, and not see anybody else. Please take care of it all for me."

I did as she asked. When I returned, she received me in something of a state: "Did you pack my little ink bottle? Wouldn't want to forget that."

By means of a strange thought-displacement process, a ten-pfennig bottle of ink had suddenly become the most important thing of all. She wouldn't rest until I had gone back upstairs again to look for this precious item. But the effort of packing proved to be redundant.

A matron appeared and commanded: "The bag stays here. Frau Schloss has not been released, only paroled for a short period of time. She's allowed to take only the clothes she's wearing."

At Frau Schloss's pleading, I was given permission to accompany her, under guard, to the mail bus.[82] I took her arm and supported her; her knees buckled with every step. But I had some difficulty standing up myself. I had grown unused to freedom. The normal signs of everyday life—the sounds of the street, the honking of an automobile horn, the loud voices of children, the barking of a dog—nearly caused me to lose my balance. Our appearance in the little town of two thousand inhabitants caused quite a stir; people cast knowing glances at one another. With a stern, expressionless face, the matron strode next to us—at a remove, of course, sufficient to emphasize the distance in status. She resembled a walking block of ice.

The mail bus stopped. How will Frau Schloss, who is completely absent-minded, ever manage this trip? I spoke quietly to a farmer's wife who was sitting, fat and happy, among her baskets of chickens and eggs. "This woman has just been informed of the sudden death of her husband and is a little confused. Please help her get onto the train to Berlin."

The farmer's wife cast a sympathetic glance toward the picture of misery in front of her. "I'll be happy to. You can count on me."

Moringen, Mid-March 1937

Twelve women have been committed here in the last few days. They bring us some frightening reports. A wave of terror is again sweeping across the country. The new People's Courts[83] are operating at full tilt. Their judges are exclusively members of the National Socialist élite, and they show themselves worthy of the trust placed in them by the state, handing down almost nothing but death penalties. It's so easy these days to get rid of unpopular people. They plant documents with Communist and treasonous content into people's apartments, and there's the evidence of their guilt.

Among the newcomers is a young student from Berlin, Ruth Abt,[84] a lively and very bright girl. She gave us details about the Schloss case, which had been much discussed in Berlin because of the circumstances surrounding it. The sons, summoned to pick up their father's body, were not allowed to enter the camp. The coffin was delivered to them outside the gate. It was soldered up with lead and closed with numerous seals. They were forbidden to open the coffin under pain of death. The burial took place in the presence of Gestapo officials, after they had confirmed that the seals were still intact.

I can't get the words of poor Frau Schloss out of my mind: "Until my dying breath I will be tormented by not knowing whether those monsters shot my husband or beat him to death. I'll never learn the truth."

The effect on the women here is extraordinarily intense. They walk around frightened and tearful, worrying constantly about their husbands, whose messages are terse and not very comfortingly worded. Hardly a word is spoken now. Our forced labor for the Winter Relief Campaign proceeds in silence. During the two free periods in the courtyard, the morgue exerts an uncanny appeal. People approach it apprehensively and withdraw apprehensively. The other day a woman collapsed with screams and convulsions. She had been seized by a sudden hallucination: the dead man in the coffin had taken on the appearance of her husband, imprisoned in Dachau.

Herta Kronau, in her desperate condition, had appealed to the administration for a visit from a chaplain. Her request was denied. I stood with her at the barred window, and we shared our concerns, our mental anguish. We talked about this latest rejection, about poor Frau Schloss, about our friend Dora Doebel, whose longing for her son Herbert is wearing her down.

A matron walked repeatedly through the room, eyeing us rudely and intently. It was our free time, so we went right on talking.

The next morning I was ordered to report to the Madam Chief Warder. "You were so very sad yesterday," she greeted me.

I was silent. I was amazed by such sensitivity to my mental state and, above all, that the matron had reported it so fast and accurately.

"Sunshine follows the rain," the Chief Warder continued. "I have good news for you. Frau Herz, you've been released."

I thought I must not have heard correctly. "Excuse me?"

"Yes, you have been released."

The director, affable and courteous, confirmed the ruling. "This time the Gestapo has done its work well," he beamed appreciatively.

A profound wave of happiness came over me so forcefully, with such a rush, that I nearly grew dizzy. "Finally, finally you may go home to your husband and your children." The jubilation swelled within me. But at the same time I was overcome by a great sadness at having to part from so many dear people here.

Apprehensively, beset by inner turmoil, I made my way slowly back to our room. I hesitated for a while, then I went in. I went up to Herta.

"The time has come. I've been released."

Herta stared at me, uncomprehending and disbelieving, then she shrank back. "I'm delighted for your sake, and I'm dismayed for my sake. You've given me so much, Frau Herz, I can't tell you how much. Now our paths must part. Let us not complicate our farewell with words. We know well we share an inner bond. Take good care."

She squeezed my hand and left the room. I followed her sadly with my eyes. I felt like Ursel Renner had. I felt like a traitor who thinks only of her own safety. How will this proud, guarded woman endure this imprisonment? She is so introspective, so solitary. Will she befriend another like-minded person?

Someone put her hand on my shoulder. Ruth Abt was standing in front of me: "Don't worry, Mother Herz. I love and admire Frau Kronau, and I think she's fond of me, too. I will do everything I possibly can to make her life here as tolerable as possible."

Her words conveyed a sense of responsibility and dependability. I felt an immense relief.

I packed my few belongings. Linens and articles of clothing I left behind for my Aryan and non-Aryan companions.

I went into the Great Hall and into the Bavaria Hall. Many hands reached out to me, and many good wishes were shared with me as well.

My last visit was to Dora Doebel. She had been summoned right after me by the director, who had informed her that her request [for a parole] had been denied.

Dora lay in bed. She was so weak that she couldn't even sit up straight. Her sweet, kind face seemed totally overcome. I sat down next to her. I couldn't speak. It was as if my throat had been sewn shut. I grasped her ice-cold hands and stroked them. Dora was speechless for a long time as well. Finally, she said softly, almost inaudibly: "Give my regards to your husband and your darling children."

My eyes became moist. "May God be with you and your brave Herbert."

Outside in front of the sleeping quarters I had to sit down on the stairs for a while. My knees were giving way under me.

I stood before the Madam Chief Warder for the last time. I signed an affidavit that I was leaving the camp in perfectly good health and would not be making claims of any sort against the state.

"Today is a day of rejoicing for the entire Herz family, and I rejoice with them," said the old woman, blustery as she was but nevertheless basically good-natured.

Frau Hobrecht, the most unpleasant of all the matrons, unlocked the gate for me, drew herself up to her full height, raised her hand, pointed straight ahead: "There." Then she wheeled around and walked back without a word of farewell.

Thus, on March 17, 1937, I left the women's camp in Moringen.

THE LITTLE LOCAL TRAIN traveled slowly. But for me it was still traveling too fast. Inwardly, I couldn't keep up. The conflict of emotions, the constant fluctuation between joy and melancholy befuddled me.

In Kreiensen, the enormous railway hub, I had to wait two hours for the express train to Berlin. I telegraphed my loved ones to expect my arrival. Why was the ticket clerk looking at me so suspiciously? Could it be that he thinks I've escaped from the camp? I bought myself some newspapers and took refuge behind a protective wall of printed paper, since I imagined that the eyes of everyone present were trained on me. A man in uniform walked through the waiting room; his loud, measured steps frightened me. The memory of Barbara Fürbringer and her rearrest in the train station immediately after her release came to mind. Is the man in uniform about to approach me and take me into custody? No, he stopped and, in a booming voice, announced the arriving and departing trains.

Finally. "Express train to Berlin. Track three."

I sat down in a corner. After a while, a fellow passenger spoke to me: "Tough, isn't it, sitting so long?" Could it be that this woman knows how long I "sat" in Moringen? No, she only wanted to find out how many hours I have already spent on the train.

I ride, I ride. Cities, villages fly past. Names resound in my ears, names that once meant a great deal to me but now ring hollow. I hear Magdeburg, Brandenburg, Potsdam. But I don't know where I am.

Then suddenly: "Berlin, Zoological Garden. Berlin, Zoological Garden."

From the other end of the platform, otherwise deserted now at midnight, my children's voices call out: "Mother! Mother!" My daughter, my son are hanging round my neck. My husband is standing in front of me. He cannot speak. Neither can I.

I HAVE WRITTEN these final pages in Berlin, in our home.[85] It's all a dream. And I am not yet awake.

Only with difficulty am I able to come to terms with my new situation. Surely it's wrong, but I am unable to enjoy my freedom. The large house with its many comfortable and attractive rooms depresses me. I still live in Moringen. I don't want to sit at our table with its bountiful, nutritious fare—in Moringen people are hungry. I don't want to take part in my visitors' often trivial conversations—in Moringen the conversations are all about the most profound of questions, about freedom, life, and death. The lovely avenues, their trees resplendent with the first green of spring, the stately villas, the wide streets, the people, all dressed up, out for a stroll—I don't want to see them. Facing me is always the suffering, the sorrow, the despair of my companions in Moringen.

GRADUALLY, BY FORCE of necessity, I find my way back to reality. I am also gradually able to help Ehm, my husband. He is expending his entire energy to press ahead with our emigration. "Let us not linger one day longer than we must," he says constantly. "Better to abandon everything here, house and belongings. Let us just get away from this land of Nazi criminality, of unfathomable barbarity."

At last. At last. Our passports, our papers have all been put in order. Tomorrow we cross the German frontier.

Notes

1. The references are to Friedrich Nietzsche, *Human, All Too Human*, preface: 8, and vol. 1: 475; see R. J. Hollingdale, trans. and ed., *Human, All Too Human* (Cambridge, 1996), 10–11, 174–75.
2. The Alexanderplatz building housed Berlin's central police authorities (the *Polizeipräsidium*), to which a Gestapo under-office (*Stapostelle*) was attached. (The Gestapo headquarters themselves were located in the Prinz-Albrecht-Strasse.) It has not been possible to identify "Room 217," but presumably it was the interrogation room used by the Alexanderplatz Gestapo officials.
3. For the regulations on "returning emigrants," see introduction, 1, 9.
4. For Ullstein, see introduction, 6.
5. Both Manfred Freiherr von Richthofen (1892–1918) and Ernst Udet (1896–1941) were German flying aces in World War I, credited with shooting down 142 enemy planes between them. Von Richthofen was killed in action in April 1918. His memoirs were published by Ullstein as *Der rote Kampfflieger* (Berlin, 1917), and revised and republished (also by Ullstein) as *Der rote Kampfflieger, eingeleitet und ergänzt von Bolko Freiherr von Richthofen, mit einem Vorwort von Reichsminister Hermann Göring* (Berlin, 1933). Udet became one of the Luftwaffe's leading planners in 1936, involved especially in aircraft design, but he lost favor when Germany failed to win the air war against Britain in 1940–41, and committed suicide in November 1941.
6. All Germans between the ages of sixteen and twenty-five were required by law to do six months' unpaid work in the National Labor Service (Reichsarbeitsdienst), usually in rural areas.
7. Erich Maria Remarque was the pseudonym of Erich Paul Remark (1898–1970). A novelist and journalist, his best-known work is *Im Westen nichts neues* (All Quiet on the Western Front, 1929); he left Germany in 1938. Carl Zuckmayer (1896–1977) was an Austrian playwright and novelist, author of *Der Hauptmann von Köpenick* (The Captain of Köpenick, 1931), among many other plays and books; he left Germany in 1938. Leonhard Frank (1882–1961) was a socialist and writer who had two periods of exile from Germany, first as

a pacifist in 1915–18, and again when the Nazis came to power. Among his many books are *Die Räuberbande* (The Robber Band, 1914) and *Carl und Anna* (1926). Lion Feuchtwanger (1884–1958) was a novelist and playwright, best known for his play *Jud Süss* (1925). In exile after 1933, he spent periods in France, the Soviet Union, and the United States. Alfred Neumann (1895–1952) was a novelist and dramaturg who emigrated to the US in 1941. Vicki Baum (1888–1960) was an editor at Ullstein who became a popular novelist. Her *Menschen im Hotel* (1929) was translated and made into the Hollywood film *Grand Hotel*. She emigrated in the 1930s.

8. The *Vossische Zeitung* was a respected liberal Berlin newspaper, published under that name from 1911 to 1934, but originating in a seventeenth-century broadsheet.

9. Herz's record of her imprisonment in the Alexanderplatz jail may be compared with that of Gerda Lerner, who was imprisoned after the Nazi takeover of Austria in a Vienna city jail in 1938; see Gerda Lerner, *Fireweed* (Philadelphia, 2002), chap. 6.

10. That is, Jehovah's Witnesses, known in Germany as "Ernste Bibelforscher"; see introduction, 27–29.

11. The "Horst Wessel Song" was the Nazi Party's official marching anthem. It was named after an SA man (Stormtrooper), who was allegedly murdered by a Communist in 1930.

12. The German Labor Front (Deutsche Arbeitsfront) was the Nazis' monopoly membership organization for workers. Established in May 1933, it replaced the banned trade unions.

13. It has not proved possible to identify the sources of these quotations or of the following group from Stalin's speeches, and some may be paraphrases rather than exact quotations. The third quotation ("Communism is the leap …") came originally from Friedrich Engels, *Socialism: Utopian and Scientific* (New York, [1882] 1972), 61. (Special thanks to Joel Hartig for his heroic efforts to locate these quotations.)

14. Karl Liebknecht (1871–1919) and Rosa Luxemburg (1871–1919) were founding members of the Spartacus League, a breakaway group from the German Social Democratic Party in 1914, and of the German Communist Party in 1918. Both were murdered by right-wing death squads during the abortive Spartacist uprising in Berlin in January 1919. Luxemburg's prison letters were published as *Briefe aus dem Gefängnis* (Berlin, 1922); translation by Eden Paul and Cedar Paul, eds., *Letters from Prison* (Berlin, 1923).

15. John Huss (c. 1370–1415) was a religious reformer in Bohemia who was burned at the stake for his heretical opinions.

16. The quotation is adapted from the play by Richard Beer-Hofmann, *Jaákobs Traum* (Berlin, 1918); see introduction, 38.

17. A mountain region in the Bohemia-Silesia region, now spanning the frontiers of Poland and the Czech Republic. For Magdalene Mewes, see biographical appendix.

18. See biographical appendix.

19. See biographical appendix.

20. For this status, see introduction, 9.

21. See biographical appendix.

22. See biographical appendix.

23. See biographical appendix.

24. The Baltic port city of Danzig was removed from German rule in 1919 and designated a free city under League of Nations supervision, with administrative rights reserved to Poland. Its status remained a point of friction between Germany, the League, and Poland. Between 1934 and 1937, Germany and Poland reached agreement about shared supervision of Danzig, but Germany renewed pressure in 1938 to restore the city to German sovereignty. Poland's refusal resulted in the German declaration of war in September 1939.

25. The identity of Anni Reiner remains unknown. The Nuremberg Laws, adopted on 15 September 1935, included a new National Citizenship Law and a Law for the Protection of German Blood and German Honor. Clause 1 (1) of the latter forbade marriages between "non-Aryans" and "citizens of German blood," and clause 2 outlawed extra-marital intercourse between

them. Clause 5 (1) of this law imposed penalties on both sexes for violation of the marriage ban, but paragraph 2 of this clause specified that only men were to be penalized for violating the regulations on extra-marital intercourse. Nevertheless, women who were found to have engaged in such illicit sexual relations were usually punished with detention under the protective custody provisions. For the text of the laws and regulations and a summary of prosecutions and sentencing practices, see Jeremy Noakes and Geoffrey Pridham, eds., *Nazism 1919–1945*, vol. 2 (Exeter, 2000), 340–47 (where the translation of clause 5 [2] is, however, incorrect in implying that it refers to both sexes).

26. For Soviet policies on marriage and the family, see Wendy Z. Goldman, *Women, the State and Revolution: Soviet Family Policy and Social Life, 1917–1936* (Cambridge, 1993), and Sheila Fitzpatrick, *Everyday Stalinism. Ordinary Life in Extraordinary Times: Soviet Russia in the 1930s* (Oxford, 1999), chap. 6.

27. See introduction, 26, 30.

28. For Centa Herker-Beimler and her husband, Hans Beimler, see introduction, 30f., and biographical appendix.

29. See biographical appendix.

30. See Hanna Elling, *Frauen im deutschen Widerstand* (Frankfurt am Main, 1981), 106.

31. See biographical appendix.

32. Evidently a misprint for Lange Strasse.

33. This habit remained with Gabriele Herz in later years, since the lavatory was also where she wrote her regular letters to her children while she was working as a hospital cleaner in Rochester.

34. Alfred Rosenberg (1896–1946) was one of the Nazi movement's chief ideologues and author of *The Myth of the Twentieth Century* (1925), a depiction of history in racialist, anti-Semitic and anti-Christian terms. Among his positions in the Nazi Party and administration after 1933, he was appointed in 1934 as the Führer's commissioner for the supervision of the total intellectual and ideological education and training of the NSDAP (the office referred to here as Reichskulturwart), and in 1941 to serve as minister for the occupied territories in the East. He was hanged at Nuremberg.

35. It has not proved possible to identify the source of this quotation.

36. Franz Gürtner (1881–1941), a member of the German Nationalist People's Party (DNVP) but a sympathizer with the Nazis since the 1920s, was minister of justice in the Nazi government. The legal provisions referred to here actually date from earlier years, viz. respectively an amendment to the penal code issued on 28 June 1935 and the Law against Malicious Attacks on State and Party of 20 December 1934.

37. See biographical appendix.

38. This is the first line of the well-known poem by Heinrich Heine (1797–1856), "Die Lorelei" (1817). Because of his Jewish ancestry, Heine's works were banned by the Nazis.

39. These are all celebrated German-Jewish scientists. August von Wassermann (1866–1925) was a physician and bacteriologist and a leading figure in the study of infectious diseases. His most famous achievement was the development of a test, commonly called the Wassermann test, for diagnosing syphilis, which is still used today. Fritz Haber (1868–1934), a chemist, is best known for the Haber Process, which synthesizes ammonia from a reaction between nitrogen and hydrogen. During World War I, he was mainly responsible for the German gas offensive and organized the manufacture of lethal gases. Under pressure from the Nazi regime, he resigned as director of the Kaiser Wilhelm Institute for Physical Chemistry in 1933 and went into exile in Britain. Paul Ehrlich (1854–1915), a bacteriologist, contributed greatly to the origination of chemotherapy, hematology, immunology, and pharmacology, and is best remembered for developing the first successful cure for syphilis. Under the Nazi regime, his widow was persecuted and his property confiscated.

40. Ernst Barlach (1870–1938) was an expressionist sculptor and writer. Although the Nazi regime attempted to suppress his "degenerate" art, he remained in Germany until his death

in 1938, continuing to produce controversial, uncompromising art and publicly rejecting the values of National Socialism.

41. Esperanto was invented in 1887 by L. L. Zamenhof, a Polish-Jewish physician, who intended it to promote international understanding. For the same reason, it was popular among socialists in Europe.

42. Presumably the workhouse physician, Otto Wolter-Pecksen. A founder-member of the local branch of the NSDAP in 1921 and a member of the SA since April 1931, he was a local official for the party's Rassepolitisches Amt (Office of Racial Politics) from September 1937; see Kuse, "Entlassungen von Häftlingen," 21–22; see also his SA membership form, in NARA Rg 242, SA Kartei (BDC Microfilm Rg 242-A3341-B0337), which gives his NSDAP membership date as May 1925, probably the date on which he rejoined the party when it was refounded after being banned following the 1923 Munich putsch. Thanks to Jan Lambertz for this reference.

43. For the Decree for the Protection of People and State, see introduction, 10f.

44. The Winter Relief Campaign was an annual charity drive instituted by the Nazi Party's welfare organization in 1933. Centering on highly public street collections, it mobilized party members and state officials to solicit donations. The campaign was intended to express the commitment of the government, the party, and the people to the welfare of the German nation.

45. See introduction, 30f.

46. The camp regulations ("Dienst- und Hausordnung für das Frauenschutzhaftlager Moringen") were modeled on the workhouse rules; in fact, they did not include corporal punishment. Typescript (incomplete) in HStA Hannover: Hann. 158 Moringen, acc. 84/82, nr. 2, 144–47.

47. German law enabled prostitutes to register with the police, in which case they had to observe regulations on health, public order, and decency. For Nazi policies on prostitution, see Julia Roos, "Backlash against Prostitutes' Rights: Origins and Dynamics of Nazi Prostitution Policies," *Journal of the History of Sexuality* 11 (January–April 2002), 67–94.

48. "Arrest" is the word Herz uses. In section 14 of the regulations, the phrase "Arrest in der Strafzelle" (confinement in the punishment cell) is crossed out and replaced by the handwritten phrase "Isolierung im Einzelraum," i.e., solitary confinement.

49. Refers to the Italian invasion of Ethiopia in 1935–36.

50. This appears to be a jocular reference either to the hero of Weber's opera *Euryanthe* (1822–23), or to the role played by the film star Hans Moser in the 1931 hit movie *Der verjüngte Adolar*.

51. From 1936, Reinhard Heydrich (1904–42) was head of the Security Police and a trusted deputy of Heinrich Himmler, by this time the chief of the SS and Gestapo. This alleged visit is not corroborated in any of the other sources or accounts, and it is not clear who might be meant here. Himmler himself visited Moringen on 28 May 1937, i.e., after Herz's release.

52. The League of German Girls, established in 1932, was the official Nazi organization for girls aged ten to twenty-one and was the counterpart to the boys' Hitler Youth (Hitler-Jugend). By 1936, it had about two million members.

53. Siemens and Halske was a leading German electrical engineering firm, established in 1847.

54. Siegfried was Jewish, and therefore Friedel's sexual relationship with him contravened clause 2 of the Law for the Protection of German Blood and German Honor. For the differential application of this law to men and women, see note 25 above.

55. For the purges and Stalin's general repression of the political opposition in the 1930s, see Barry McLoughlin and Kevin McDermott, eds., *Stalin's Terror: High Politics and Mass Repression in the Soviet Union* (Basingstoke, 2003), and Robert W. Thurston, *Life and Terror in Stalin's Russia, 1934–1941* (New Haven, 1996).

56. See biographical appendix.

57. The small Silesian town of Jauer housed a penitentiary to which numerous women were sent between 1933 and 1945.

58. For the Soviet campaign against religion in this period, see William B. Husband, *"Godless Communists": Atheism and Society in Soviet Russia, 1917–1932* (De Kalb, 2000).
59. This hymn, written in 1597 to celebrate a Dutch military victory, underwent many later adaptations and translations. In Germany, the most famous was Karl Budde's "Wir treten zum Beten" (1897); its militaristic marching tone made it popular among nationalists and later with the Nazis, who played it before party events and rallies. Played as a march, it is titled "Wir treten zum Beten"; played as a hymn, the "Nederlandisches Dankgebet." (The melody is known in the US as "We Gather Together," traditionally played at Thanksgiving.)
60. Johann Wolfgang von Goethe, "An Lida" (1794). Written in 1781, the poem was dedicated to Charlotte von Stein, with whom Goethe was involved in a long and apparently platonic relationship. Either Ehm or Gabriele has adapted or misremembered the original, with the effect that a theme of loss is substituted for Goethe's original portrayal of unattainable courtly love. The original reads:

> Den Einzigen, Lida, welchen du lieben kannst,
> Forderst du ganz für dich, und mit Recht.
> Auch ist er einzig dein.
> Denn seit ich von dir bin,
> Scheint mir des schnellsten Lebens
> Lärmende Bewegung
> Nur ein leichter Flor, durch den ich deine Gestalt
> Immerfort wie in Wolken erblicke:
> Sie leuchtet mir freundlich und treu,
> Wie durch des Nordlichts bewegliche Strahlen
> Ewige Sterne schimmern.

61. The arrival of a group of new inmates offers Herz another opportunity to interpolate a summary of some of the major events and problems in international relations during this period.
62. See biographical appendix.
63. See biographical appendix.
64. An agreement not to intervene in the Spanish Civil War, accepted by all European powers (except Spain, Portugal, and Switzerland) in August 1936 and supervised by a committee under the League of Nations. It was honored more in the breach than the observance, but although it did not stem the flow of arms and fighters into Spain, it may have prevented the war from becoming a more general conflict.
65. The term "Rome-Berlin Axis" was first used by Mussolini in a speech on 1 November 1936. It refers to the partnership between Germany and Italy signaled in their agreement of 23–24 October 1936 on common interests and spheres of influence in the Mediterranean and Eastern Europe. It was premised on the close personal relationship between Hitler and Mussolini and was solidified into a military alliance, the Pact of Steel, in May 1939.
66. The five International Brigades, recruited under the auspices of the Communist International, fought on behalf of the Spanish Republic between 1936 and 1938. They were composed of volunteers from European and American Communist Parties and numbered about 40,000 in total, including about 5,000 from Germany.
67. The "Polish Corridor" was the strip of land carved by the Treaty of Versailles from the German territory of West Prussia and assigned to the restored state of Poland in order to give it access to the Baltic Sea. Its population was predominantly Polish, but the loss of the territory (which separated East Prussia from the rest of Germany) and the tribulations of the German minority under Polish rule were sources of intense friction between Germany and Poland. The status of the city of Danzig (see note 24 above) only added to the dispute. Hitler's unexpected conclusion of a non-aggression pact with Poland in January 1934 was a short-term policy directed against Russia and did not signal a permanent intention to abandon these issues.

68. Two regions of Germany subjected to special provisions by the Treaty of Versailles (1919). The Rhineland region was to be occupied by Allied troops for fifteen years, while east of the river a demilitarized zone was established in which Germany was forbidden to station troops. Under the Locarno agreements in 1925, Germany achieved the evacuation of the Allied occupation forces from the Rhineland between 1926 and 1930, i.e., before Hitler came to power. In March 1936, Hitler moved German troops into the demilitarized zone, in violation of the Versailles and 1925 treaties. Further south, the coal-rich Saar region, which had been placed under League of Nations administration in 1920 for fifteen years, was restored to German sovereignty after a landslide plebiscite in 1935.

69. The reference here is to the history of Russo-German rapprochement since the early 1920s, initiated by the Treaty of Rapallo signed in April 1922, which established diplomatic and commercial relations between Germany and Soviet Russia and which provided for collaboration in economic and military matters. This treaty was confirmed and extended in the Treaty of Berlin (April 1926), which was renewed in 1931 and again in 1933.

70. This is slightly misleading in suggesting that Hitler was issuing a threat. The correct version of this speech, given by Hitler to the muster of the German Labor Front on 12 September 1936, is as follows: "If the Urals with their immeasurable wealth of raw materials, Siberia with its rich forests, and the Ukraine with its immeasurable plains of wheat lay in Germany [*in Deutschland lagen*], this [country] would be swimming in plenty under National Socialist leadership"; see Max Domarus, *Hitler. Reden und Proklamationen 1932–1945*, vol. 2 (Leonberg, 1973), 642.

71. Lev Kamenev (1883–1936), Grigory Zinoviev (1883–1936), and Karl Radek (1885–?1939) were Old Bolsheviks who held leadership offices in Russia after the Revolution, but were eliminated by Stalin in the power struggles of the later 1920s and 1930s. After show trials, in which they were accused as "terrorists" or "Trotskyists," Kamenev and Zinoviev were executed, while Radek received a ten-year sentence and died in captivity.

72. Shortly before his death in January 1924, Lenin dictated a series of advisory notes on political strategy and structure, known as his "Testament": these included a warning against Stalin's defects and praise for Trotsky's qualities. See Moshe Lewin, *Lenin's Last Struggle* (London, 1975), 77–89.

73. Georgy Dimitrov (1882–1949), a Bulgarian Communist and an official of the Communist International, was tried for complicity in the Reichstag Fire (27 February 1933) but was acquitted in a major blow to the prestige of the Nazi regime. Maksim Litvinov (1876–1951), the Soviet commissar for foreign affairs from 1931 to 1939, led Russia's search for collective security in the 1930s. Vyacheslav Molotov (1890–1986), an Old Bolshevik and Stalinist, served as premier (1930–41), and, as Litvinov's successor, he signed the Russo-German non-aggression pact in August 1939.

74. The "Old Guard" (*alte Kämpfer*, literally, Old Fighters) were members of the Nazi Party who had joined before 1928.

75. Friedrich von Schiller (1759–1805) was one of Germany's most celebrated writers. Encompassing poems, plays, and philosophy, his works were centrally concerned with the concept of freedom, both political and spiritual, and it is this influence to which Herz refers here.

76. Moses Mendelssohn (1729–86) was a German Jewish philosopher and translator of the Torah whose work upheld the principles of both Judaism and the Enlightenment. He was a founder of the Haskala (Reason) movement, which initiated Jewish engagement with secular European culture and helped pave the way to the integration of German Jews into bourgeois culture.

77. Herz is probably referring to the projects developed in the 1920s by national, international, and private organizations for repatriating or resettling refugees displaced from their homelands by the upheavals of World War I and its aftermath. Attempts to negotiate an international agreement for Jewish emigration from Germany, notably the American Rublee Plan of 1938–39, either failed or were cut short by the war; see Claudena Skran, *Refugees in Interwar Europe: The Emergence of a Regime* (Oxford, 1995), esp. 245–55.

78. See biographical appendix.
79. See biographical appendix.
80. Julius Streicher (1885–1946) was among the early members of the NSDAP and became Gauleiter of Franconia in 1928. He founded and edited the viciously anti-Semitic paper *Der Stürmer* in 1923. Notorious for his extreme brutality, corruption, and factionalism, he was relieved of his party offices in 1940. He was hanged at Nuremberg for crimes against humanity.
81. These are all prominent public figures in different fields who were critical of the Nazis but reached various levels of compromise with the regime. Gerhart Hauptmann (1862–1946) was one of Germany's most celebrated writers. Although privately critical of the Nazis, he was among the few literary luminaries to remain in Germany and have his plays produced during the Nazi period. Goebbels frequently mentioned Hauptmann's continued residence in Germany during public speeches. Richard Strauss (1864–1949) was the most famous German composer in the first half of the twentieth century. Appointed by Goebbels as president of the Reich Music Chamber in 1933, he shared several goals with the Nazis, such as fighting what was perceived as "atonal music." His relations with the regime deteriorated after 1935, when he was accused of associating with and befriending members of the Jewish faith. However, Strauss remained a prominent composer in Germany, composing the "Olympic Hymn" for the 1936 Winter Games. Wilhelm Furtwängler (1886–1954), best known as a conductor, was appointed director of the Berlin State Opera and vice-president of the Reichsmusikkammer in 1933, and remained in Germany throughout the Nazi era. While Furtwängler rose to positions of prominence under the Nazis, he also refused to identify himself with National Socialists publicly, and supported musicians, including Jews, who were attacked and publicly persecuted by the authorities. Ferdinand Sauerbruch (1875–1951) was a prominent surgeon, famous for his treatments and operations on war injuries during World War I. He publicly supported the Nazi regime and was recognized as the leading surgeon in Germany, operating on the Nazi elite, including Hitler and Goebbels. Despite his prominence, he made some efforts to dissociate himself from the intellectual goals of the regime and had contacts with resistance circles. Field Marshal Werner von Blomberg (1879–1946) served the Nazi regime as defense minister and war minister (1933–38), but became increasingly critical of Hitler's foreign policy. He was forced to resign in 1938 during Hitler's purge of the military and political establishment. Werner von Fritsch (1880–1939) was appointed army commander-in-chief in 1934 and helped develop the Wehrmacht into a powerful military force. Also critical of the regime's foreign policy and military strategy, he was forced into resignation in 1938.
82. The mail bus combined mail collection and delivery with public transport in rural areas.
83. The People's Court (Volksgerichtshof) was created in April 1934 to try cases of treason and high treason. Its powers were expanded in January 1936 to include military sabotage, espionage, and other offenses related to the military and war. Its six members were nominated by Hitler and included representatives of the police, army, and NSDAP formations, as well as professional jurists. Herz's pluralization ("People's Courts") probably indicates a confusion of this court with the network of Special Courts (Sondergerichte), established in March 1933, which tried mainly political offenses. Both the Volksgerichtshof and the Sondergerichte were notorious for their draconian and politicized procedures and verdicts (against which there was no right of appeal). During the war they imposed about sixteen thousand death sentences between them.
84. See biographical appendix.
85. For the more probable circumstances of the memoir's composition, see introduction, 36–38.

Biographical Appendix

<hr/>

This APPENDIX INCLUDES the major figures mentioned in the *Memoir*, listed alphabetically by the pseudonym adopted by Herz, and followed by the correct name. Further references and biographical details are given where possible. Many identifications were made by Ursula Krause-Schmitt and published in her article "Im 'Judensaal' des Frauenkonzentrationslagers Moringen," *Dokumente. Rundbrief der Lagergemeinschaft und Gedenkstätte KZ Moringen e.V.* 19 (2000): 6–11 (referred to below as K.-S.).

"Ruth Abt": Ruth Arzt, a Berlin student detained in Moringen from December 1936 to September 1937 as a "returning emigrant." After her release, she emigrated to Palestine (K.-S., 11).

"Fritz Baimler": Hans Beimler (1895–1936), Communist Reichstag member, party leader in southern Bavaria, and resister. Killed during the Spanish Civil War (see introduction, 30f.).

"Zenta Baimler": Centa Herker-Beimler (1909–2002), Communist activist and resister; married Hans Beimler in 1929. She was first arrested in Munich in April 1933 and held in the Munich-Stadelheim prison. She was transferred to Moringen in January 1936, released in February 1937, but detained again from November to December 1938. Arrested once more in 1942, she was released pending trial and conviction for high treason in 1944. Her jail sentence was commuted to probation. In 1945, she married her second husband Hans Herker, a Communist resister whom she had met while in Gestapo detention (see further references in introduction, 30f.).

"Frau Berns": Frau Rehren, chief warder of the women's camp in Moringen, previously in charge of the workhouse women's wing (description by ex-inmate Anita H., 14 September 1947, in BA-SAPMO: BY5/V 279/84).

"Dora Doebel": Viktoria Hösl (1902–53), Communist activist and member of the Bavarian Landtag since 1932. She served a prison term in Stadelheim from March 1933 to March 1936 and was then held in Moringen. After her release, she joined a resistance group, was rearrested in 1942, and sentenced to prison again in June 1944. During her Moringen imprisonment, her son Herbert (born 1923) was cared for in the Clemens Maria Children's Home in Munich (K.-S., 10).

"Gusti Folander": Anni Nolan Pröll (1916–), member of Communist youth movement and resister. Arrested and imprisoned for the first time in 1933–35, she was rearrested in July 1935, sentenced to solitary confinement, and then detained in Moringen from May 1936 to June 1937. She remained active in the resistance through 1945.

"Ilse": Lotte Katz (1921–?), a student from Vienna detained in Moringen from November 1936 to March 1937. She was unable to emigrate and is thought to have been deported and murdered in Minsk (K.-S., 9).

"Herta Kronau": Herta Kronheim (1893–?), Communist activist. She was arrested in October 1933 and, after serving a fifteen-month sentence in the prisons of Aichach and Landshut, was sent to Moringen in April 1936. Her later fate is unknown (K.-S., 6).

"Axel Lark": Hugo Krack (1888–1962), the director of the Moringen workhouse (see introduction, 22, 24f.).

"Ilse Lipinski": Ilse Gostynski (1909–?), Communist activist and resister. She was sent to Moringen in January 1936 and was subsequently transferred to Lichtenburg and Ravensbrück. After her release in May 1939, she emigrated to Britain (K.-S., 6).

"Vera List": Gerda Lissack (1904–?1942), graphic artist from Berlin; disabled. She was transferred to the police prison in Berlin in June 1937, and is thought to have been killed in Ravensbrück in January 1942 (K-S., 10).

"Anna Löser": not identified. The KPD Reichstag members known to have been in Moringen at this time are Helene Overlach (1936–37) and Lisa Ullrich (from March 1936), both of whom were transferred to Lichtenburg in 1938. See *Reichstags-Handbuch, VI. Wahlperiode 1932* (Berlin, 1932), 165, 243; Martin Schumacher, ed., *Das Ende der Parlamente 1933 und die Abgeordneten der Landtage und Bürgerschaften der Weimarer Republik in der Zeit des Nationalsozialismus. Politische Verfolgung, Emigration und Ausbürgerung 1933–1945. Ein biographischer Index,* 3rd ed. (Düsseldorf, 1994), 352, 534; and Heide-Marie Lauterer, *Parlamentarierinnen in Deutschland 1918/19–1949* (Königstein-Taunus, 2002), 266–75.

"Gerda Loss": Gerda Rose (1914–99), member of the Communist youth organization in Braunschweig, arrested in 1933 and sentenced to three months'
imprisonment. Arrested again in October 1934, she was sentenced to a further
prison term and then detained in Moringen from March 1936 to March 1937.

"Gertrud Mannheim": thought to be Gertrud Herrmann (1889–?), detained
in Moringen as a "returning emigrant" from September 1936 to October 1937
(K.-S., 7).

"Maxe": Maria (Maxi) Dengler (1910–), Centa Herker-Beimler's sister, arrested
in September 1933 and imprisoned with Centa in Munich-Stadelheim. She was
transferred with her to Moringen in January 1936 and released in June 1937.

"Magdalene Mewes": Jehovah's Witness, not identified for certain and possibly a composite figure. See K.-S., 8–9, and Hans Hesse, "Zur Identifizierung
der im Bericht von Gabriele Herz erwähnten Zeuginnen Jehovahs," *Informationen* 52 (November 2000) (Studienkreis Deutscher Widerstand, Frankfurt
am Main): 39.

"Käte Moser": Katharina Thoenes (1904–?), Jehovah's Witness. She was arrested
and sentenced to prison in October 1935 and again in July 1936. She was then
detained in Moringen from August 1936 to June 1937, and served a further
prison term on her release (see Hesse, "Zur Identifizierung").

"Ursula Renner": Hedwig Laufer (1908–2001), member of the Communist
youth organization in Nuremberg, held in "protective custody" from March
1933 and detained in Moringen from March 1936 to January 1937 (K.-S., 8).

"Sophie": possibly Hertha Eichholz, who worked as a governess in Barcelona
in 1936 and was arrested on her return to Germany. She was released from
Moringen in July 1937 and emigrated to Palestine (K.-S., 9).

"Matilde Urban": not identified. Although Herz describes her as a Communist
Reichstag member, her biographical details do not match any of the KPD
Reichstag members known to have been in Jauer and Moringen. The closest
fit appears to be Friedel Malter, although she was a member of the Prussian
Landtag, not the Reichstag (see Lauterer, *Parlamentarierinnen in Deutschland
1918/19–1949*, 266–72).

"Hilde Weber": Hilde Gerber (1915–), member of the Communist youth organization in Nuremberg, arrested in 1933, sentenced to eight months' imprisonment in October 1934, then held in "protective custody." She was sent to
Moringen in fall 1935 and released in May 1937 (K.-S., 7–8).

Bibliography

Allen, M. T. *The Business of Genocide: The SS, Slave Labor, and the Concentration Camps.* Chapel Hill, 2002.

Amesberger, H., and B. Halbmayr, eds. *Vom Leben und Überleben. Wege nach Ravensbrück: Das Frauenkonzentrationslager in der Erinnerung.* 2 vols. Vienna, 2001–2.

Anonymous. *Als sozialdemokratischer Arbeiter im KZ Papenburg.* Moscow, 1935.

Apel, L. *Jüdische Frauen im Konzentrationslager Ravensbrück 1939–1945.* Berlin, 2003.

Arendt, H. *The Origins of Totalitarianism.* 2nd ed. New York, 1958.

Arndt, I. "Das Frauenkonzentrationslager Ravensbrück." In *Studien zur Geschichte der Konzentrationslager,* ed. H. Rothfels and T. Eschenburg, 110–53. Stuttgart, 1970.

Ayass, W. "Vagrants and Beggars in Hitler's Reich." In *The German Underworld: Deviants and Outcasts in German History,* ed. R. Evans, 210–37. London and New York, 1988.

———. *Das Arbeitshaus Breitenau. Bettler, Landstreicher, Prostituierte, Zuhälter und Fürsorgeempfänger in der Korrektions- und Landarmenanstalt Breitenau (1874–1949).* Kassel, 1992.

———. *"Asoziale" im Nationalsozialismus.* Stuttgart, 1995.

Barkai, A. *From Boycott to Annihilation: The Economic Struggle of German Jews 1933–1943.* Hanover, NH, 1989.

Beer-Hofmann, R. *Jaákobs Traum.* Berlin, 1918.

Beimler, H. *Four Weeks in the Hands of Hitler's Hell-Hounds: The Nazi Murder Camp of Dachau.* London, 1933.

Benz, W., and B. Distel, eds. *Terror ohne System: Die ersten Konzentrationslager im Nationalsozialismus 1933–1935.* Berlin, 2001.

———. *Der Ort des Terrors. Geschichte der nationalsozialistischen Konzentrationslager* (Munich, 2005–).

Bock, G. *Zwangssterilisation im Nationalsozialismus. Studien zur Rassenpolitik und Frauenpolitik.* Opladen, 1986.

———. *Herrschaft und Gewalt: Frühe Konzentrationslager 1933–1939.* Berlin, 2002.

Bromberger, B., H. Elling, J. v. Freyberg, and U. Krause-Schmitt. *Schwestern, vergesst uns nicht. Frauen im Konzentrationslager: Moringen, Lichtenburg, Ravensbrück 1933–1945.* Frankfurt am Main, 1988.

Broszat, M. "The Concentration Camps 1933–1945." In H. Krausnick, H. Buchheim, M. Broszat, and H-A. Jacobsen, *Anatomy of the SS State,* 397–504. New York, 1968.

———. *The Hitler State: The Foundation and Development of the Internal Structure of the Third Reich.* Trans. J. W. Hiden. London and New York, 1981.

Brückner, W. *"Arbeit macht frei." Herkunft und Hintergrund der KZ-Devise.* Opladen, 1998.

Buchheim, H. "The SS—Instrument of Domination." In H. Krausnick, H. Buchheim, M. Broszat, and H.-A. Jacobsen, *Anatomy of the SS State*, 127–301. New York, 1968.

Burleigh, M. *Death and Deliverance: "Euthanasia" in Germany, 1900–1945*. Cambridge and
New York, 1994.

Burleigh, M., and W. Wippermann. *The Racial State: Germany 1933–1945*. Cambridge and
New York, 1991.

Caplan, J. "Political Detention and the Origin of the Concentration Camps in Nazi Germany,
1933–1935/6." In *Nazism, War and Genocide: Essays in Honour of Jeremy Noakes*, ed. N.
Gregor. Exeter, 2005.

Crew, D. F. *Germans on Welfare: From Weimar to Hitler*. Oxford and New York, 1998.

Crowther, M. A. *The Workhouse System 1834–1929: The History of an English Social Institution*. London, 1981.

Daners, H. *"Ab nach Brauweiler ...!" Nutzung der Abtei Brauweiler als Arbeitsanstalt, Gestapo-
gefängnis, Landeskrankenhaus*. Pulheim, 1996.

Deutschland-Berichte der Sozialdemokratische Partei Deutschlands (Sopade) 1934–1940.
Frankfurt am Main, 1980.

Dickinson, E. R. *The Politics of German Child Welfare from the Empire to the Federal Republic*.
Cambridge, MA, 1996.

Distel, B. "Im Schatten der Helden. Kampf und Überleben von Centa Beimler-Herker und
Lina Haag." *Dachauer Hefte* 7 (1991): 21–57.

Domarus, M. *Hitler. Reden und Proklamationen 1932–1945*. 4 vols. Leonberg, 1973.

Drobisch, Klaus. "Frauenkonzentrationslager im Schloss Lichtenburg." *Dachauer Hefte* 3
(November 1987): 101–15.

———. "Hinter der Torschrift 'Arbeit macht frei'. Häftlingsarbeit, wirtschaftliche Nutzung
und Finanzierung der Konzentrationslager 1933 bis 1939." In *Konzentrationslager und
deutsche Wirtschaft 1939–1945*, ed. H. Kaienburg, 17–27. Opladen, 1996.

———. "Frühe Konzentrationslager." In *Die frühe Konzentrationslager in Deutschland. Aus-
tausch zum Forschungsstand und zur pädagogischen Praxis in Gedenkstätten*, ed. K. Gie-
beler et al., 41–60. Bad Boll, n.d.

Drobisch, K., and G. Wieland. *System der NS-Konzentrationslager 1933–1939*. Berlin, 1993.

Eksteins, M. *The Limits of Reason: The German Democratic Press and the Collapse of Weimar
Germany*. London and New York, 1975.

Elling, H. *Frauen im deutschen Widerstand 1933–1945*. 3rd ed. Frankfurt am Main, 1981.

Engels, F. *Socialism: Utopian and Scientific*. New York, [1882] 1972.

Eschebach, I., and J. Kootz, eds. *Das Frauenkonzentrationslager Ravensbrück. Quellenlage
und Quellenkritik. Tagungsdokumentation*. Berlin, 1997.

Finzsch, N., and R. Jütte, eds. *Institutions of Confinement: Hospitals, Asylums, and Prisons in
Western Europe and North America, 1500–1950*. Cambridge, 1996.

Fitzpatrick, S. *Everyday Stalinism. Ordinary Life in Extraordinary Times: Soviet Russia in the
1930s*. Oxford, 1999.

Frei, N., S. Steinbacher, and B. C. Wagner, eds. *Ausbeutung, Vernichtung, Öffentlichkeit. Neue
Studien zur nationalsozialistischen Lagerpolitik*. Munich, 2000.

Freidenreich, H. P. *Female, Jewish, and Educated: The Lives of Central European University
Women*. Bloomington, 2002.

Freyberg, J. v., and U. Krause-Schmitt, eds. *Moringen. Lichtenburg. Ravensbrück. Frauen in
Konzentrationslager 1933–1945*. Frankfurt am Main, 1997.

Friedländer, H. "Kategorien der KZ-Häftlinge." In *"Am mutigsten waren immer wieder die
Zeugen Jehovas." Verfolgung und Widerstand der Zeugen Jehovahs im Nationalsozialismus*,
ed. H. Hesse, 15–20. Bremen, 1998.

Friedländer, S. *Nazi Germany and the Jews. Vol. 1: The Years of Persecution, 1933–1939*. New
York, 1997.

Füllberg-Stolberg, C., M. Jung, R. Riebe, and M. Scheitenberger. *Frauen in Konzentrations-lagern—Bergen-Belsen, Ravensbrück.* Bremen, 1994.

Garbe, D., ed. *Die vergessenen KZs? Gedenkstätten für die Opfer des NS-Terrors in der Bundes-republik.* Bornheim-Merten, 1983.

———, *Zwischen Widerstand und Martyrium. Die Zeugen Jehovahs im "Dritten Reich."* 2nd ed. Munich, 1994.

Gellately, R. *The Gestapo and German Society: Enforcing Racial Policy, 1933–1945.* Oxford, 1990.

———. "The Prerogatives of Confinement in Germany, 1933–1945: 'Protective Custody' and Other Police Strategies." In *Institutions of Confinement: Hospitals, Asylums, and Prisons in Western Europe and North America, 1500–1950,* ed. N. Finzsch and R. Jütte, 191–211. Cambridge, 1996.

———. *Backing Hitler: Consent and Coercion in Nazi Germany.* Oxford, 2001.

Gellately, R., and N. Stoltzfus, eds. *Social Outsiders in Nazi Germany.* Princeton and Oxford, 2001.

Genschel, H. *Die Verdrängung der Juden aus der Wirtschaft im Dritten Reich.* Göttingen, 1966.

Giles, G. "'The Most Unkindest Cut of All': Castration, Homosexuality and Nazi Justice." *Journal of Contemporary History* 27, no. 1 (January 1992): 41–61.

Goldman, W. *Women, the State and Revolution: Soviet Family Policy and Social Life 1917–1936.* Cambridge, 1993.

Graf, C. *Politische Polizei zwischen Demokratie und Diktatur. Die Entwicklung der preus-sischen Politischen Polizei vom Staatsschutzorgan der Weimarer Republik zum Geheimen Staatspolizeiamt des Dritten Reiches.* Berlin, 1983.

Grau, G., ed. *Hidden Holocaust? Gay and Lesbian Persecution in Germany, 1933–45.* New York, 1995.

Grossmann, A. *Reforming Sex: The German Movement for Birth Control and Abortion Reform, 1920–1950.* New York, 1995.

Gruner, W. *Der geschlossene Arbeitseinsatz deutscher Juden: Zur Zwangsarbeit als Element der Verfolgung 1938–1943.* Berlin, 1997.

Guse, M., A. Kohrs, and F. Vahsen. "Das Jugendlager Moringen—Ein Jugendkonzentrationslager." In *Soziale Arbeit und Faschismus,* ed. H.-U. Otto and H. Sünker, 321–44. Bielefeld, 1986.

Hackett, D. A., ed. *The Buchenwald Report.* Boulder, CO, 1995.

Harder, J., and H. Hesse. "Die Zeuginnen Jehovahs im Frauen-KZ Moringen: Ein Beitrag zum Widerstand von Frauen im Nationalsozialismus." In *"Am mutigsten waren immer wieder die Zeugen Jehovas." Verfolgung und Widerstand der Zeugen Jehovahs im National-sozialismus,* ed. H. Hesse, 35–62. Bremen, 1998.

Harvey, E. *Youth and the Welfare State in Weimar Germany.* Oxford, 1993.

Hellfeld, M. v., and W. Breyvogel, eds. *Piraten, Swings und junge Garde. Jugendwiderstand im Nationalsozialismus.* Bonn, 1991.

Henry, F. *Victims and Neighbors: A Small Town in Nazi Germany Remembered.* South Hadley, MA, 1984.

Herbermann, N. *The Blessed Abyss: Inmate #6582 in Ravensbrück Concentration Camp for Women.* Ed. H. Baue and E. R. Baer. Detroit, 2000.

Herbert, U. "Arbeit und Vernichtung. Ökonomisches Interesse und Primat der 'Weltanschau-ung' im Nationalsozialismus." In *Ist der Nationalsozialismus Geschichte?* ed. Dan Diner, 198–236. Frankfurt am Main, 1988.

Herbert, U., K. Orth, and C. Dieckmann, eds. *Die nationalsozialistische Konzentrationslager. Entwicklung und Struktur.* 2 vols. Göttingen, 1998.

Herz, E. *Denk ich an Deutschland in der Nacht. Die Geschichte des Hauses Steg.* Berlin, 1951; new ed., Warburg, 1994.

———. *Before the Fury: Jews and Germans before Hitler.* New York, 1966.

Hesse, H., *Hoffnung ist ein ewiges Begräbnis. Briefe von Dr. Hannah Vogt aus dem Gerichts-gefängnis Osterode und dem KZ Moringen 1933.* Bremen, 1998.

———. "Zur Identifizierung der im Bericht von Gabriele Herz erwähnten Zeuginnen Jehovahs," *Informationen* 52 (November 2000) (Studienkreis Deutscher Widerstand, Frankfurt am Main): 39.

———, ed. *Persecution and Resistance of Jehovah's Witnesses during the Nazi Regime 1933-1945.* Bremen, 2001.

———. *Das Frauen-KZ Moringen 1933-1938.* Moringen, 2002.

Hesse, H., and J. Harder, *"… und wenn ich lebenslang in einem KZ bleiben müsste." Die Zeuginnen Jehovas in den Frauenkonzentrationslagern Moringen, Lichtenburg und Ravensbrück.* Essen, 2001.

Hong, Y.-S. *Welfare, Modernity and the Weimar State, 1919-1933.* Princeton, 1998.

Howard, E. F. *Across Barriers.* London, 1941.

Husband, W. B. *"Godless Communists": Atheism and Society in Soviet Russia, 1917-1932.* De Kalb, 2000.

Kaienburg, H. *Die Wirtschaft der SS.* Berlin, 2003.

Kaminski, A. J. *Konzentrationslager 1896 bis heute. Geschichte, Funktion, Typologie.* Munich, 1990.

Kaplan, M. A. *Between Dignity and Despair: Jewish Life in Nazi Germany.* New York, 1998.

King, C. E. *The Nazi State and the New Religions: Five Case Studies in Non-Conformity.* New York and Toronto, 1982.

Kogon, E. *Der SS-Staat.* Stockholm, 1947.

Kosthorst, E. "Die Lager im Emsland unter dem NS-Regime 1933-1945. Aufgabe und Sinn geschichtlicher Erinnerung." *Geschichte in Wissenschaft und Unterricht* 6 (1984): 365-79.

Kosthorst, E., and B. Walter. *Konzentrations- und Strafgefangenenlager im Dritten Reich. Beispiel Emsland. Dokumentation und Analysen zum Verhältnis von NS-Regime und Justiz.* 3 vols. Düsseldorf, 1983.

Krause-Schmitt, U. "Im 'Judensaal' des Frauenkonzentrationslagers Moringen." *Dokumente. Rundbrief der Lagergemeinschaft und Gedenkstätte KZ Moringen e.V.* 19 (2000): 6-11.

Krause-Vilmar, D. *Das Konzentrationslager Breitenau: Ein staatliches Schutzhaftlager 1933/34.* 2nd ed. Marburg, 2000.

Kuse, M. "Entlassungen von Häftlinge aus dem Frauenkonzentrationslager Moringen 1934-1938." Master's thesis, University of Bremen, 1999.

———. "Hugo Krack. Ein 'Zivilist' als KZ-Direktor?" *Dokumente. Rundbrief der Lagergemeinschaft und Gedenkstätte KZ Moringen e.V.* 20 (July 2001): 8-11.

———. *Zwischen Kooperation und Konflikt. Hugo Krack als Werkhaus und KZ-Direktor in Moringen.* Bremen, 2003.

KZ Moringen. Männerlager—Frauenlager—Jugendschutzlager. Eine Dokumentation. Die Gesellschaft für christlich-jüdische Zusammenarbeit Göttingen e.V. und dem evangelischen-lutherischen Pfarramt, ed. Göttingen-Moringen, 1983.

Lauterer, H.-M. *Parlamentarierinnen in Deutschland 1918/19-1949.* Königstein-Taunus, 2002.

Lerner, G. *Fireweed.* Philadelphia, 2002.

Lewin, M. *Lenin's Last Struggle.* London, 1975.

Lotfi, G. *KZ der Gestapo: Arbeitserziehungslager im Dritten Reich.* Stuttgart, 2000.

Luxemburg, R. *Briefe aus dem Gefängnis.* Berlin, 1922; trans. Eden Paul and Cedar Paul, eds., *Letters from Prison.* Berlin, 1923.

Mallmann, K.-M. "Zwischen Denunziation und Roter Hilfe. Geschlechterbeziehungen und kommunistischer Widerstand 1933-1945." In *Frauen gegen die Diktatur. Widerstand und Verfolgung im nationalsozialistischen Deutschland,* ed. C. Wickert, 82-97. Berlin, 1995.

Mason, T. W. *Social Policy in the Third Reich: The Working Class and the National Community*. Ed. J. Caplan. Providence and Oxford, 1993.

McLoughlin, B., and K. McDermott, eds. *Stalin's Terror: High Politics and Mass Repression in the Soviet Union*. Basingstoke, 2003.

Meyer, C. "Abschreckung, Besserung, Unschädlichmachung: Die Disziplinierung gesellschaftlicher Randgruppen im Werkaus Moringen (1871–1944)." Master's thesis, University of Göttingen, 2000.

Milton, S. "Deutsche and deutsch-jüdische Frauen als Verfolgte des NS-Staates." *Dachauer Hefte* 3 (November 1987): 3–20.

———. "Die Bedeutung von Photodokumenten als Quelle zur Erforschung der NS-Konzentrationslager." *Revue d'Allemagne* 27, no. 2 (1995): 175–87.

Mlynek, K. "Der Aufbau der Geheimen Staatspolizei in Hannover und die Errichtung des Konzentrationslagers Moringen." In *Hannover 1933. Eine Grosstadt wird nationalsozialistisch*, ed. A. Dietzler et al., 65–80. Hanover, 1981.

Morsey, R. *Das "Ermachtigungsgesetz" vom 24. Marz 1933. Quellen zur Geschichte und Interpretation des "Gesetzes zur Behebung der Not von Volk und Reich."* Düsseldorf, 1992.

Muth, H. "Das 'Jugendschutzlager' Moringen." *Dachauer Hefte* 5 (November 1989): 223–52.

Neugebauer, M. *Der Weg in das Jugendschutzlager Moringen. Eine entwicklungspolitische Analyse nationalsozialistischer Jugendpolitik*. Mönchengladbach and Godesberg, 1997.

Nietzsche, F. *Human, All Too Human*. Trans. and ed. R. J. Hollingdale. Cambridge, 1996.

Noakes, J. "Nazism and Eugenics: The Background to the Nazi Sterilization Law of 14 July 1933." In *Ideas into Politics*, ed. R. J. Bullen, H. Pogge von Strandmann, and A. B. Polonsky, 75–94. London, 1984.

Noakes, J., and G. Pridham, eds. *Nazism 1919–1945*. 4 vols. Exeter, 1983–98.

Ofer, D., and L. J. Weitzman, eds. *Women in the Holocaust*. New Haven, 1998.

Orth, K. *Das System der nationalsozialistischen Konzentrationslager. Eine politische Organisationsgeschichte*. Zürich and Munich, 1999.

Peukert, D. *Die Edelweisspiraten. Protestbewegung jugendlicher Arbeiter im Dritten Reich. Eine Dokumentation*. Cologne, 1980.

———. *Die KPD im Widerstand. Verfolgung und Untergrundarbeit an Rhein und Ruhr 1933 bis 1945*. Wuppertal, 1980.

———. *Volksgenossen und Gemeinschaftsfremde. Anpassung, Ausmerze und Aufbegehren unter dem Nationalsozialismus*. Cologne, 1982.

Peukert, D., and J. Reulecke, eds. *Die Reihen fast geschlossen. Beiträge zur Geschichte des Alltags unterm Nationalsozialismus*. Wuppertal, 1981.

Philipp, G. *Kalendarium der Ereignisse im Frauen-Konzentrationslager Ravensbrück 1939–1945*. Berlin, 1999.

Pingel, F. *Häftlinge unter SS-Herrschaft: Widerstand, Selbstbehauptung und Vernichtung im Konzentrationslager*. Hamburg, 1976.

Proctor, R. N. *Racial Hygiene: Medicine under the Nazis*. Cambridge, MA, 1988.

Richter, G., ed. *Breitenau. Zur Geschichte eines nationalsozialistischen Konzentrations- und Arbeitserziehungslagers*. Kassel, 1993.

Richthofen, Baron B. von. *Der rote Kampfflieger*. Berlin, 1917.

Riebe, R. "Frauen im Konzentrationslager 1933–1939." *Dachauer Hefte* 14 (1998): 125–40.

Roos, J. "Backlash against Prostitutes' Rights: Origins and Dynamics of Nazi Prostitution Policies." *Journal of the History of Sexuality* 11 (January–April 2002): 67–94.

Sachsse, C., and F. Tennstedt. *Geschichte der Armenfürsorge in Deutschland*. Vol. 2: *Der Wohlfahrtsstaat im Nationalsozialismus*. Stuttgart, 1992.

Schikorra, C. *Kontinuitäten der Ausgrenzung. "Asoziale" Häftlinge im Frauen-Konzentrationslager Ravensbrück*. Berlin, 2001.

Schmitt, H. A. *Quakers and Nazis: Inner Light in Outer Darkness*. Columbia, MO, 1997.

Schumacher, M., ed. *Das Ende der Parlamente 1933 und die Abgeordneten der Landtage und Bürgerschaften der Weimarer Republik in der Zeit des Nationalsozialismus. Politische Verfolgung, Emigration und Ausbürgerung 1933–1945. Ein biographischer Index.* 3rd ed. Düsseldorf, 1994.

Schwarz, G. *Die nationalsozialistichen Lager.* Frankfurt am Main, 1990.

Sedlaczek, D. "Wir haben keine KZ-Opfer zu bedauern oder zu beklagen." *Dachauer Hefte* 19 (2003): 128–51.

Skran, C. *Refugees in Interwar Europe: The Emergence of a Regime.* Oxford, 1995.

Sneeringer, J. *Winning Women's Votes: Propaganda and Politics in Weimar Germany.* Chapel Hill, 2002.

Sofsky, W. *Die Ordnung des Terrors. Das Konzentrationslager.* Frankfurt am Main, 1993.

Steinbacher, S. *Dachau, die Stadt und das Konzentrationslager in der NS-Zeit: Die Untersuchung einer Nachbarschaft.* Frankfurt am Main and New York, 1993.

Strauss, H. A. "Jewish Emigration from Germany: Nazi Policies and Jewish Responses." *Leo Baeck Institute Year Book* 15 (1980): 313–61.

Suhr, E. *Die Emslandlager. Die politische und wirtschaftliche Bedeutung der Emsländischen Konzentrations- und Strafgefangenenlager 1933–1945.* Bremen, 1985.

Szepansky, G. *Frauen leisten Widerstand: 1933–1945. Lebensgeschichten nach Interviews und Dokumenten.* Frankfurt am Main, 1983.

Terhorst, K.-L. *Polizeiliche planmässige Überwachung und polizeiliche Vorbeugungshaft im Dritten Reich.* Heidelberg, 1985.

Thurston, R. W. *Life and Terror in Stalin's Russia, 1934–1941.* New Haven, 1996.

Tillion, G. *Ravensbrück.* Paris, 1997.

Tuchel, J. "'Arbeit' in den Konzentrationslagern im Deutschen Reich 1933–1939." In *Arbeiterschaft und Nationalsozialismus—in Memoriam Karl Stadler,* 455–67. Vienna and Zürich, 1990.

———. *Konzentrationslager. Organisationsgeschichte und Funktion der "Inspektion der Konzentrationslager" 1934–1938.* Boppard am Rhein, 1991.

———. *Die Inspektion der Konzentrationslager 1938–1945. Das System des Terrors. Eine Dokumentation.* Berlin, 1994.

Tuchel, J., and R. Schattenfroh. *Zentrale des Terrors. Prinz-Albrecht-Strasse 8. Hauptquartier der Gestapo.* Berlin, 1987.

Tutas, H. E. *Nationalsozialismus und Exil. Die Politik des Dritten Reiches gegenüber den deutschen politischen Emigranten.* Munich and Vienna, 1975.

Ullstein, H. *The Rise and Fall of the House of Ullstein.* London, 1944.

Union für Recht und Freiheit. *Der Strafvollzug im III. Reich. Denkschrift und Materialsammlung.* Prague, 1934.

Vogt, H., ed. *KZ Moringen. Männerlager. Frauenlager. Jugendschutzlager. Eine Dokumentation.* Göttingen, n.d.

Wachsmann, N. "'Annihilation through Labor': The Killing of State Prisoners in the Third Reich." *Journal of Modern History* 71, no. 3 (September 1999): 624–59.

———. "Between Reform and Repression: Imprisonment in Weimar Germany." *Historical Journal* 45, no. 2 (June 2002): 411–32.

———. *Hitler's Prisons: Legal Terror in Nazi Germany.* New Haven, 2004.

Wadle, A. *Mutti, warum lachst du nie? Erinnerung an Zeiten der Verfolgung und des Krieges.* Ed. L. Walz. Dreisteinfurt, 1988.

Wagner, P. *Volksgemeinschaft ohne Verbrecher. Konzeptionen und Praxis der Kriminalpolizei in der Zeit der Weimarer Republik und des Nationalsozialismus.* Hamburg, 1996.

———. *Hitlers Kriminalisten: Die deutsche Kriminalpolizei und der Nationalsozialismus zwischen 1920 und 1960.* Munich, 2002.

Weinmann, M., ed. *Das nationalsozialistische Lagersystem (CCP).* Frankfurt am Main, 1990.

Werle, G. *Justiz-Strafrecht und polizeiliche Verbrechensbekämpfung im Dritten Reich.* Berlin and New York, 1989.

Wetzel, J. "Auswanderung aus Deutschland." In *Die Juden in Deutschland 1933–1945: Leben unter nationalsozialistischer Herrschaft*, ed. W. Benz, 413–98. Munich, 1988.

Wetzell, R. F. *Inventing the Criminal: A History of German Criminology 1880–1945.* Chapel Hill, 2000.

Wickert, C. "Frauen im Hintergrund—das Beispiel von Kommunistinnen und Bibelforscherinnen." In *Das "andere Deutschland" im Widerstand gegen den Nationalsozialismus. Beiträge zur politischen Überwindung der nationalsozialistischen Diktatur im Exil und im Dritten Reich*, ed. H. Grebing and C. Wickert, 200–225. Essen, 1994.

Wieland, G. "Die normativen Grundlagen der Schutzhaft in Hitlerdeutschland." *Jahrbuch für Geschichte* 26 (1982): 75–102.

Wilhelm, F. *Die Polizei im NS-Staat: Die Geschichte ihrer Organisation im Überblick.* Paderborn, 1997.

Wisskirchen, J. "Das Konzentrationslager Brauweiler 1933/1934." *Pulheimer Beiträge zur Geschichte und Heimatkunde* 13 (1989): 153–96.

Zorn, G. *Widerstand in Hannover. Gegen Reaktion und Faschismus 1920–1946.* Frankfurt am Main, 1977.

Index

Note: Individuals mentioned in the *Memoir* are normally indexed under the pseudonyms used by Herz, which are enclosed in quotation marks. The correct names, where identified, are cross-referenced to the relevant pseudonyms. In a few cases where individuals are also extensively discussed in the introduction under their correct names, those references are indexed under this name. For further details on all identified pseudonyms, see the biographical appendix.